# AFRICAN TRADITIONAL RELIGION AND CHRISTIAN RELIGION

*Integration of Spiritual Powers*

COLLIS GARIKAI MACHOKO

PublishAmerica
Baltimore

First printing



Hardcover 978-1-4512-7431-8
Softcover 978-1-4512-7430-1
PUBLISHED BY PUBLISHAMERICA, LLLP
www.publishamerica.com
Baltimore

Printed in the United States of America

This book is dedicated to the following people: Margaret Munorwei Machoko (my wife), Marerudzeni Mangwayana Dhamu Zininga Machoko (my late mother), Garikai Machoko (my late father), Dzito Mutandazuri Machoko (late brother), Fred Munorwei (late father-in-law), Mugurwi Nyapfumbi Munorwei (late mother-in-law), Shumbireni Caltus Munorwei Mbanda Zininga (late aunt) and Patience Rhodha Tazira Musoni (late cousin) and Kufahakusiyani Kubvobvo Mangwayana Dhamu Zininga (late grandmother).

# ACKNOWLEDGEMENTS

First and foremost I am grateful to God (*Mwari)* my Heavenly Father, Jesus Christ (*Mudzimu Mukuru* par excellence) my Lord and Savior, and the Holy Spirit (*Mweya Anoyera/ Mudzimu Anoyera)* my giver of life, guide, and comforter for giving me this transitory life, for making me a pilgrim on this planet. I am also grateful to my parents—my father, the late Garikai Machoko, and my mother, Marerudzeni Mangwayana Dhamu Zininga Machoko—who, as traditional Shona and Shona USPG Christians, combined ATR and USPG Christianity and thus enriched my life with our Shona traditional values, practices, and beliefs as well as nourished me with inculturation even before I was conscious of it.

Special thanks go to my former bishop Dr. Peter Ralph Hatendi. His constant understanding, support, encouragement, and above all his fatherly love contributed much to the realization of this work. I express my indebtedness and special gratitude to Professor F. J. Verstraelen for his scholarly advice during the writing of this book. His support, guidance, constructive criticisms, scholarly comments, academic challenges, constructive dialogue, love, and patience were an invaluable inspiration in the completion and quality of this book. To Professor H.P. Gundani who advised me during the corrections of this book, I say thank you, and keep it up! A very good, lasting friendship which started during our student days at the University of Zimbabwe (UZ) has been greatly strengthened. To Dr. J. L. Cox, a phenomenologist who was a lecturer in the Department of Religious Studies at the UZ, with his intellectual depth, mental acumen, and wisdom, I say thank you; he too inspired me in the very early stages of the writing of this book. I wish also to express my gratitude to Dr. E. C. Mandivenga and Dr. J. Kurasha who, as lecturers and chairmen of the Department of Religious Studies, Philosophy, and Classics at the University of Zimbabwe gave me great love and encouragement during and after the writing of this book. To Drs I. Mukonyora and Aynos Moyo both of the UZ Department of Religious Studies, I say thank you very much for helping me with some relevant reference books during the correction of this book. To Bishop Dr. S. Bakare of Manicaland (Mutare), who was Senior Ecumenical Chaplain at the UZ, I say thank you. Keep it up! With his love and encouragement, he made my task of writing this book much easier.

Last but not in any way the least important, I would like to thank my family: Margaret Machoko my wife, Anesu Machoko and Nyasha Machoko my sons, Plaxcedes Munorwei (now Mrs P. Chakwana) my wife's youngest sister (*amainini*), and the late Patience Musoni our niece for bearing with me during the hard times when this book was written. God and His Christ bless them now and always.

# INTRODUCTION

This introductory chapter has seven parts: the problem, objectives, approaches, research methods, criteria of analysis, literature review, and an overview of the chapters.

The problem I address is the tensions and antagonisms that exist between the missiologies of United Society for the Propagation of the Gospel (USPG) missionaries in Zimbabwe and the missiologies of African Traditional Religion (ATR), which were retained by the Shona Anglican bishops, priests, and Shona USPG Christians. My aim is to integrate these two opposing missiologies into a new soteriological paradigm. The term *missiology* refers to the propagating of a religious faith, in this case the Christian faith. Mission is evangelism—preaching the Good News of Jesus Christ. By preaching the Good News of Jesus Christ or by being involved in humanitarian work, one is involved in mission. The end product of missiology (evangelism) is soteriology (salvation). We are involved in mission to save people. Soteriology is the doctrine of saving people. Soteriology has to do with the saving action and works of Jesus. Jesus Christ is the Savior of the world. Christology has to do with the Person, Being, and Identity of Jesus Christ. Nobody can separate Jesus' Being from His actions (works). What one does is what one is. For example, in the Old Testament, who is God? God is the One who redeemed Israel. God is what God does. God is known by His works and actions. Who is Jesus? Jesus, like God, is also identified by His works and actions; hence, Jesus is identified as Savior (soteriology).

The Christian understanding of Jesus goes to and from Christology to soteriology; that is, from Being to action. Mission is the starting point, and soteriology is the end product. Through His works of preaching the Kingdom of God (mission), healing the sick, and raising the dead (salvation), Jesus was involved in both mission and soteriology. One is involved in missiology (evangelism), and the end result of that evangelism is soteriology (salvation) of both the preacher (one involved in mission) and the people evangelized. I am going to use the term missiology (mission) when I am talking of evangelism (preaching the Good News of Jesus Christ), and I am going to use the term soteriology when I am talking of salvation (saving people). Ecclesiocentric soteriologies hold the belief that explicit knowledge of Jesus Christ and membership of the Church is required for salvation. Christocentric soteriologies hold the belief that Jesus Christ is the way to salvation for all people, even those outside the Church.

For Christocentricism, salvation is possible for those people outside the Church through the working of the Holy Spirit *(Mweya Anoyera/* Mudzimu *Anoyera*) which flowed from the Church. Pneumatocentric soteriologies hold the belief that the theology of religions is based on the recognition of the universal presence and action of the Holy Spirit; the Spirit of God has been universally present throughout human history and remains active today outside the boundaries of the Christian fold. Theocentric soteriologies hold the belief that Jesus Christ is the way to salvation for Christians only, while other religions of the world—for example, African Traditional Religion (ATR), Hinduism, and Islam—constitute a way for others. Theocentric soteriologies advocate that Jesus Christ and his saving mystery no longer stand at the center of God's saving design for religious traditions. Theocentric and pneumatocentric soteriologies seem to produce inculturation (Christ of culture) even to the point where Christian identity is dissolved into ATR, while ecclesiocentric and Christocentric soteriologies seem to produce a clear separation between USPG Christianity and ATR. Why do pneumatocentric and theocentric soteriologies seem to produce inculturation even to the point where Christian identity is dissolved into ATR? That is, why do theocentric and pneumatocentric soteriologies seem to produce a Christ of culture, and ecclesiocentric and Christocentric soteriologies seem to produce a clear separation between USPG Christianity and ATR?

The USPG, the biggest missionary society of the Anglican Church, was formed in 1701 to look after the spiritual welfare of the British settlers in the British colonies. It started and developed the Anglican Churches first in the British colonies and then in other countries all over the world. There are Christological, missiological, and soteriological tensions between the USPG missionaries and Shona Anglican bishops, Shona Anglican priests and Shona Anglican (USPG) laity in Zimbabwe. Today, the USPG gives financial support and human resources in the form of clergymen to the Anglican dioceses in the developing countries, Zimbabwe included (for a history of the USPG, see chapters 2 and 3). The Christ of culture takes everything in a culture and calls it Christian (see chapter 5 for a discussion of Niebuhr's *Christ and Culture*). For those who believe in the Christ of culture, Christ is the supreme example of universal human goodness and the fulfillment of cultural aspiration. The majority of Shona Anglican bishops and priests in the Anglican Church in Zimbabwe have opted for pneumatocentric and theocentric soteriologies which have produced a Christ of culture. However, the majority of European and American Anglican priests in Zimbabwe, who have been heavily influenced by the USPG, have opted for ecclesiocentric and Christocentric soteriologies which seem to have produced a clear separation between USPG Christianity and ATR (see chapters 3 and 4). These two different soteriological and Christological approaches, one by the Shona Anglican bishops and priests and the other one by USPG missionaries, have created the tensions we now see in the Zimbabwean church.

Four objectives have guided me in writing this book. First, I intend to find out the types of soteriologies employed by the traditional Shona people in Zimbabwe as adherents of ATR before the coming of the USPG missionaries and then compare them with the soteriologies employed by the USPG missionaries in Zimbabwe in order to determine the effect on evangelism (mission) in relation to ATR. Second, I intend to integrate ATR and USPG Christianity into Christ understood as the Greatest Ancestor par excellence (*Mudzimu Mukuru* par excellence) through a transformation process which is different for each religious (ATR and USPG Christianity) interpretation. USPG Christianity has to introduce the concept of the Greatest Ancestor par excellence, while ATR has to give a new eminent and superior meaning to the concept of Greatest Ancestor par excellence, with Christ integrated into the Trinity. Third, I intend to incarnate Jesus Christ understood as the Greatest Ancestor par excellence (*Mudzimu Mukuru* par excellence) into ATR by way of integrating USPG Christianity and ATR to produce a synthesis—inculturated practical Christianity and inculturated practical worship in Zimbabwe which is salvific, particular, and worldwide. Fourth, I intend to integrate the Greatest Ancestor par excellence *(Mudzimu Mukuru* par excellence) into the Trinity in order to save the value of a Christian faith interpretation of God as a Trinitarian Being.

The approaches I use in this book are the historical, the participant-observation, the hermeneutical, the comparative-functional, the appropriational and inculturational, and the theological. I use them for the purpose of arriving at an inculturated, dynamic, and salvific *Mudzimu Mukuru* par excellence Christology.

**Historical Approach:** the history of Christology is an attempt to find the reality of incarnation. The test of Christology is how it renders, clarifies, and protects the facts of Christology. The logic of salvation (soteriology) says there are two poles, one of God (Divine) and another of human beings. Salvation history involves the God who acts and human beings who respond to God's actions either positively or negatively. One cannot emphasize the Divine and neglect the human. I will use both equally. I describe the historical forces that shaped the Anglican Church in Zimbabwe, Shona Anglican bishops, Shona Anglican priests, Shona Anglican (USPG) lay people and USPG missionaries in Zimbabwe. A Christology is created within the context of the existing store of historical knowledge on the subject matter. Although USPG Christianity in Zimbabwe is not a result of historical factors, historical factors did influence it. It is for this reason that the rich lessons provided by the histories of ATR and USPG Christianity in Zimbabwe are instructive. The historical approach also sheds light on ATR among the Shona people and the USPG mission among the Shona people in Zimbabwe. The history of the USPG sheds light on its missiology (evangelism) in Zimbabwe. The historical approach forces me to obtain accurate historical facts and results of USPG missionary activities in Zimbabwe. However, while the historical method concerns itself with events and change, the relationship between history and the Church is theological. As McBrien argues, "it has to do with the presence of grace in the world, with the direction and destiny of the world toward the Kingdom of God, and with the role of the Church in proclaiming, exemplifying, and saving the reality of grace."[1]

**Participation-Observation Approach**: This is an inside approach whereby one studies from the adherents of a religion themselves. I am a Shona, was born in ATR, live in and practice ATR, and I speak the Shona language. I know the traditional Shona culture, traditions, and taboos. I have my cultural roots in ATR. The fact that I am a Shona Anglican priest qualifies my method to be called participant-observation; hence, data were collected from interviews with Shona Anglican bishops, priests, and lay Christians. I am studying the problem with the adherents of ATR and USPG Christianity.

**Hermeneutical Approach:** The hermeneutical process of analyzing and interpreting data was used. This was done by relying on interviews and observations of believers, by reflecting believers' perspectives, and then by using a hermeneutical process which is consistent with, or at least not offensive to, the believers' own points-of-view. I recorded the number of Shona Anglican bishops, Shona Anglican priests and Shona Anglican lay people who accepted or rejected ATR and Shona ancestors. Since an interpretation is involved, however, the conclusion presented will not necessarily be identical with what a believer would consciously state. The hermeneutical approach supplements the participant-observation approach. It systematizes the facts and the data which the Shona Anglican bishops, Shona Anglican priests, and Shona USPG Christians are not aware of or which they do not want to reveal. The systematization and interpretation of the data and facts are in chapters 5, 6, and 7.

**Comparative Approach:** The comparative-functional approach has been used since 1875 in a specialized way. It has both the historical and comparative perspectives and is used in this book in three specialized senses. First, I compare the main features and doctrines of USPG Christianity and ATR. I want to investigate points of intersection between ATR and USPG Christianity. For example, Jesus Christ is understood as the New Adam, hence an Ancestor. Third, the method is used to compare USPG Christianity and ATR in a general manner. It is used to compare Christian and ATR symbols and data to see which features are common to both religions and to restrict oneself to those few features. The whole idea is that Christianity is not superior to ATR. One should not denigrate, reject, or condemn ATR in favor of USPG Christianity. Both USPG Christianity and ATR are important and should be cross-fertilized to produce a hybrid Christology—a *Mudzimu Mukuru* par excellence Christology.

**Appropriational and Inculturational Approach:** Inculturation cannot be divorced from the adherent, for he or she worships, prays, and sacrifices in a distinct way. These are the activities of the Shona Anglican bishops, priests, and laity. African anthropology and African traditional religious beliefs and practices are included in this book. The people are the bedrock of any inculturation process. The contributions of the people interviewed matter very much in the production of the inculturated *Mudzimu Mukuru* par excellence Christology. The two core concepts of appropriation and inculturation are central to my thesis. The *Mudzimu Mukuru* par excellence Christology must embody the personal, cultural, and ultimate dimensions of Christianity. I use the New Testament (NT) as the central critical agent and the lens for looking into African anthropology and African traditional religious beliefs and practices. The NT as central and critical agency challenges the process of appropriation and inculturation (see chapters 6 and 7).

The believers—Shona Anglican bishops, priests, and lay people, USPG missionaries, and Shona traditionalists—are my primary sources of data (see Appendix 4). Shona ATR believers must be understood and respected in order to avoid imposing on them my own value judgments, and, thus, this study aims to understand the traditional Shona perceptions of a core concern, which is Shona ancestors. However, by putting this approach into practice, I endeavor to do full justice to ATR and Shona ancestors from the "inside view" in order to arrive at an empirical description with testable conclusions.

**Theological Approach:** A theological perspective is inevitable when the study tackles issues like inculturation of the Gospel of Jesus Christ and the Church. Issues like justice, peace, liturgy, ethics, spirituality, catechism, pastorality, and evangelism involve theology and have a theological perspective. However, theological references and arguments will be used only as they serve to highlight the thoughts that link the historical, inculturational, and the soteriological processes that we are concerned with. I adopt the theological approach in which the theological aspects of the Anglican Church in Zimbabwe and the various Christological and soteriological positions are studied in relation to African traditional religious beliefs and practices. By choosing the theological method, I am involved in the evaluation of the described and analyzed facts of history on the basis of Christian faith. The theological approach forces me to make careful theological analyses of the results of the various USPG Christological and soteriological positions and of the basic concepts of USPG Christian practices and also of ATR practices before I investigate whether a Trinitarian Christology that transforms USPG Christianity and ATR by integrating them into Christ is useful for the development of Christianity in Zimbabwe.

My primary research method was the personal interview (see Appendix 1). The extensive interviews I conducted from January 1990 to February 2000 of Shona Anglican bishops, priests, and laity are the essential data of this empirical study (see chapter 4 for a report of the interviews). All other analyses depend on this invaluable material. The face-to-face oral interviews are easy to carry out, confidential, and straightforward to analyze. Most people probably will never write down the details of the most personal and inspirational parts of their lives, but they often will talk their histories—enthusiastically and in marvelous detail. Instead of worrying about stylistic niceties in sentences and paragraphs, my interviewees concentrated more on remembering and relating their stories of being devotees of both ATR and USPG Christianity. A phone call home gives a fuller account than does a letter. It is the same with an oral history. In conversation, the colorful, brief, vivid descriptions, episodes, and trivialities are told. The interviewer and interviewee interaction helps in clarification, lessens suspicion, and builds good will. When the interview is tape recorded, one gets a history preserved in the person's own voice, filled with his or her unique expressions, emotions, and personality. Hearts and minds are better brought together, family relationships deepened, and generation gaps closed through conversations. In conjunction with a transcript, oral history carries enormous impact. At the touch of a button, we can recall hopes, fears, and joys. Oral interviews can provide glimpses into the lives and ideas of everyday Anglican Shona bishops, priests and laity. They offer personal perspectives not often found in traditional written sources. This methodology also gave me, the researcher, opportunity to ask highly specific questions about USPG Christianity directly to the Zimbabwean Shona Anglicans who live it. As the interviewer, I also worked collaboratively with Zimbabwean Anglicans, who are the historical actors, to construct their interpretations of USPG Christianity in Zimbabwe.

Oral historians face potential problems, such as faulty or embellished memories. They also have the disadvantage of the possibility of competing versions of events told by several interviewees. And interviewees may give false information in order to win the sympathy of the interviewer. However, these potential challenges are more than made up for by the richness of historical insight afforded by the craft. The challenges can be accounted for through careful analysis. My methodology is worth noting, for it relates the historical material about the Anglican Church in Zimbabwe—which I got from both the primary and secondary sources—with the situations on the ground. Those situations are the practicing of both ATR and USPG Christianity by Shona Anglican bishops, priests, and laity at different times. The interviewees brought the everyday into history and theology. We see theology and church history written by the devotees of both ATR and USPG Christianity and not by the USPG missionaries.

Oral evidence helps us to better understand very difficult realities. The interviews reveal the often unsuspected oppressive nature of USPG Christianity. USPG Christianity is being used by missionaries to oppress ATR and its adherents, Zimbabwean Shona people. Interviewing Zimbabwean Shona Anglican bishops, priests, and laity makes them participants in the history and theology of Christianity in Africa. The problems and limitations of interviews are of linking them to archival documents—Church documents and Commission Reports of the Anglican Diocese of Harare. Sensitive information was given by Shona Anglican bishops, priests, and lay people only when I promised to keep their identities anonymous because they fear for their job security, they fear being sued in law courts, and they fear for their welfare within the Church.

I also used a questionnaire (see Appendix 1) to gather responses from Shona Anglican bishops, priests, and lay people. The advantages of a questionnaire are that it is considered an effective tool of gathering information, it clearly articulates the research problem, it can be cost-effective, and it can be constructed with assurance of confidentiality. The disadvantages of a questionnaire are that it can have numerous non-responses, confusing responses, and leeway for the respondent to provide false information. Questions can be too difficult or overly abstract for popular participation, too comprehensive and therefore inaccessible to the less educated, of little use with an illiterate or semi-literate population, and can be expensive if the questionnaire is mailed.

These research methods, the interview and the questionnaire, still require decisions about whom to interview—the "sampling units". These decisions can be subject to interviewer bias. Two factors affect the quantity of information contained in the sample and hence affect the precision of my inference-making procedure. First is the size of the sample selected from the population. Second is the amount of variation in the data. These problems can be controlled by the method of selecting material from the sample—simple random sampling. A researcher should appeal to overwhelming evidence. Without such evidence, the quality of contributions is problematic. Firstly, the people deciding on the quality of Christianity in the Anglican Church in Zimbabwe are predominantly Shona Anglicans and would definitely see their ancestorcentric, Christological position as being of better quality than USPG ecclesiocentric and Christocentric positions. Secondly, "the quality of contributions" thesis requires that I support my recommendations from the "majority" positions and not from "minority" positions. The contributions from the people interviewed include graphic and detailed descriptions of their involvement in ATR and Shona ancestors. This is why I use such expressions as "overwhelming evidence" or "incontrovertible evidence". The advantages of simple random sampling are that it is less subjective, lacks researcher-bias, gives every element being sampled equal chances of selection, and obtains much diversified and hence rich information about a population. The disadvantages of simple random sampling are that it needs to correctly determine the population size before selecting the sampling units, it can be time-consuming and imprecise, it can be very costly especially if sampling is done over a very large area or a very large population, and can be severely affected by the problem of unavailability of the selected sample unit.

My criteria of analysis are the following. First, a particular soteriology is defective if it produces separation between USPG Christianity and ATR; that is, when a particular Christology produces a Christ against Shona ancestors (ATR). A soteriology is also defective if it produces a Christ of Shona ancestors; that is, when Christian identity—the non-negotiables of the divinity, the humanity, the cross and the resurrection of Christ—are dissolved into ATR. Second, a particular Christology or soteriology is good if it views Jesus Christ as the Greatest Ancestor par excellence (*Mudzimu Mukuru* par excellence). It is good if it produces an inculturated Zimbabwean Christology or soteriology (integrates Christ and transforms USPG Christianity and ATR). The produced inculturated Zimbabwean Christology should result in a change of dominion from the evil old dominion of Satan the greatest wizard or witch (*muroyi mukuru*) to the good new dominion of *Mudzimu Mukuru* par excellence, and this change of dominion should be accompanied by changes in the soteriological, eschatological, and ethical perspectives by the one who uses the inculturated Zimbabwean Christology. Finally, a particular Christology or soteriology is good if Christianity maintains its identity whenever inculturation takes place. Christian identity should become part of ATR after inculturation. Both the universality of Jesus Christ and the uniqueness (particularity) of Jesus Christ should be maintained, but there should be no separation between Christianity and ATR and no dissolution of the Christian identity into ATR.

In this literature review, I would like firstly to hold a dialogue with some non-African Christologies in order to show how I could profit from them but also how my Zimbabwean *Mudzimu Mukuru* par excellence Christology could complement their work. Paul Tillich (1953) advocated a Christocentric soteriology. For him the God revealed in Jesus Christ is truly speaking through voices other than that of Jesus. Tillich argues that "Jesus Christ is the New Being. The problem of human beings is that of alienation from God. Jesus Christ helps human beings to overcome that alienation. Jesus Christ is the Answer for all human problems."[2] Karl Barth (1963) pleaded for an Ecclesiocentric Christology, for he says that "Christianity is the only true Religion. Revelation and salvation are offered only in Jesus Christ. Jesus Christ is the Word of God—the Revelation of God."[3] Barth rejected liberal theologies which were based on reason, for example on science, technology, and philosophy. He says that theologies based on reason are idolatry. He advocated the preaching of the Word of God—Jesus Christ who is the Revelation of God. Beker (1988) is an exponent of an Ecclesiocentric type of Christology, for he says that Christ alone represents not only the total fullness of God but also the all-sufficient fullness of life and salvation for Christians. Christ cannot be supplemented with other divine agencies, for that would constitute a betrayal of the triumph of Christ. Christ, by His death and resurrection, has annulled the supplements. Christ alone is the exclusive basis of Christian life. The worship of other powers in addition to Christ manifests a religious anxiety and uncertainty on the part of Christians that contradicts the joyful thanksgiving, knowledge and wisdom of the Christian life (Col. 1: 15-20, 2: 6-23).[4]

Schleiermacher (1960) also related the Christian tradition to the modern world of secularism, science, and technology. The social situation in the world today is dominated by a culture strongly influenced by the Enlightenment. European culture and Christianity were fused to form "Christian" Europe. Fitzmyer, S.J. (1968) is a Roman Catholic Jesuit who advocated a Christocentric soteriology. He maintains that the use of *Kyrios* for Jesus in the early Church bestowed on him the ineffable name of *Yahweh* in its LXX form. In effect it suggests that Jesus is on a par with *Yahweh* himself. The equality is spelled out in detail in the hymn of Philippians 2: 6-11, the reason why the name given to Jesus is above every name is that it is *Yahweh's* own name, *Kyrios*. It is the early Church's way of expressing its faith in the divinity of Christ. Though it is predominantly a functional title, expressing Christ's dominion over men and his present vital influence in their lives and conduct, yet it also denotes an equality of Christ with the Father. The titles Father and Son, being relational words, suggest distinction and even subordination. But *Kyrios* ascribes both *Yahweh* and Jesus a dominion over creation and a right to the adoration of all creation.[5]

Jones (1968) is also Christocentric in his approach to theology, for he asserts that "Christ is the ultimate goal of the universe. The world, then, begins, continues, and ends in Christ. This gives the cosmic significance of Christ which is based on Colossians 1: 15-20."[6] And Stauffer (1964) is Christocentric; he states that "Jesus Christ has come, with all the authority of God. He issues a summons to His people. The *Ego* (I) alone validates His word. Christ is on earth the fully authorized representative and executor of God. All God's work is done through Jesus Christ. Christ is the Mediator of the whole world and the Mediator of revelation."[7] Alongside the absolute Subject God there comes a second Subject in a unique Thou-relationship, namely, that of the Son who is known by the Father alone and who alone can know the

Father. There is no knowledge of God except through the Son. The Christ of the New Testament replaces not only the wisdom (*Sophia)* but all the intermediaries of Jewish theology, uniting their office in one. All historical and cosmic lines intersect in His ego. He stands at the heart of the times and in the center between God and the world. "The Christological *ego* of the New Testament Gospels expresses the claim of Jesus to absoluteness. Jesus Christ is the Absolute, He is not relative."[8]

Oepke (1964) is an exponent of Christocentric Christology, for he reasons that" all mediations between God and human beings are through Jesus Christ. Christ is the Mediator of human beings' activities towards God."[9] Christ also mediates the actions of God to human beings. For example, Christ mediates in creation (Jn. 1:3, Col. 1:16), the revelation of salvation and reconciliation (Jn.1:17,3:17), miracles (Acts 2:22), and judgment (Rev. 2:16). God takes the initiative in all mediations through His action in Christ and thus makes all human judgments superfluous and excludes any intermediate authority. Kittel (1964) advocates for Christocentricism, for he says that the use of the term *logos* has an awareness that preaching of what has taken place in the person of Jesus is preaching of the Word and that reception of the Word implies faith in Jesus. Kittel states that the Epistle of St. Paul to the Colossians makes it clear that the content of the logos cannot be anything other than the fact of Christ. This fact of Christ is the Word of God, the Word which God has spoken to His saints. In Christ was enacted "Yes" (11 Cor.1:19). The Word "Yes" has taken place in Jesus Christ, which means that He is this Word "Yes" in His historical person. Christ is the Word "*Amen*" (Rev. 3:14). Christ took part in creation. In Jesus Christ, the Word of God has taken place in truth.[10]

The Word is the Christ event which has taken place in Jesus.

Rahner (1974), a distinguished Roman Catholic theologian, states that there is no conflict between Scripture and culture (tradition) since Scripture itself is the fundamental moment in the Church's tradition. Scripture is the Church's book. Rahner demonstrates that what we know from the Gospel is that God is generous, and His Grace is everywhere. His Grace is not confined to Christianity alone. Rahner pleaded for Christocentricism. God has a universal salvific will. Grace without which salvation is impossible should be offered to all human beings. He believed in the salvific value of other religions. He pleaded for religious pluralism. For Rahner, Christ's Grace cannot be confined to Christianity only, for God is greater than human beings and the Church. Adherents of other world religions are anonymous Christians. Here Rahner agrees with Snook (1986) and Panikkar (1981), who also advocate for an Anonymous Christ in all world religions. Panikkar pleaded for an Unknown Christ of Hinduism. For Rahner, there is a saving Grace within other world religions, but also this Grace is Christ's:

> Christ is the constitutive cause of salvation. Christ is the final cause of God's universal salvific will. Jesus Christ is the final Goal, the End-Product of the entire process of universal revelation and Grace. Christ is the Absolute Perfection and Guarantee of God's love and Grace, the greatest support and source of confidence for committing oneself to God. Christ is the final cause of Salvation.[11]

Pannenberg (1970) states that the historical foundation of Jesus is the resurrection. For him, the resurrection is historical and is a unique event with no parallel in history. He did not want to get rid of the historical basis on which his theology was based. Theology is not like mathematics. The truth of Christianity and theology cannot be justified independent of history. Christian and theological truths are based on history. Pannenberg and Moltmann (1988) argue for a Christocentric Christology. They argue that any claim for superiority or normativity in Christian revelation cannot stand until it is verified through a dialogue with the revelation found in other world religions. Both Pannenberg and Moltmann explain that Jesus Christ is the End (the *Eschaton*). They disagreed with Barth. They argue that no theologian can claim to have knowledge of Jesus Christ from revelation. Pannenburg states that the category of eschatology is an essential part of the structure of Christian faith and should play a major role in any discussion of revelation. Eschatology is not one element of Christianity, but is the medium of Christian faith as such. The eschatology cannot really be only a part of Christian doctrine. Rather, the eschatological outlook is characteristic of all Christian proclamations, of every Christian existence and of the whole Church. Christian hope is based on the eschatological events. The message of Jesus Christ and the whole Christian faith have an eschatological core. Jesus Christ is the only eschatological hope. The eschatological hope is talk of the Kingdom of God here and now and also in the future. Jesus has the message of the eschatology, which is the Kingdom of God as the basic starting point for any Christology or doctrine of salvation (soteriology).[12]

Pannenberg (1970) and Moltmann attest to the transformation and renewal of history represented by the idea of judgment. Both believe the resurrection is historical. In history there is a forward-looking event. The End is Jesus Christ. For Christians all things will end in Christ. The resurrection event has meaning and is the disclosure of the end. Jesus Christ is the beginning and the end, the Alpha and the Omega (Rev.1: 8, 21: 6, 23: 13). Moltmann (1988) speaks of the future as a new paradigm of transcendence. The future can be a paradigm of transcendence only by bringing into the present something qualitatively new. That something qualitatively new is Jesus Christ. Jesus Christ is the Transcended Future who brings about revolutionary transformations in human life. He destroys evil and brings about good to all who believe in Him as the End (*Eschaton)*.[13]

For Pannenberg the starting point of theology is the historical Jesus. He appealed not to the enlightenment but to Jesus Christ who is the End, the *Eschaton*. What is there in Scripture that gives meaning to history? In Scripture, history is apocalyptic. One looks at the end. Pannenberg believes in the Scriptural view of history. The meaning of history should be seen at the end. History by itself is meaningless, but if one's world view is apocalyptic, history is meaningful. Only if one's view of history is apocalyptic can one overcome hopelessness. W. Kasper (1976) agrees with Pannenberg and Moltmann, for he also argues for Christocentricism, and he also says that Jesus Christ is the Messiah anointed of the Spirit, the Saviour of the world, and the eschatological fulfillment of history. For Kasper, the basis and meaning of the Church is Jesus Christ. He states thatt he many Churches and communities and groups within the Church, however much they differ among themselves, all agree on one thing: their claim to represent Jesus Christ—His Word and work. Jesus Christ is the starting point and centre of Christianity. "Jesus is the Christ" is the basic statement of Christian belief, and Christology is no more than the conscientious elucidation of that proposition. When we say that Jesus is the Christ, we maintain that this unique, irreplaceable Jesus of Nazareth is at one and the same time the Christ sent by God.[14]

Jesus Christ is the only mediator between God and human beings.

Cobb (1962, 1975) and Cobb Jr. (1983) advocate for Christocentricism. Christ is at the centre of all world religions. Cobb Jr. claims that when Christianity moved into the Greek world, it was Hellenized. If Christianity can be Hellenized, it can also be Africanized, Europeanized, Americanized, or Asianized. There can be African, Shona, American, Canadian, Asian, European, and Australian Christians. Cobb states that the human predicament is chaos and disorder. Human beings need creative transformation. A process theologian, he claims that creation is not pre-determined and static. It is dynamic. Chaos and disorder were brought by human beings because they misused their freedom. For Cobb, salvation means turning people away from destruction and turning them to the direction God wants the world to move. Cobb establishes that Christian faith is really faith in Jesus Christ.[15] The meaning of Christ is to call human beings from destruction to creative transformation. Christ calls human beings from destruction to a life full of peace and prosperity. But human beings have the freedom to frustrate that call. God directs the world but does not control it. God's call does not destroy the freedom of human beings. Cobb testifies that Christ is the Logos. He propounds a Logos Christology. God became flesh. Jesus releases God's power for salvation. Christ is the enfleshed principal of all creation, which has been there from the beginning. Christ is the way God orders the world. When people have faith in Christ, they intensify God's purpose in their own lives.

Schillebeeckx (1977, 1983) has a hermeneutical approach to Christology. He contends that one cannot know exactly the scientific history of Jesus, but there are some things about Jesus we can know today. For example, Jesus was a founder of a new movement which was a mass movement. This is an historical fact. The problem is how to interpret the historical material faithfully and honestly. What does the historical material mean to us today? There are philosophical, political, soteriological, and theological interpretations about Jesus today. A diversity of interpretations about Jesus existed from the beginning, and there is still a wide diversity of interpretations today. Jesus is interpreted differently in South Africa, Zimbabwe, Nigeria, Britain, America, Russia, China, Japan, Australia, and elsewhere. Not all interpretations can be sustained. So there is an element of judging the different interpretations. The hermeneutical approach of Schillebeeckx argues the New Testament texts are historical. Therefore, how does one interpret them in a way which is honest? Schillebeeckx maintains that there is something historical about Jesus. It is historical that Jesus associated with the poor, got a lot of moral and material support from the outcasts of society, had religious and social controversies with the Pharisees on interpreting the Scriptures, and was involved in religious controversies. Schillebeeckx asserts that the human predicament is isolation—broken relationships. He reasons that any view of salvation must co-ordinate the social, economic, political, and psychological relationships. For Schillebeeckx, theology is a discipline of relationships. Schillebeeckx believes that "Jesus Christ is the Reconciler in all human relationships. Jesus Christ is the focal point in all good human relationships."[16] This is a social and natural view of Christology. Schillebeeckx's Christology changes the narrow view of reconciliation to a wider view of reconciliation. Any view of Christ which excludes nature is inadequate. For example, the building of Lake

Kariba on the Zambezi river on the border of Zambia and Zimbabwe is a work of reconciliation and is also a religious project and not an economic project only. Human beings also survive because of nature.

Hick (1985) calls for a Copernican revolution in theology. For Hick, all world religions are centered on God. He pleaded for theocentricism. He explains that "religion should move from Christocentric to theocentric. All religions are based and centred on God and not on Jesus Christ. Christ is not the centre of the world but God is the centre of the world."[17] For Hick, Christians should continue to adhere to Christ as their unique Savior without having to insist that He is necessarily unique or normative for others. According to Hick, by understanding the incarnation as a myth, Christians can declare that God is truly to be encountered in Jesus, but not only in Jesus. Panikkar (1981), Samartha (1991), Knitter (1985), Krieger (1991) and Bosch (1991) also advocate theocentricism. Panikkar insists on the importance of diversity among religions, for he argues that "recognizing the presence of God in other religions is equivalent to proclaiming the presence of Christ in them, for in him all things subsist."[18] Panikkar challenged the definitive normativity of Christ. He has a non-normative Christology by making distinctions between the universal *Logos* or Christ and the historical Jesus. With Rahner and Cobb, Panikkar affirms that the *Logos* or Christ, eternal and universal, has been incarnated in Jesus of Nazareth.

For all liberation theologians—for example Moltmann (1984), Fiorenza (1983), Gutierrez (1974), Muguez Bonino (1975), Sobrino (1978), Segundo (1976), and Cone (1969, 1979, 1986)—the lens and litmus test for all Christologists is praxis. Every Christology should be examined using the lens and litmus test of praxis to see how it is building up the Kingdom of God. For Gutierrez, the subject of liberation theology is not theology but liberation. All liberation theologians have a theocentric Christology because liberation comes through many different figures, not only through Jesus Christ. Jesus Christ is not the only Liberator or Savior. Shona ancestors are also liberators and saviors. Gutierrez states that

For liberation theology, normative claims about Jesus are not attainable. The only thing necessary for a Christian to carry on the job of theology is commitment to the Kingdom of God's vision of liberating redemptive action. Christians, on the basis of their praxis, know that the vision and power of Jesus of Nazareth is a means for liberation from injustice and oppression, that it is an effective, hope-filled, universally meaningful way of bringing about God's Kingdom.[19]

Liberation Christology allows, even requires, that Christians recognize the possibility of other liberators and other incarnations.

If liberating praxis is the foundation and norm for authentic divine revelation and truth, then Christians must be open to the possibility that in their dialogue with other world religions, they may encounter religious figures—for example Shona ancestors—whose vision offers a liberating praxis and promise of the kingdom equal to that of Jesus. In view of their fruits of praxis, such saviors as African ancestors have to be recognized and affirmed. The existence of such saviors would in no way have to jeopardize the universal relevance of Jesus' vision or lessen one's commitment to it. "Anyone who is not against us is with us" (Mk. 9:40). I am not going to leave these non-African scholars out. I know what they wrote and what they talked about. Schreiter is an American who wrote about African views and African Traditional Religion (ATR). A non-African knows and can argue and write about issues involving ATR.

My thrust is African Christology, theology, and ATR. I am going to pick up African Christologians and some non-African theologians and scholars on ATR and leave others out. On African and Shona ancestors, I refer to Bourdillion (1987, 1993); he argues that "the traditional Shona concept of *Mwari* is that He is not up there, where He sits, but is in constant touch with the people through the ancestors."[20] Chigwedere (1980) mentions that "Tovera and Sororenzou are both Shona gods and at the same time Shona ancestors."[21] For Chigwedere, the traditional Shona regard *Mwari* as the highest peak imaginable in the hierarchy of ancestors. Beach's view (1980) is that "the traditional Shona High God (*Mwari)* is a combination of sky-God and ancestral spirits."[22] Daneel (1970) argues for the *Mwari* cult in Zimbabwe. Mutswairo (1983) says that *Mwari* is the Ancestor God for the traditional Shona people. Shona ancestors are the mediators between *Mwari* and the traditional Shona people. The spirit of *Mwari* possesses the diviners (*n'angas*): ancestral spirit mediums (*masvikiros*), tribal ancestral spirit mediums (*mhondoros-midzimu mikuru*), family ancestral spirit mediums (*midzimu yepamusha),* and alien spirits (*mashave*), but not the avenging spirits (*ngozi*). The *ngozi* are the embodiment of the devil, according to Chavhunduka.

On the role of African ancestors, I rely on Pobee (1979) who says that "ancestors, in theory at any rate, operate *loco Dei* and *pro Deo*, but in practice, ancestors are treated as ends in themselves, as real givers of good things in life."[23] According to Kirwen (1987), the ancestors are the judges of all things done by the traditional Africans. Every traditional African knows that within a reasonable time the ancestors will intervene and right the evil done. Mbiti (1969) euphemistically calls the African ancestors "the living dead". The authors who wrote about the roles of Shona ancestors and African ancestors are all of the opinion that African ancestors are at the centre of ATR and play a salvific role in ATR, and without the African ancestors there is no ATR.

On USPG, I drew on the invaluable works of Pascoe (1900), Dewey (1975), Thompson (1951), and Walls (1977) who are in total agreement that the USPG was not formed primarily to spearhead and bless British colonialism but to meet the spiritual needs of the British settlers in the British colonies and also to be involved in mission (evangelism) among the indigenous people of the British colonies. Dewey states that "Jesus Christ is at the centre of USPG missionary activities. For the USPG missionaries Christianity is the only religion, African ancestors are irrelevant and Jesus Christ is the only mediator between God and mankind."[24] On USPG missionary attitudes against Shona ancestors (ATR), I used Church documents and Commission Reports of the Anglican Diocese of Harare (1891-1995); see

Appendices 2 and 3. I also draw on the work of Knight-Bruce (1895), Paget (1926), Evans (1945), Broedrick (1953), Peaden (1970), Steere (1973) and Farrant (1974). All these authors highlighted the fact that there were tensions and antagonisms between USPG Christianity in Zimbabwe and Shona ancestors (ATR). The USPG missionaries in Zimbabwe, in conformity with the USPG missiology, condemned and rejected Shona ancestors. This motivated me to develop an inculturated African Christology for Zimbabwe in particular and the rest of the world in general.

I am interested in theology, ecclesiology, and Christology as propounded by Dupuis (1991) and Samartha (1991), but I am very much interested in ATR, African Christian theologies, ecclesiologies, Christologies, and soteriologies as propounded by the various African Christian theologians and ATR scholars. For example, I am indebted to the works of Dickson (1969, 1975), Kato (1974, 1975, 1976), Pobee (1979, 1992), Tieonou (1982), Nyamiti (1984, 1989), Mugambi (1989), Magesa (1989), Bediako (1990, 1992, 1995), Wachege (1992), and Bujo (1992). I am also very interested in Zimbabwe African Christian theologians and ATR scholars such as Banana (1980, 1991, 1996), Moyo (1983), Muzorewa (1990), and Bakare (1994, 1996, 1998). These authors are culturally, deeply rooted in African ancestors (ATR). At one time in their lives they either practiced ATR or directly came into contact with ATR, and benefitted from the ministry of ancestors, or lived among the traditional Africans who practiced and venerated African ancestors. They wrote about African ancestors because they were born into ATR and are Christians. They also wrote Christology in an African context, pleading for the appropriation and inculturation of African traditional religious beliefs and practices into the Christian Gospel. African Christian theologians give Jesus Christ different images (faces)—for example Ancestor, Elder Brother, Ideal Elder, Chief, Master of Initiation, Healer, King, Prince, Priest, and Liberator—which are all embodied in the African ancestor concept. They are trying to incarnate Jesus Christ into ATR and to develop an inculturated African Christian theology which remains basically Christian—that is, salvific, particular, and worldwide without dissolving Christianity into ATR. The African Christian theologians are developing inculturated Christologies and soteriologies which are appealing to the African Christians. They are developing theologies which are making Africans truly Christians and truly Africans at the same time without compromising their Africanness which includes their ancestors. They are giving Jesus Christ African faces (images) in order to clarify the soteriological functions of Jesus Christ among the Africans. They are trying to integrate African ancestors and Christianity. The only two exceptions are Kato and Tienou who condemn and reject African ancestors and ATR outright.[25]

In this book I am contributing to the Christological, missiological, and soteriological debate into which American, European, Third World, and African Christian theologians are involved, for example Barth, Tillich, Pannenberg, Hick, Cobb, Schillebeeckx, Moltmann, Kriegr, Panikkar, Snook, Rahner, Kasper, Kittel, Pobee, and Nyamiti, just to mention a few. In my theological and Christological assessment and analysis in chapter 6, I followed Niebuhr (1951), who delineated Christ against culture, Christ of culture, Christ above culture, Christ and culture in paradox, and Christ the transformer of culture as the starting point. The USPG missionaries seem to use European theology, ecclesiology, Christology, missiology, and soteriology, which they seem to regard as at all times final.

I am interested in rethinking and rewriting Christology in both the African and Zimbabwean context, for I am part of a search of African and Zimbabwean theologians especially in the Anglican Church in Zimbabwe. I intend to search for a new Christology which challenges African, Asian, European, and American Christian theologians. The Christological and soteriological problems have always been at the heart of Christian theology. They remain so today. Dupuis (1991) and Samartha (1991) are of the opinion that, as Samartha states, "an ecclesiocentric soteriological position is too narrow a perspective to account for the presence of God and of His saving grace outside the Church. A theocentric soteriological position is intrinsic in the Christocentric itself; hence the two should not be construed as distinct paradigms."[26] Dupuis agrees with Samartha, for they both believe that ecclesiocentricism, Christocentricism, pneumatocentricism, and theocentricism are not exclusive of each other. The four cannot be theologically separated, but in practice they can be separated. They are not exclusive, for Jesus Christ, who is God (Jn. 20:28), who with the Holy Spirit, is greater than the Church. These authors are relevant to my topic in that they do not plead for exclusive world religions but advocate inclusive world religions, for example ATR with Jesus Christ, the Son of God, at the centre. Jesus Christ, the Greatest Ancestor par excellence, is in every world religion, ATR included. Hence there is a relation between Christianity and other world religions. Samarth and Dupuis also say that the task confronting theology, missiology, Christology, and soteriology lies in the appropriation, integration, inculturation, and transformation of the many seemingly conflicting revelations of God in the different world religions.

On contextual Christian liturgy, I draw on Price and Weil (1979), who plead for a contextual Christian worship. I also advocate an inculturated practical liturgy and ethics in the Anglican Church in Zimbabwe which are salvific, particular, and worldwide. Non-African Christologies help me to shape my study and analysis in that they give Jesus Christ different faces. For example, Barth and Kittel give Jesus Christ the image of the Word or Revelation of God. E. Stauffer, Oepke, and Kasper give the image of Mediator of the whole world. Rahner, Cobb, and Panikkar give Jesus the image of *Logos*. Pannenberg and Moltmann give Jesus the image of the End (The *Eschaton*). Schillebeeckx gives Jesus the image of Reconciler. All liberation theologians give Jesus Christ the image of Liberator. African Christologians also give Jesus Christ different faces, just as non-African theologians do.

I am giving Jesus Christ an image of the *Mudzimu Mukuru* par excellence. I am doing exactly what has been done by non-African and African theologians and Christian scholars but in a different context so as to sharpen my Christological analysis. Both non-African and African Christian scholars and theologians are exponents of ecclesiocentric and theocentric soteriologies. Shona Anglicans in

Zimbabwe fit very well into all these Christological paradigms. For the Shona Anglicans in Zimbabwe, there are no theological distinctions but only practical distinctions among all these Christological paradigms. This is very helpful in shaping my thesis. I am not leaning to any one theological or Christological school of thought. I combine them all in my *Mudzimu Mukuru* par excellence Christology in order to produce a synthesis. The methodologies of African Christian scholars and theologians are relevant to my study. I am attracted to them, for I share an African cultural, religious (ATR), economic, social, and political experience with them.

This book is divided into four parts. After this introduction, part one provides the historical background of ATR and USPG (chapters 1 and 2). Part two analyzes ATR and USPG Christianity and their different approaches to salvation (chapters 3 and 4). Part three deals with evaluation and integration of both approaches into the *Mudzimu Mukuru* par excellence Christology (chapters 5 and 6). Part four looks into the applications of the *Mudzimu Mukuru* par excellence Christology (chapter 7).

# CHAPTER 1

## *God the Center of African Traditional Religion and Shona Ancestorhood*

The aim of this chapter is to investigate whether African traditional ancestorhood is deeply integrated into ATR and in traditional Shona social life. It also aims to investigate whether Shona traditional ancestorhood was relevant to the traditional Shona in the past and is still relevant to the Shona people in Zimbabwe today and in the future. This chapter also investigates the types of soteriologies which were advocated by the traditional Shona people who practiced ATR. I am going to develop a thesis that ATR is ancestorcentric, pneumatocentric, and theocentric, which will help me to develop my inculturated transformative Trinitarian *Mudzimu Mukuru* par excellence Christology which leads Zimbabwean Christians to be involved in the process of appropriation and inculturation and to follow pneumatocentric and theocentric paths. Ancestorcentric, theocentric, and pneumatocentric aspects help me elucidate my overall thesis of developing a *Mudzimu Mukuru* par excellence Christology.

In this chapter I also elucidate my own understanding of Shona traditional culture, practices, and beliefs (ATR), which in many cases are transparent to me. I present traditional Shona myths as they are understood by me, for I am familiar with them. I find support for my understanding of the material I have used. The limitations are that ATR varies from one region to another. One example is in the way God (*Mwari*) is perceived. In Northern Zimbabwe, the ancestor cult is emphasized, whereas in the South the *Mwari* cult is emphasized. Another variation is in the traditional ritual of the bringing-back-home (*kurova guva/ chenura*) ceremony, which transforms a deceased traditional Shona adult into an ancestor. This varies within families, villages, ethnic groups, and regions (see Tabona Shoko, "Health and Well Being: A Phenomenological Quest for the Essence of the Karanga Religion, Dissertation." Harare: University of Zimbabwe, 1993; and Paul Henry Gundani, "The Second Vatican Council and Beyond: A Study of The Transformation Process, Power Transfer And Sharing in The Roman Catholic Church in Zimbabwe (1965-1985), Dissertation." Harare: University of Zimbabwe, 1994).

This chapter also helps me to find a synthesis between ATR and USPG Christianity. Hence this chapter helps me to develop an inculturated transformative Trinitarian *Mudzimu Mukuru* par excellence Christology. I am not going to write in detail about ATR among the traditional Shona people of Zimbabwe, for that was done very well by other scholars—for example, M.L. Daneel in *God of the Matopo Hills* (Mouton: The Hague, 1970); M. F. C. Bourdillon in *The Shona People* (Gweru, Mambo Press, 1973) and in *Where are the Ancestors? Changing Culture in Zimbabwe* (1993); S. M. Mutswairo in *Mapondera: The Soldier of Zimbabwe* (Harare: Longman Zimbabwe Ltd, 1983); and Tabona Shoko (1993) and Paul Henry Gundani (1994).

## WARNING AGAINST FOSSIL SHONA TRADITIONAL RELIGION

A traditional Shona person of 1890, before the coming of the USPG missionaries into Zimbabwe, was very different from a Shona person of 2010. The reason is that traditional Shona culture—and ATR—was dynamic. Even now it is not completely static because of science, technology, and intercultural activities with other peoples of different nationalities and cultures. We should ask how indigenous is indigenous, and how traditional is traditional? This warns us against fossil traditional Shona culture and fossil Shona traditional religion. I wish to hold the past, present, and future Shona culture together by saying that the traditional Shona view of time is not linear but cyclic.

How have the traditional Shona people changed in both culture and religion since 1890, lest I waste time developing a *Mudzimu Mukuru* par excellence Christology for thc Christianity in Zimbabwe of 1890, which no longer exists? My Christology should answer the existential problems faced by an African Christian of 2010 and beyond. Christology emerges from, among other things, a historic community and a people's experiences. The traditional Shona people are continuously growing in stature mentally, economically, politically, socially, technologically, culturally, and religiously.

## TRADITIONAL SHONA WORLD-VIEW

The traditional Shona world-view is basically pneumatocentric, ancestorcentric, and theocentric. *Mwari* and Shona ancestors, who are spiritual beings, are at the center. There is a holistic approach to everything in life. Trees, mountains, rocks, animals, rivers, flowers, pools, grass, and people are holy and are possessed by spirits. ATR is a way of life. It is African traditional culture. One cannot separate ATR and African culture. They are one and the same thing. The state is theocratic: the chief is the chief justice, chief administrator, and the religious leader. There is no traditional Shona atheist, for every person is born an African traditionalist; that is, born into ATR. There is no conversion into ATR. As far as membership of ATR is concerned, it is based on an all-or-nothing rule. The traditional Shona world-view is full of spirits—some good and some evil.

In Shona traditional religion, what are the connections among God *(Mwari),* ethnic/regional/territorial spirits (*mhondoro),* family ancestral spirits (*midzimu yepamusha*) and alien spirits (*mashave*)? Also, what are the connections among pneumatocentricism, theocentricism, and ancestorcentricism? There is a center. Ancestors are the center. Ancestors, who manifest themselves as spiritual beings, possess some traditional Shona people and make them their pockets (*homwe*). Pneumatocentricism is at a very low level of ancestors (*midzimu*) and alien spirits (*mashave*). The spirit of God (*Mwari)* does not possess any ordinary traditional Shona person. The spirit of *Mwari* possesses only the high priests of *Mwari*, who dwell at Matopos/ Matonjeni/Njelele. The voice of *Mwari* speaks through his possessed high spirits at Matonjeni. This is why messengers, when there is a drought or a national disaster, are sent to Matonjeni by their chiefs to consult *Mwari*, who speaks at Matonjeni through his high priests only. The spirit of *Mwari* does not possess family ancestors *(midzimu yepamusha)*, ancestral spiritual mediums (*masvikiro*), and ethnic or regional spirit mediums (*mhondoro*), who are the junior gods. These are possessed by ancestral spirits or alien spirits only.

The concept of the Trinity is not there in ATR. It is foreign. The name of *Mwari* is not invoked when family ancestors (*midzimu yepamusha*), territorial ancestors *(mhondoro*, the junior gods), and alien spirits *(mashave*) are propitiated. There is no traditional Shona ritual where the name of *Mwari* is directly invoked except the rain-making ceremony *(mukweverera)*, where the rain-making alien spirits (*majukwa*) are invoked. The *Jukwa* spirit is related to *Mwari* in the rain-making ceremony (*mukweverera)*. The spirits are associated with the pool totems, *Chirorodziva* and *Dzivaguru*. They are also associated with fertility, reproduction, and procreation. The *mukweverera* ritual is also associated with *Dzivaguru* and *Chirorodziva*—hence associated with fertility and procreation. If the *mukweverera* is not efficacious—for example, if rain does not come—a delegation is sent by a traditional chief to Matonjeni to consult *Mwari*, who speaks through his high priests who are permanently based at Matonjeni.

*Mhondoro* are associated with particular regions or chiefdoms. At the family level, there are family ancestral spirits (*mudzimu yepamusha*). These are ordinary *midzimu*, not chieftainships. No reference is made to God (*Mwari)* when these are venerated/ propitiated and worshipped (*kunamatwa/kuteurwa*). Unlike Christianity, the traditional Shona people, as families, cannot worship *Mwari* individually or directly, but do so as a community through the intermediation of ancestors. God is only invoked directly at national or ethnic/regional rituals—for example at the *mukweverera* ceremony by the *majukwa*. The territorial or regional spirits (*mhondoro*) have reference to *Mwari*.

ATR is full of relevance to the lives of traditional Shona people. Traditional Shona thought is interested in a lived, reflective world-view which affects day-to-day life directly. A traditional Shona person is interested in issues and problems which affect his or her existence only. ATR cannot perceive of a God *(Mwari*) who is not a solution to human existential problems. The concept of *Mwari* is that He must be involved in day-to-day lives through the intermediation of the ancestors. This view is similar to that of the Luo tribe in Tanzania, which was observed by M. C. Kirwen; he explained that "our God is not remote from humanity. God created the lesser deities, the sun, the *Iryoba*, and the moon, *Nyamanga*, to watch over and care for humanity.... The surety of the rising sun by day and the moon by night are the cornerstone reminders of the warm and caring presence of *Kimet.*"[1] The traditional Shona concept of *Mwari* is that He is not up there, where He sits and shows no interest in people, but He is in constant touch with the people through ancestors. *Mwari* is the Creator and Sustainer of the universe. In this created universe, human beings are anthropocentric; that is, they are at the center. Other creatures were created for the sake of human beings. M. F. C. Bourdillion asserts that the Shona people believe in a High God...*Mwari* is now the most common name for the High God....Although *Mwari* is known under different names, He is believed to be God of all men....He is considered to have made the white people as well as the black. *Mwari* is far removed from family spirit elders who are intimately concerned with the private affairs of their descendants. The High God is too remote and his interests are too broad for Him to concern Himself with private individuals and their problems.[2]

But *Mwari* is not remote. He is present among the traditional Shona people through the ancestors. *Mwari* is the Supreme authority above the ancestors to whom He has delegated most of His functions and duties. The ancestors are directly involved in the day-to-day aspects of life. *Mwari's* remoteness does not mean that He is not concerned. He works through the ancestors. *Mwari* is in the ancestors, and the ancestors are in *Mwari*. *Mwari* concerns Himself with the daily affairs of the people through the ancestors. Bourdillion applied to *Mwari* the term "remote high God" in contrast to Daneel and Abraham, who state that *Mwari* was far from being *Deus otiosus* or *Deus remotus.*[3] Abraham reasons that *Mwari* was not totally lost sight of. In the composite picture of Shona traditional religion He did become the Personal Being beyond and above the hierarchies of the ancestral spirits, accessible to man only through the mediation of the senior regional ancestors (*mhondoro-midzimu mikuru*), or through His messengers who came from afar to the Matopos shrines to hear *Mwari's* pronouncements about the community of man. To the individual who in everyday life had to depend on his friendly ancestors for his well being, this God of fertility was the transcendent being who spoke far off at Matonjeni.... Private prayers were directed to family ancestors (*midzimu yepamusha),* and these judged whether they could give direct solace or whether such petitions should be forwarded to the senior territorial spirits and ultimately to *Mwari. Mwari* entered the routine life of the ethnic community mainly by way of oath and invocation.[4]

Daneel maintains that, just as senior regional spirits could be approached through the *masvikiro,* so *Mwari* could eventually be consulted at His shrines.[5]

## THE *MWARI* CULT IN SOUTHERN ZIMBABWE

According to T. O. Ranger, before the late 19th century the *Mwari* cult was central and associated with the Southern Zimbabwe Shona people only. This is Ranger's Bantu Migration Theory. Ranger contends that the first people to settle in Southern Zimbabwe were the Dziva people, whose totem *(mutupo)* is the pool *(dziva)* or the

Zimbabwe fish eagle (*shiri yehungwe*), or fish (*hove*), or the Save river which is associated with the pool. Ranger claims that *Mwari* is the name used for the oracular High God of the Matopo Hills.[6] The *Mwari* cult is associated with the fertility of the land, animals, and human beings. The *Mwari* cult is associated with the *chinamwali* fertility rite of the Cewa tribe in Malawi. *Mwari* is referred to as an unmarried young woman *(mhandara)*, which points to a female goddess. Van der Merwe reported that, in Manicaland, he was told that words like *Mwari* and *mhandara* (a young girl who has reached the age of puberty) are used interchangeably.[7] *Mwari* is associated with the reproductive cycle and with agricultural feasts—for example, the feast-of-the-first-fruits *(kurumagore),* which is presided over by the chief *(ishe/ mambo/ changamire)* who represents the ancestors of the land *(mhondoro).* The feast-of-the-first-fruits is a festival where every adult traditional Shona person who owns a field *(munda)* brings in every ripe first fruit from his or her field to be consecrated by the chief to the ancestors and then the fruits are consumed after the consecration ceremony. After the ceremony the traditional Shona people are then allowed to go and eat the ripened crops from their fields.

In Southern Zimbabwe, there are sub-cults in each region. For example, the nature fertility cult called Fruit *(Karuva)* which is found in Southern Manicaland Province in Chief Musikavanhu's and Chief Mutema's areas. The Rassa cult is in the Masvingo area in Chief Gutu's area; Makumbi is the chief priestess of that cult. The Grass *(Vuhwa)* cult is found in the Mberengwa area. The Ntabazikamambo, Dula, and Njelele cults are found in the Kalanga area. *Dula* in Kalanga and *Dura* in Shona are granaries where harvested crops are stored. These cults are associated with harvest, hence fertility. Sub-cults of different regions are associated with Umtonjeni (Matonjeni), where the *Mwari* cult is currently centered. *Umtonjeni* means a place where you fetch water. The Karanga call the place Matonjeni (*Mahwe Adziva*), meaning a rocky place where there are pools *(madziva)* of water. H. von Sicard argued that the idea of the *Mwari* High God had come from the Kalanga area after the period of initiation or fertility rite religion, and in purifying opposition to it.[8] The Big Pool *(Dzivaguru)* cult is found in

Mashonaland West Province among the Korekore people at Chinhoyi Caves (*Chirorodziva*), chief Zvimba's area. The Chinhoyi Caves (*Chirorodziva*) are connected to the rain-making (*majukwa)* spirits and are associated with pools *(madziva)*. They are also related to the *Mwari* cult centered at Matonjeni.

In Southern Zimbabwe, chiefs work very closely with related spirit mediums (*masvikiro/ mbonga*). The *masvikiro* advise the chiefs. Every traditional Shona chief, in times of regional disasters or calamities such as droughts, plagues, and pestilences, sends messengers (*vatumwa/ manyusa)* who accompany the spirit mediums (*masvikiro)* to consult *Mwari* at Matonjeni. Every chief in Southern Zimbabwe collects finger-millet (*zviyo/rukweza/rapoko*) from every household every year. The *zviyo* can be harvested from a community field called *zunde ramambo*. The harvest from the *zunde ramambo* is also used each year to feed the poor in the community. The *rapoko* is sold, and the money is sent to Matonjeni, to the high priests and priestesses of *Mwari* by the messengers who are accompanied by the *masvikiro*. The messengers to the Mwari cult at Matonjeni are the chief's representatives. The gifts (collections) from the people, and the *zviyo* from *zunde ramambo*, are associated with the rain-making (*mutoro/ mukweverera*) ceremony. The chief and the spirit mediums (*masvikiro)* are central in the *mukweverera* ceremony.

At Matonjeni, messengers from the different regions, the chiefs, and the *masvikiro/ mbonga* with their gifts meet together and are addressed by the high priests and priestesses of *Mwari*. The voice of *Mwari* addresses all the messengers and spirit mediums from the different chiefs and regions. Each region has access to Matonjeni as the center of *Mwari*. In Southern Zimbabwe, there are family ancestral spirits (*midzimu yepamusha/ homwe*) at the family level, which is the lowest level. Next are the senior territorial spirits (*makombwe/ masvikiro)* which are not related to the chief. Next is *Mwari* (God) at the apex. There are no territorial/regional spirit mediums (*mhondoro)* in Southern Zimbabwe, only *makombwe/ masvikiro* and priests and priestesses of *Mwari*. The *Mwari* cult is very strong in Southern

Zimbabwe but not in Northern Zimbabwe, which is dominated by the *mhondoro* cult.

## THE ANCESTOR-TERRITORIAL/REGIONAL (*MHONDORO*) CULT IN NORTHERN ZIMBABWE

In Northern Zimbabwe, especially among the Zezuru ethnic group, there is a very strong emphasis on the territorial/ethnic/regional (*mhondoro)* ancestor cult and not on the *Mwari* cult. There is no clear concept of *Mwari.* The territorial spirit (*mhondoro*) is related to, attached to, and associated with, the chief's family. There is a pyramidal hierarchy of ancestors according to their seniority. At the lowest level is the family spirit medium (*midzimu yepamusha*). Next is the territorial spirit medium (*mhondoro).* The most senior ancestors are at the apex. The *mhondoro* cult is related to the Chaminuka cult. Chaminuka is one of the great Shona ancestors. Chaminuka was a miracle worker. It is believed that, as the Shona crossed the Zambezi River from the land of tall grass (*Guruuswa*) in East Africa, they heard a voice (*izwi).* It was an apotheosis (an elevation to a divine status or deification). Fortune reports that Chief Chirau (Shava Mwendamberi) of Zvimba argues that his ethnic group was guided and protected by *Mwari. Mwari* was a Voice (*Izwi/ Shoko*) which was heard but the speaker was never seen.... Chief Samuriwo (Moyo Wakaipa) of Marandellas (Marondera) asserted that the great ancestral spirit of his founding father which accompanied them on their journey from Guruuswa was *Mwari* of the Rozvi. The Spirit spoke its commands and was obeyed. All the people in this country were ruled by the Rozvi and, through them, by *Mwari.*[9]

The voice was that of Chaminuka, who was regarded as a god.

I regard the so-called Matabele war of 1893-94 as the first war of liberation in Zimbabwe (Chimurenga I). After the demise of the Rozvi Empire, during the second war of liberation (Chimurenga II, 1896-97) the process of nationalizing the *Mwari* cult began during the time of

Nehanda and Kaguvi. *Mwari* became a national Zimbabwean cult. Northern Zimbabwe was incorporated into the *Mwari* cult based at Matonjeni. All the Shona ancestors became junior gods. In Southern Zimbabwe, the *masvikiro* are not related to the chief and are independent of the chief, but they work with the chief. In Northern Zimbabwe the *mhondoro* are the ancestors of the chiefs. What then is the connection between God (*Mwari*), territorial spirits (*mhondoro*), family ancestral spirits (*midzimu yepamusha)* and alien spirits (*mashave)*? Also, what is the connection between pneumatocentricism, theocentricism, and ancestorcentricism? Shona ancestors connect them all together. In the pyramidal hierarchy of ancestors, ancestors manifest themselves as spiritual beings and make people their pockets (*homwe)*. At the family level, there are family ancestral spirits (*midzimu yepamusha)*. These are ordinary *midzimu*, not chieftainships. No reference is made to God (*Mwari)* when these are venerated or worshipped. *Mhondoro* are associated with particular regions or chiefdoms and have reference to *Mwari*.

As far as pneumatocentricism is concerned, one is speaking about God *(Mwari*) who is a Spiritual Being. This is not at the family level. Chigwedere, an ancestral spirit medium (*svikiro*), former government Education Minister and former Provincial Governor, argues that the next personality to be remembered—somewhat more clearly than Mambiri of the Mbire people—is Tovera. This name is well known to many branches of the Mbire family in this country but they are not sure whether he is *Mwari* or an ancestor. This emerged clearly at a meeting of the Shona Cultural Association held at the Methodist Hall in Remembrance Drive in the Township of Mbare in Harare. A Church Minister was asked by the chairman to say a short prayer before the proceedings. The priest directed the prayers to Tovera. One wonders whether the Minister appealed to Tovera as God or as ancestor. Tovera is regarded as the Shona High God or God of Matopos. Tovera is treated as God but he is an ancestor of the Mbire family. My impression was that he thought of Tovera as the original Shona name for God. Certainly Tovera is deified in this country, but I must state categorically that he is an ancestor and not God in the true sense of the word.[10]

Tovera is a junior god for the Mbire people, whose totemic animal is baboon/monkey (*gudo/tsoko/shoko*). Hence, Shona ancestors are at times regarded as gods, for the Shona have a saying: your God is your ancestors (*Mwari wako ndiye midzimu yako*). The traditional Shona people believe that they are surrounded by a host of ancestors.

*Mwari* is not confined to one locality but is omnipresent, omniscient, and omnipotent. *Mwari* existed before all creation and is all powerful, blessing or destroying both good and bad. *Mwari* is Spirit and is closely related to other spirits, such as ancestors and other spiritual forces. *Mwari* is concerned with individual and family affairs through the family ancestors (*midzimu yepamusha*) and tribal ancestors (*mhondoro/ midzimu mikuru*). *Mwari* is also concerned with national issues, such as droughts, wars, rain, epidemics, and earthquakes, through the *midzimu mikuru.* Ancestral spirits (*midzimu yepamusha/masvikiro*), alien spirits (*mashave*), and ethnic spirits (*mhondoro*) are mediators between *Mwari* and human beings. *Mwari* is a spirit (*Mudzimu Anoyera/Mweya Anoyera*), for Chigwedere contends that the Shona High Spirit at Matopos, popularly known as the Shona God, is the God of Matopos, or the Hamitoid Mbire High God described by the European scholars.[11] Ancestors are spiritual beings. Tovera is regarded as the Shona High God or *Mwari* of the Matopos. Chigwedere states that "when we examine the position of the Matopos religious centres later, we shall find Tovera treated as God, but he is an Ancestor of the Mbire family."[12] If it is true that Sororenzou is the traditional Shona High Spirit, or an ancestor, and not God in the Christian sense of the word, how is it that he is referred to as *Mwari*? God (*Mwari*) is the Shona High Spirit, who is also called by many names, including *Nyadenga* (he who dwells in the sky), *Musikavanhu* (he who creates human beings), *Musiki* (the Creator), and *Chidzachepo* (one who was there from the beginning and will be there forever). The God of the Matopos, *Mwari,* the Hamitoid Mbire High God, and the Shona High Spirit are all Sororenzou.[13]

The traditional Shona approach to an elder or important person is summarized by the saying *kukwira gomo kupoterera*, which literally means that when you try to go up to the peak of a mountain, you should never try to go straight up. You should go round and round until you get to the peak. Similarly, when you try to negotiate a marriage deal with a prospective traditional Shona father-in-law (*vatezvara*), it is unthinkable that you should make a direct approach to him: he is the peak of the mountain and must be approached indirectly until the message gets to him. In other words, the whole negotiation must be done through his juniors. Likewise, if you want to approach a chief on some matter, you must realize that he is the peak of the mountain and can only be approached through his juniors until the message gets to him. This was aptly summarized by a Portuguese observer who watched the representatives of the regional chiefs presenting themselves to the northern Korekore Mutapa. Aplers wrote that when the Ambassador reaches his determined place...he offers the present...and presents his embassy not to the Emperor but to the lowest ranking of his grandees who then relays the message up through the ranks until it reaches the most important of all the nobility and it is he who communicates the embassy to the Emperor and his reply descends to the same junior grandee....[14]

The story is true when it comes to ATR. For instance, if a traditional Shona wants to offer ritual sacrifices of a black bull and prayers to his or her great-grandfather, he or she cannot sacrifice to him directly as if he had no juniors. The great grandfather is the peak of the mountain. He must be approached indirectly. In this case then, if one's elder brother is dead, one presents the black bull and one's prayers to one's dead elder brother. Next one asks him to present the offerings to one's dead father. The dead father will present them to the grandfather. Finally the grandfather is asked to present them to his own father, the great-grandfather. The great-grandfather will present them to his seniors in the family ancestral hierarchy until finally the black bull and one's prayers are presented to *Mwari*. Traditional Shona look upon *Mwari* as the highest peak imaginable, the last in the pyramidal hierarchy of ancestors. The traditional Shona people look upon themselves as very close to *Mwari* but far too small and inferior to have direct contact with

Him. The family ancestral spirits *(midzimu yepamusha)* are also not too far and not too small; they are somewhat nearer. The territorial ancestral spirits (*mhondoro*) are bigger and nearest to *Mwari*. They are big enough and nearest enough to have direct contact with *Mwari*. *Mwari* is national and all pervading. As such only ethnic/regional ancestral spirits (*mhondoro*) can have direct contact with *Mwari*.

*Mhondoro (midzimu mikuru)* themselves have a hierarchy of their own, starting with the youngest and the most numerous at the bottom and the greatest *mhondoro* at the top, in a pyramidal form. The traditional Shona further believe that they do not know *Mwari*. They believe that he who is nearest to *Mwari* knows *Mwari* or knows Him better than they do. In the traditional Shona world-view, the greatest known ancestor is the one nearest to *Mwari* and is the only one in the whole hierarchy of their creation who may know enough about *Mwari*. What the traditional Shona know is that ancestors are junior gods to *Mwari* in the hierarchy of ancestors. So the traditional Shona pass their messages to ancestors for delivery to *Mwari*. Likewise, *Mwari* sends his replies to the people through ancestors. This immediately establishes ancestors as mouthpieces of *Mwari* and at the same time as the spokesmen/women of the traditional Shona people. Ancestors have no power in themselves. They get all their power from above, from *Mwari*. Because of this hierarchy of ancestors in ATR, traditional Shona people venerate the junior gods (Shona ancestors).

In this way, the traditional Shona believe that all they get from ancestors is from *Mwari*, since the ancestors are *Mwari's* spokesmen/women and junior gods. Indirectly, therefore, the voices, the messages of ancestors are the Voice of *Mwari* and contacts with ancestors are contacts with *Mwari*. Therefore, it is not surprising to find Chigwedere saying that "Matonjeni and Matopos are referred to as '*Mwari's* Caves' and the voice that speaks there is the 'Voice of *Mwari*'."[15] But Daneel notes that "very rarely if at all is the name *Mwari* ever mentioned in all proceedings at the cave or during the offering of ritual sacrifices and prayers at home."[16] *Mwari* is not an object of direct worship. Worship and ritual sacrifices reach *Mwari* through the Shona ancestors and not from the traditional Shona people. After creation, *Mwari* maintained direct contact with His creation through the ancestors. The Shona ancestors are venerated and are the ones in direct contact with both *Mwari* and human beings. *Mwari* has delegated authority to the ancestors to deal with all affairs of human beings. Creation and sustaining the universe are the most important tasks; hence they are under the direct control of *Mwari*. The rest are relatively trivial affairs of human beings, which *Mwari* deals with through the hierarchy of Shona ancestors. Pobee concludes, "thus the ancestors, in theory at any rate, operate *loco Dei* and *pro Deo*."[17]

However, I must add that, as a matter of fact, the average traditional Shona supplicant is oblivious of *Mwari* and treats the Shona ancestors as ends in themselves. To that extent there is the danger of treating the Shona ancestors as the Ground of Being (*Mwari*). There is the danger of idolatry if one uses Christian value judgment. *Mwari* is rarely invoked. Only Shona ancestors are mentioned by name, starting with the junior and ending with the most senior. *Mwari* is not far away. He is the Highest and Greatest Being, and no human being can dream of talking or appealing to Him directly. Hence traditional Shona people send their ritual sacrifices, prayers, and worship to *Mwari* through the hierarchy of Shona ancestors.

ATR seems to be ancestorcentric, yet it is both pneumatocentric and theocentric. The traditional Shona people seem to have regarded Tovera as God, for Beach, an historian at the University of Zimbabwe, argues that "by the eighteenth century, we know that earlier political formulations such as those of the Tovera or of Musikavanhu (he who creates human beings) in the southeastern highlands were beginning to gain recognition by the dominant lineages as religious entities."[18] But for the traditional Shona people, *Mwari* is the only one who creates human beings. If Tovera was referred to as Musikavanhu, Tovera was also regarded as *Mwari* but not in the sense that he was the real *Mwari* but in the sense that he was the nearest Shona ancestor to *Mwari*. Tovera is a junior god nearest to *Mwari* and thus uses the power and authority of *Mwari*. Beach believes that the traditional Shona God is a combination of sky-god and ancestral spirit, for he explains that "the specifically Rozvi high-god *Mwari,* a combination of sky-god and ancestral spirit, seems to have been of importance in the northeast where the Rozvi had originated and of course in the Changamire State."[19] This makes ATR both pneumatocentric and theocentric, for *Mwari* is a combination of the Rozvi ethnic Sky god and Shona ancestral spirits. Mutswairo claims that the spirit medium of Nehanda once told Mapondera, who was one of the leaders in the second war of liberation from 1896-97 in the Mazowe Valley, that our country is built upon a spiritual foundation. We believe in the ever-existing and watchful eyes of our invisible ancestor spirits. Now we know that *Mwari*, our ancestor God, is with us, for he has sent in our midst, not only spirit mediums, like myself and others, but great soldiers like you, Mapondera, and like Kunzvi Nyandoro.[20]

*Mwari*, and not the ancestors, was and still is the center of worship for the traditional Shona.

Ancestral family spirit mediums (*midzimu yepamusha*) and regional ancestral spirit mediums (*mhondoro*) were referred to as Bandadzi ra*Mwari* (God's spokesmen/women). This is clearly shown by the following statement:

I am Muhwati, Mhanduwe, son-in-law to Mutinhima, the Rozvi Paramount of Gweru, whose daughter Tengera I married. They call me *Bandadzi raMwari* (God's spokesman/woman) to the nation of the Rozvi, Mbire central Mamboland, because I am the chief mediator between *Mwari* and the ancestors and the people.[21]

Ancestors are regarded as junior *mwari* in that once one is in good standing with one's ancestors, one is automatically in good standing with *Mwari.* Then one is open to receive blessings from *Mwari* through one's ancestors. If one offends one's ancestors, one automatically offends *Mwari,* and one is liable to receive curses from *Mwari* through one's ancestors.

# THE CULT OF ANCESTORS AT THE CENTER OF SHONA TRADITIONAL RELIGION

The cult of ancestors is something that we find in religious systems throughout the world, especially where extended families live together and co-operate together politically, socially, and economically. The traditional agrarian Shona society is one such society. Traditional Shona social organization is centered on the ancestors' extended families within an ethnic system. It is structured hierarchically and includes past members of the family and ethnic group—family ancestors (*midzimu yepamusha*) and ethnic/territorial/regional ancestors (*mhondoro/ midzimu mikuru). Mwari* Himself, as well as the *Mwari* represented by ancestors, is the giver of good things in life, and, at the same time, *Mwari*, through Shona ancestors, opens "doors" for bad and evil things to happen to people. *Mwari*, through Shona ancestors, is the Protector and Savior of the people in every respect. One must be careful not to offend one's ancestors for fear of retribution from *Mwari* through the ancestors. Unusual and strange occurrences are often attributed to ancestors. In times of trouble, such as famine, war, pestilence, drought, unemployment, car accidents, divorce, failure at school, or impotence, ancestors are consulted and propitiated/ worshipped by beseeching their help in controlling the evil forces which cause these calamities. These propitiations are led by diviners *(n'angas*) and the elders as representatives of the living community. Traditional Shona ritual sacrifices and prayers are attempts to reunite a lineage with the offended *Mwari* through Shona ancestors who are punishing them for their misdeeds. In ATR theology, *Mwari* is the Ancestor in a more superior and pre-eminent manner than Shona ancestors. From Christian theology, God is God, and there is no other god besides God (Ex. 20:3).

The regional ancestors (*mhondoro/ midzimu mikuru*), who are nearest to *Mwari*, are the guardians of public order. They are the ones who have the power to fend off the evils and epidemics that affect the whole community, evils such as sudden deaths, war, starvation, and epidemics such as cholera and HIV/AIDS. They are the owners of the land, the source of life, and it is under their careful guidance that humankind strives to keep in step with the harmony and order of creation. The roles of Shona ancestors are as *Mwari's* liberating messengers, reconcilers, and guardians of religion and the land. They are leaders and rulers. They are family establishers and promoters of healthy relations among traditional Shona people. Shona ancestors shepherd their families and tribes, reconcile their family and regional members, and unite their families and ethnic groups. Shona ancestors are the judges and teachers of their families and ethnic groups.

Shona ancestors are not absolute. They are answerable to *Mwari*, who is absolute. The powers of Shona ancestors are limited. Shona ancestors conceive *Mwari* as unique. They are strictly monotheistic. Shona ancestors have sacred shrines: trees (Mutiusinazita near Marondera and the Buhers District) and mountains (the Great Zimbabwe and Matopos/Matonjeni). Shona ancestors offer ritual sacrifices, libation, and prayers to *Mwari*. Shona ancestors have power to bless and curse. Shona ancestorhood penetrates the whole of ATR and Shona traditional culture. Shona ancestorhood as a process begins with childhood rituals like naming, marriage, and all other rituals which take place within ATR. The importance of ATR rituals is that no one can become an ancestor unless he or she had undergone such childhood rituals. However, the gender of the child is irrelevant to future Shona ancestorhood. These are preliminary and indispensable steps towards successful ancestorhood in the traditional Shona social life. Another important element in Shona ancestorhood is marriage. Traditional Shona social structure is particularly linked with matrimonial life. It is in marriage that the vital relational and communal elements of Shona traditional life emerge strongly and spontaneously. It is in marriage that one's fecundity is proved. Marriage affects ancestorhood as a necessary ancestral status indicating strongly that an ancestor is primarily a promoter of life, interpersonal relationships, and life in the community. Besides, in most cases, no one can become an ancestor in the traditional Shona society unless he or she is married and has left descendants.

The traditional Shona believe in an extended family, not in a nuclear family. A traditional Shona family includes all the living members and the ancestors, the "living dead". In a sense, one cannot be an ancestor without having a family. It is within a family or ethnic context that a Shona ancestor proves himself or herself to be a promoter of life. In the traditional Shona world-view, promoting of life is a determining factor for ancestral qualities. Just as ancestorhood is integrated in the birth of an individual (the starting of life), it is also integrated in his or her death (the end of earthly life). A Shona ancestor understands death as an inevitable event marking entrance into the realm of ancestors, which is the spirit world (*nyikadzimu*). They see the peaceful calm manifested by a dying traditional Shona elder and the deep religiosity and solemnity in the farewell rituals where he or she calls his or her people, blesses them, divides his or her property for their inheritance, exposes his or her hidden properties, and pronounces his or her last will and wishes. Within the traditional Shona social order, death empowers, in a certain sense, the Shona ancestors to be more alive since those they leave behind keep them in their memory. By dying, they join the company of ancestors in the *nyikadzimu*, whose life is fuller.

The fact that marriage is a very important aspect in African ancestorhood does not necessarily mean that there are no celibates in ATR. Some individuals are called to a life of permanent or temporary celibacy by the ancestors so that they can serve the community better. Permanent celibate priests and priestesses do exist in ATR, and also temporary married ones, who must abstain from sexual relations for a few days, weeks, or months when they celebrate their rites. Those scholars of ATR, for example Oyeronke Olajubu, who argue that for the African mentality celibacy is inconceivable, are telling an untruth.[22] Celibate priesthood is not foreign to ATR. The m*akumbi*, who are the chief priestesses of the Rassa cult in the Masvingo area in chief Gutu's area, are permanent celibates. Temporary celibacy can also be taken within marriage. One is made a celibate by ancestors. In ATR, celibacy is not voluntary, for it can be forced on one by a religious quest or when observing religious rituals. Some regional spirit mediums are rain-makers (*majukwa).* The regional spirit mediums have their assistants called the *ngonya/makumbi*. The *ngonya/makumbi* are not married for life. They are initiated into permanent celibacy. Traditional African celibates, in answering their call, answer it on behalf of their entire family, community, and the ancestors whom they embody in their life.

Therefore, when African traditionalists are set apart to be celibates, they do not come as mere individuals with little significance and no influence. They become celibates who deserve great respect and honor. Celibates in ATR are not alienated people. They become celibates in order to serve the community as rain-makers (*majukwa*), diviners (*n'anga)*, and healers (*n'anga/varapi*). The ancestors call celibates through an entire network of relationships between the living and the ancestors. This gives celibates a great sense of support and responsibility. To know that they bear the spirit of a deceased beloved father, mother, grandmother, grandfather, uncle, or aunt in their life makes the path of celibacy less precarious, less lonely, and more meaningful. Second, it gives the celibates a great sense of dignity and worth. They respect their call. This applies also to the whole community. Celibacy does not in any way contradict ATR and African traditional cultural communalism. Celibacy favors a life of communion and not individualism. Celibates live corporate lives and are not just persons in their endeavors but an embodiment of the whole history—a network of persons, experiences, aspirations, feelings, hopes, a family-community.

Celibates in ATR are married to the ancestors, and the whole community is their family and children. They are married and have procreated that way. The Shona people of Zimbabwe would say that celibates are married to the ancestors, and all people in the community are their children. Therefore, celibacy is a message to traditional Africans that the vocation they hold in high esteem (matrimony) is not absolute, not meant for all men and women. There is a minority called to perpetual virginity "for religious purposes", for the sake of the community. The African cultural emphasis on fecundity reminds the celibates of an aspect of their charisma, that virginity also implies parenthood or spiritual fruitfulness. By it, the celibate "begets life" for the community and hence assures continuous succession of descent. This agrees with the cultural sense and concern for family continuity. The difference lies in the fact that one is temporal, the other spiritual. Celibacy is a calling from the ancestors which both the individual and the community do not reject, for the decision to make one a celibate is not theirs but the ancestors' in consultation with God (*Mwari*). A traditional African who remains single does so because the ancestors have called him or her to a higher office of rain-making, divination, and healing in the community. When an African is called to a life of celibacy, he or she is called to be deeply rooted in ATR and to be a priest/priestess in ATR.

Shona ancestorhood is deeply integrated in ATR. *Mwari* is the Creator and Sustainer of the universe. These concepts of *Mwari* help the Shona ancestors in the sense that conceiving *Mwari* through such attributes enables them to accept and appreciate that whatever sacred powers they have are rooted in *Mwari* as the primordial source. For Shona ancestors, then, it is *Mwari* who gave them all authority and power over the traditional Shona people. That is why Shona ancestors are necessarily imbued with Godliness in practically everything. Thus, they are called junior gods. In their approach to *Mwari*, in the going round and round until they reach the peak (*kukwira gomo kuporerera*), Shona ancestors play a priestly role in sacrificial rituals and prayers as the ordinary officials. Such conceptions challenge the Shona ancestors to remain guardians of ATR, the land, and the people's welfare as a whole. The ancestors have a higher status and are more sacred than people still living on earth. By virtue of being in the *nyikadzimu*, the *midzimu* are believed to be nearer *Mwari* and hence are more sacred and more powerful. That is why the ancestors command respect and expect worship, propitiation, and ritual offerings such as the pouring of libations to them. On account of their proximity to *Mwari,* the traditional Shona consider the ancestors as stronger and more sacred than they are. That is why ancestors are not ignored in fulfilling their roles as reconcilers, leaders and rulers, establishers, and promoters of unity and healthy interpersonal relationships.

Despite the fact that the traditional Shona world-view has undergone some big changes due to colonization, borrowing from other cultures, modern education, science, economy, technology, foreign systems of government administration, Christian and Muslim influences, as well as the creation of inter-racial and inter-ethnic and international communities, Shona ancestors and ATR have a future role to play in Zimbabwe. Shona ancestorhood is relevant for today and tomorrow. Bourdillion (1993) argues that ancestors are there in ATR, among the traditional Shona people. But, he asks, as Zimbabwe changes, where are the ancestors? Why can't they stop all this change? Ancestors cannot stop all these technological, scientific, political, economic, and social changes taking place in Zimbabwe because the ancestors, like ATR, are dynamic. For example, traditionally, ancestors used to make one a hunter (*muvhimi*), but now in modern times ancestors can make one a general manager of a company or a member of parliament. African ancestors are now members of the global village, for Africans are now found in almost every country in the world, and Africa is a very active member of the global village. ATR is now being practiced in America, Europe, Australia, and Asia by Africans in the diaspora and some of the people in these countries seek mental and physical healing from traditional African healers or medicine men and women.

Libation is an important and prominent aspect of ATR. A libation is poured to secure the goodwill of *Mwari* through the ancestors. Libation has two parts: first, the act of pouring the drink, and, second, the words which declare the intention of the pouring of the drink. Obviously the pouring of the drink as a religious rite is by itself neutral. So the crux of the matter is the accompanying words which express the intention. Normally the words ask for blessings from *Mwari* through the ancestors. But before or after they are mentioned, there is no invocation of the Supreme Being (*Mwari*). The words of invocation reach *Mwari* through the hierarchy of ancestors. Libation presupposes the idea of the Communion of Saints. However, this is in dispute. Traditional Shona people agree that they worship their ancestors. But

African Christian theologians do not want to say that ancestors are worshipped. They say that ancestors are venerated. In this case, traditional Shona people agree with Pobee, who says, "much as I am most sympathetic to this theory as a method of missionary strategy, I am yet reluctant to accept it as a description of fact, because for all practical purposes the ancestors are treated as ends in themselves, as the real givers of the good things in life."[23] Pobee is reluctant to accept that ancestors are venerated. As a method of Christian evangelization, more harm might be caused if one says the traditional Shona worship ancestors, but from the practical and observational points of view, there is more worship of ancestors than veneration. The fact that ancestors are worshipped means that Shona ancestors are junior gods.

In ATR, there are some ancestors that the traditional Shona people know exist in the spirit world, but people do not know their names. In traditional prayers, sacrifices, and petitions to their ancestors (*vachipira kana kunamata midzimu yavo*) the traditional Shona people say: "Will you please make our prayers reach those in the spirit world (*nyikadzimu*) that we do not know by name. (*Tisvisireiwo mipiro neminamato yedu kune vari kumhepo avo vatisingazivi mazita avo).*" During prayers and sacrifices, only the names of known and very junior ancestors at the very bottom of the pyramidal hierarchy of ancestors are mentioned. As one goes up the pyramidal hierarchy of ancestors, the names of the ancestors become unknown, and the ancestors also do not possess the living human beings (*midzimu yacho haichasutsi vanhu).* The known ancestors who no longer possess people are Tovera, Sororenzou, and Dzivaguru. In ATR, there is the concept of known but anonymous ancestors (*midzmu inozivikanwa kuti iriko asi iyo isingazivikanwi mazita ayo).*

## CHRIST AND THE SHONA ANCESTORS

The connection between Christ and the Shona ancestors is that Christ is the Creator and Sustainer of the universe. The Christ of faith and not the historical Jesus is God (*Mwari).* He is pre-existent, and He is at the apex of the pyramidal hierarchy of the Adamic ancestorhood.

Christ was there before all creation (Col. 1:15). He created and sustained Shona ancestors. He is at the apex of the pyramidal hierarchy of all human ancestorhood. Christ the *Mudzimu Mukuru* par excellence is greater than Tovera, Sororenzou, and Dzivaguru. As *Mwari* the Creator, Christ created Tovera, Sororenzou and Dzivaguru. God (*Mwari*) is an Ancestor. *Mwari* is the *Mudzimu Mukuru* par excellence. At the ontological level, Christ is God (*Mwari*) and is greater than ancestors who possess human beings (*midzimu inosutsa*). Christ as *Mudzimu Mukuru* par excellence has creative powers. He was there at creation. Behind God (*Mwari)*, there is Christ, who is part of *Mwari.* Christ, who is *Mwari*, does not possess any traditional Shona person. He is an Ancestor who does not possess *(Mudzimu usingasutsi*). Tovera, Sororenzou, and Dzivaguru are remote Shona ancestors who no longer possess any person (*midzimu isingasutsi*). Christ is a very remote *Mudzimu Mukuru* par excellence who is *Mwari* and who does not possess any traditional Shona person (*Kirisito Mudzimu usingasutsi).*

What values of service, charity, and welfare, did Christ the *Mudzimu Mukuru* par excellence bring to the traditional Shona people? Traditional Shona culture discovers and acknowledges that Christ the *Mudzimu Mukuru* par excellence is *Mwari* who brings values of service to Shona families. Christ serves the welfare of the traditional Shona people. Therefore, there is no point in rejecting Him. Christ the *Mudzimu Mukuru* par excellence does not destroy traditional Shona welfare. Christ who is *Mwari* is there to fulfill traditional Shona culture and not to destroy traditional Shona culture together with its ancestors. Christ accepts traditional Shona vessels (culture and ancestors). He is to fulfill the Shona vessels. "Think not that I have come to abolish the law and the prophets. I have come not to abolish them but to fulfill them" (Mt.5:17). Christ is the *Mudzimu Mukuru* par excellence who no longer possesses human beings (*Mudzimu usingasutsi)* but is active just like Tovera, Sororenzou, and Dzivaguru. There is no inculturation when one destroys Shona vessels of service, welfare, and charity.

In ATR, no ancestors are left out of prayers and sacrifices. After invoking the names of all the ancestors who are known by name, supplicants end their prayers by saying, "please send this prayer or sacrifice to those of our ancestors who are in the spirit world (*nyikadzimu)*, whom we do not know by name (*tisvisireiwo minamato yedu kune avo vese vari kumhepo (nyikadzimu) vatisingazivi mazita avo)*." Christ is in the spirit world (*nyikadzimu)* and is not known by name. All ancestors whose names are known and the anonymous ancestors are invoked during prayers and sacrifices. This makes ATR all inclusive. Christ is accommodated anonymously in ATR. Here ATR agrees with Rahner (1974) and Panikkar (1981), who speak of the Unknown Christ of Hinduism, and Snook (1986), who speaks of the Anonymous Christ.

What is required in ATR is to pronounce the name of Christ just as Paul did to the Greeks at Athens in Acts 17:24-25: "What, therefore, you worship as unknown this I proclaim to you. The God who made the world and everything in it, being the Lord in heaven and earth, does not live in shrines made by man, nor is He served by human hands, as though He needs anything, since He Himself gives to all men life and breath and everything." The Greatest Ancestor (*Mudzimu Mukuru*) par excellence, who the traditional Shona know exists but who is anonymous, is Jesus Christ. Christ should be proclaimed and made known to the Zimbabweans as the *Mudzimu Mukuru* par excellence.

## SPIRIT POSSESSION

No traditional Shona person is possessed by the Spirit of God (*Mwari*). No traditional Shona person is possessed by God's Spirit (*Mudzimu waMwari*). The rain-making spirits (*majukwa*) are associated with pools (*madziva*) related to the *Mwari* fertility cult. This is the closest a traditional Shona can get to *Mwari*. The Kalanga people have messengers (*mahosana*), but they do not hear the Voice of *Mwari*. The Voice of *Mwari* is only heard at Matonjeni by the high priests/ priestesses of *Mwari*. The priests and priestesses communicate the message of *Mwari* to the people. Nevertheless, the high priests and priestesses of *Mwari* are not possessed by the Spirit of *Mwari*.

At the upper echelons of ATR, there is God (*Mwari*). Therefore, the traditional Shona people are theocentric. The God of the Jews—not *Mwari* the God of the traditional Shona people whose Voice speaks from Matonjeni—possesses Christians as the Holy Spirit (*Mweya Anoyera/Medium Anoyera*). The God of the Jews possesses everybody but not *Mwari* of the Matonjeni. Shona Christians accepted the new concepts and attributes of Yahweh, God of the Jews. Shona Christians adopted Yahweh and called him *Mwari*. At the upper echelons of ATR, Shona Christians replaced the *Mwari* of Matonjeni with Yahweh. At the lower level, the ancestors have not been replaced. They are still very intact and efficacious. Shona Christians have replaced *Mwari* of Matonjeni—who possesses no one—by the God (*Yahweh)* who possesses everybody. Therefore, they have become pneumatocentric. At the ancestor level, the traditional Shona are both pneumatocentric and ancestorcentric because the ancestors (*midzimu*) possess them. The traditional Shona are not pneumatocentric at the divine (*Mwari*) level, for the *Mwari* of Matonjeni possesses nobody.

## THE DIVINER (*N,ANGA*) AS MEDIATOR BETWEEN ANCESTORS AND THE PEOPLE IN ATR.

Because of the life-sharing, life-protecting, and life-saving role of *Mwari* through the Shona ancestors, it is necessary that both *Mwari* and Shona ancestors be contacted on a regular basis so as to know their wills and desires. Diviners (*n'angas*) mediate the wills and desires of *Mwari* through Shona ancestors to the living in order to ensure that the primal order of creation is maintained. The diviners (*n'anga*) also detect the breaking of ethnic rules or family rules such as incest, murder, and violating the traditional day of rest (*chisi*). These misdeeds provoke *Mwari* and the ancestors into sending suffering and even death until the immorality is corrected. Hence the *n'anga* are able to decipher the past, the present, and the future as well as uncover the human and the spiritual causes of events and the possible solution to the problems of life.[24] Diviners are consulted about every aspect of life. Parrinder puts it this way:

> If anything is lost, if a barren woman desires children, if there is a mysterious disease, if a man is troubled by strange dreams and for many other causes, the diviner is sought out and he has recourse to geomancy. The diviner may be called in at all the important crises of life, at birth discover the appropriate name to give to a child, at the betrothal to find the right husband, at death to find who has caused death. In some places, the diviner draws up a horoscope for adolescents, and this is treasured by them, the rest of their lives showing their fate. The horoscope is inscribed on a piece of calabash and any competent diviner should be able to read it.[25]

Aylward Shorter's investigation led him to a similar conclusion. In his words, "Some diviners seem to have powers of telepathy because they appear to be able to tell the client facts about himself and the purpose of his visit at the very start of the interview."[26] Divination (*kushopera*) for the traditional Shona is an important means of unraveling the mystery surrounding the uncertainties of life. The purpose of consulting a *n'anga* is to obtain a solution to a problem, to know the minds of Shona ancestors and of *Mwari*.

## THE SOURCE OF EVIL

*Mwari* created a moral, good, and rational world. The world was created without evil. *Mwari* cannot do evil, does not permit evil, nor is he involved in any way in evil. Evil cannot be found in any plan of *Mwari*. *Mwari* is the source of blessings, life, fertility, and happiness. Evil is caused by the immorality of the living, and that immorality must be neutralized if the moral order is to be restored. This is why unjustifiable suffering triggers in people's minds the thought that there is some immorality at work—either their own personal evil deeds, or some violation of the social order that has made the ancestors angry, or the action of a perverted human being who—whether a man or a woman—is called a witch.[27] Evil does not come from *Mwari* but from the disorder in creation caused by people and evil spirits who act immorally. The source of the ancestors' power is *Mwari*, to whom the ancestors appeal to ward off the evil that plagues mankind. Everyone knows that within a reasonable time the ancestors will intervene and right the evil done.[28] Thus, prosperity must be a sign that one is in harmony with one's neighbors.

Consequently, even if one abuses one's neighbors, everyone knows that within due time the ancestors will intervene and right the evil done. It is the role of *Mwari* through the Shona ancestors to maintain the order of creation by chastising and punishing the living for their evil deeds and by neutralizing evil caused by other created spirits. Traditional Shona people ask *Mwari*, through the Shona ancestors, to make definite attempts to repair evil before it gets out of control. Witches (*varoyi*), sorcerers (*varoyi)*, and wizards (*varoyi)* are human agents that cause evil. Sorcerers operate both day and night. Parrinder has a typical description of what Africans believe about sorcerers:

> The sorcerer deliberately tries to harm his enemies, or those of his clients who have paid him, by evil magical means. He may use suggestive magic only, or true poison. Harmful ingredients may be put in a cooking pot or drinking gourd. The soul of the enemy may be pinned down with pegs, or a clay image made of his body and thorns stuck in the vital organs. The enemy will then feel pain in those spots and may die....[29]

As a matter of fact, for many traditional Shona people, there is no such thing as an accident in the real sense of the word. The goblin (*zvikwambo/tokoloshis*) type of witchcraft, very common in Zimbabwe, makes its owners rich by causing economic, social, and physical harm to their victims. What appears to be an accident is, to a traditional Shona person, the result of a spell cast by an evil man or woman or the result of the anger of *Mwari* and the ancestors whose taboos have been violated.

## ATR IS BASICALLY PNEUMATOCENTRIC, ANCESTORCENTRIC, AND THEOCENTRIC

The fact that all traditional Shona people have exclusive knowledge of their family and ethnic ancestors, are members of a family and a tribe and know their totem (*mutupo*), makes pneumatocentricism and theocentricism very appealing to them because they are inclined towards *Mwari* through their family and regional spirits. ATR is both pneumatocentric and theocentric because the Shona Ancestral High Spirit at Matopos is the same Shona God at Matopos. In ATR, ritual sacrifices, worship, and prayers are offered starting from the ancestors who are spiritual beings to *Mwari* who is also a Spiritual Being. ATR is full of spirits, some good and some evil. ATR is pneumatocentric because the traditional Shona people refer to God (*Mwari*), the Shona High Spirit, as *Mudzimu Anoyera* or *Mweya anoyera*. ATR is theocentric and pneumatocentric because of the hierarchy from family ancestors (*midzimu yepamusha*), to territorial ancestors (*midzimu mikuru* the *mhondoro*), and finally to *Mwari* the *Mudzimu Anoyera.* ATR is theocentric because *Mwari* is the Creator and Sustainer of the universe. *Mwari* is the overall power in creation. Shona ancestors protect and save their family and ethnic members only. They also punish and withdraw blessings from their family and ethnic members only. Ancestors of a particular family and of a particular ethnic group should not be worshipped by foreigners (*vatorwa*). There is no mutual protection and saving of different families and different ethnic groups. The traditional Shona people have a song which clearly shows that there is no mutual protection and saving of different families and ethnic groups by Shona ancestors who are not members of that family and ethnic group. The song is *Mudzimu mukuru chirega chinya, zvaunouraya vana vako, tarisa vana vevamwe vanofara, mudzimu mukuru chirega chinya.* (Greatest ancestor (*mudzimu mukuru*) do not be angry with your children. You kill your children. See the children of other ancestors are very happy). This song refers to the greatest ancestor (*mudzimu mukuru,* the *mhondoros*). The *mudzimu mukuru* is the regional spirit. This song clearly shows that each Shona ancestor is believed to look after the affairs of his or her family and ethnic members only. The traditional Shona people approach *Mwari* through the ancestors. Each family and each ethnic group has its own family and territorial ancestors, but all the different families, all the different ethnic groups, and all the different ancestors were created by one *Mwari*, are sustained by one *Mwari*, and are answerable to one *Mwari*.

The ancestors are at the centre of ATR, of traditional Shona culture and religion. Ancestors permeate every aspect of traditional Shona culture and religion. Ancestors act on behalf of *Mwari*. *Mwari*'s attributes are open-ended and inexhaustible. The traditional Shona place a lot of emphasis on the omnipresence of *Mwari* and the consequent sacramental nature of the universe. For the traditional Shona, there is no demarcation between the sacred and the profane (secular). The traditional Shona live in the omnipresence of spiritual realities who, in accordance with their political-social set up, are *bona fide* Vicars of the Creator-God (*Mwari*). In that case, traditional Shona worship of ancestors is tantamount to a virtual worship of the Creator, *Mwari*. Traditional Shona are aware of the omnipresence, omnipotence, and omniscience of *Mwari* in every aspect of the universe. In the traditional Shona world-view, whatever a person does or thinks is done in the very presence of *Mwari* as represented by His spiritual agents, the ancestors. The awareness of this fact leads the traditional Shona to practice the *UBANTU* philosophy (life relationships) in their relationships with society and community. The *UBANTU* philosophy is basically the statement: I am because we are. I am here because of the community, and without the community I die. The community is more important than the individual. There is no individual salvation outside the community or family. Human beings are created not for themselves but for the community. Shona proverbs provide one form for communicating these realities. A person is a person through other people (*Munhu vanhu*). A chief is a chief because of people (*Mambo vanhu*). Life is when you are with others; alone you are like an animal: *Upenyu kunge une vamwe vanhu, kana uri wega uri mhuka*. Consequently, any time a traditional Shona person feels that he or she has violated the norms of the society and of the spiritual entities who are the ancestors, that person becomes conscience stricken. This usually leads to functional and physical indisposition. The person is then seized with the inner urge to confess and make amends. In order to express their inner feelings, people generally consult the *n'anga* by which they are ordered to confess their violations and make sacrifices and prayers to *Mwari* through the ancestors so as to atone for the wrongs done or the moral norm violated.

The fact that ATR is both pneumatocentric and theocentric makes ATR a very fertile ground for the processes of appropriation and inculturation of the Gospel of Jesus Christ in the Church in Zimbabwe. ATR makes it possible for me to develop my inculturated transformative Trinitarian *Mudzimu Mukuru* par excellence Christology. This chapter has made it clear that one cannot understand traditional Shona ancestorhood if one does not take into account the intimate link it bears to social and religious life. Shona Ancestorhood embodies and consolidates Shona people. Shona ancestorhood was and is still relevant today. There seems to be enough fertile ground now to develop a Trinitarian transformative *Mudzimu Mukuru* par excellence Christology of integration of USPG Christianity and ATR into Christ.

# CHAPTER 2

## *History and Missiology of the USPG with Special Reference to Zimbabwe*

The aim of this chapter is to describe how the United Society for the Propagation of the Gospel (USPG) came into being and developed and to investigate what types of Christologies, missiologies, and soteriologies the USPG missionaries used in their mission. USPG Christocentric and ecclesiocentric soteriologies affect the Shona people who have become Christians. I am going to develop a thesis that USPG missionaries were Christocentric and ecclesiocentric, in their approach to mission. This chapter also investigates whether the concept of ancestor is found in USPG soteriologies. The aspects which will help me to elucidate my thesis are explicit knowledge of Jesus Christ, membership of Christ's Church, the centrality of Jesus Christ in the order of Salvation, the presence of the Holy Spirit in the Church and among Christians, and God as the Creator and Sustainer of the universe. I would like to build a strong foundation for the effects of Christocentric and ecclesiocentric soteriologies on ATR and Shona USPG Christians in Zimbabwe.

The USPG was formed in 1965 out of a post-colonial merger of the Society for the Propagation the Gospel in Foreign Parts (SPG), founded in 1701, and the Universities' Mission to Central Africa (UMCA), founded in 1857 after David Livingstone's appeal for Christianity, commerce, and civilization in Africa. The SPG and the UMCA were both launched with the formal backing of the

Convocation of the Church of England (Anglican). The USPG is a missionary society with very wide authority to enable the Anglican Church's mission through its own enthusiasm, administrative machinery, experience, and money. The family history of the USPG, its collective memory, begins in 1701. I will therefore sometimes use the name USPG to refer to ways of thinking that predate it. However, the 1965 merger did result in changes of insights, missiology, and theology. A more aggressive policy of adaptation (accommodation) was soon pursued by the USPG.

## SPG MISSIONARY MOTIVES: GO INTO ALL THE WORLD, AND PREACH THE GOSPEL TO ALL NATIONS (MATTHEW 28:19-29)

The major aim of the formation of the SPG was to carry out the commission of Our Lord Jesus Christ to His disciples, a little before His departure, when He said, "Go therefore and make disciples of all nations, baptizing them in the name of the Father and of the Son and of the Holy Spirit, teaching them to observe all that I have commanded you, and lo, I am with you always, to the close of the age" (Mt. 28:19-20). From the beginning, two objectives were identified. The minutes of the Lower House of Convocation of the Province of Canterbury show that on March 13, 1701, a committee was set up to "consider the promotion of the Christian religion according to the doctrine, discipline, and worship of the Church of England as by law established."[1] The first meeting of the Committee of Convocation was held on the 15th of March 1701, and within the next three weeks Dr. Thomas Bray appealed to King William III for the formation of the SPG in the following terms: "in many of the colonies thereof, more especially on the continent, they [the colonists] are in very much want of instruction in the Christian Religion, and in some of them utterly destitute of the same."[2] King William III responded positively to Dr. Bray's request, and the Royal Charter for the formation of the Society for the Propagation of the Gospel in Foreign Parts (SPG) was given. On

June 16, 1701, the Great Seal of England was affixed to the Charter, and the SPG was born. However, at a Bicentenary of the SPG in Exeter Hall on the 19th June, 1900, the Marquis of Salisbury stated: "but though its primary aim has been to save our fellow Christians (British subjects in the colonies) from lapsing into Pagans, the work of converting Pagans into Christians has gone simultaneously from the first." [3]

Initially, the priority was to preach the Gospel to the British subjects in the British colonies overseas and only secondarily to preach the Gospel to the indigenous peoples of the British colonies: "But while the Society's first duty is to the peoples within the Empire, its work of propagating the Gospel in foreign parts has extended to the regions beyond Greater Britain, so that our own kith and kin, wanderers from home, are enabled to sing the Lord's song in strange lands."[4] The Dean of Lincoln, in the first anniversary sermon, February 1702 argued that the design in the first place, to settle the state of Religion as well as may be among our own people there, which by all accounts we have, very much wants their Pious care; and then to proceed in the best methods they can towards the conversion of the Natives. The breeding up of Persons to understand the great variety of languages of those countries in order to be able to converse with the Natives and preach the Gospel to them.[5]

In 1710 it was laid down by the Society that that branch of its design which related to the "conversion of heathens and infidels" ought to be prosecuted preferably to all others. Though this proposed exclusive policy was not pursued, the Society throughout its history has sought to convert the heathen as well as to make spiritual provision for the Christian Colonists and according to its ability. Neither duty has ever been neglected by it.

The SPG wanted to convert the British settlers first and to make them a missionary Church, which would in turn evangelize the indigenous people of the British colonies. In 1899, the President of the SPG, Archbishop Temple, addressing the officers of the SPG, reasserted that "Jesus Christ is an universal Saviour, and hung on the

Cross not only for Englishmen, wherever they may be found, but also for the whole world."[6] Mission to the indigenous people in the British overseas colonies was to be a slow process, but mission to the British settlers was clearly urgent.[7]

The SPG Supplementary Charters and the Lambeth Conferences occurred when the SPG missionaries came into contact with the traditional religions and traditional cultures of the indigenous people in the British colonies. The SPG missionaries were constantly confronted with new situations and cultures. These contacts called for some positive changes within the SPG as a missionary organization and within Anglicanism. The Lambeth Conferences were born in 1868 out of controversies within Anglicanism. The Lambeth Conferences are the Anglican Communion's family consultations to resolve differences within Anglicanism. The 1701 Charter restricted SPG missionaries "to the dominions of the British Crown and its greater apparent concern for the British immigrants than for 'the heathens'."[8] The SPG had been born during a period prior to the rapid expansion of Christianity in the late eighteenth century. The Supplementary Charters and Lambeth Conferences made the SPG and Anglicanism dynamic so as to address themselves to the ever-changing political, social, economic, and cultural norms in the world. The Supplementary Charters and the Lambeth Conferences brought about new developments and new attitudes towards Islam, Hinduism, and ATR and also towards different cultures.

The SPG Supplementary Charters and the Lambeth Conferences also resulted from a shift in membership and leadership. From its formation in 1701, the financial burden of the SPG was on the wealthy British people. By 1879, the financial support was shifting from the wealthy few to the countless ordinary British people at the grass roots. In 1882, the first Supplementary Charter from Queen Victoria gave executive power to the Standing Committee, each diocese having a representative from the laity.[9] In 1921, the SPG obtained from King George V a Second Supplementary Charter. In addition to admitting women as Incorporated Members, the Charter opened the SPG missionary activities to all nations:

It shall be and shall be deemed always to have been lawful for the Society to carry on the work of the Society in all or any parts of the world as the Society may from time to time think proper, and to carry on such work among and for the benefit of persons wheresoever resident and whether British subjects or not and whether at home or abroad, and also to carry on Medical Mission work at home and abroad.[10]

The SPG had now a view of mission as primarily evangelizing individuals and of planting the Church where it did not yet exist. Dewey describes the development of this idea through the Lambeth Quadrilateral:

The scandal of Christian disunity proved a major obstacle to the Gospel. In 1888, the Lambeth Conference proposed as a basis for Christian unity the 'Lambeth Quadrilateral': the Scriptures as the basis of Christian faith, the Apostles' and Nicene Creeds as sufficient statements of it, the Gospel sacraments of Baptism and the Lord's Supper and the historic episcopate.[11]

Dewey adds that "a third Supplementary Charter in 1956 gave more flexibility in investment and more freedom in transferring overseas property to overseas Churches."[12] The 1958 Lambeth Conference proclaimed: "every generation needs to be evangelised, and to this all-important task we summon the People of God in every land."[13] In 1959, the SPG wrote a letter to all English incumbents from the eleven recognized missionary societies asking "what answer is to be given to the evident call of the Holy Spirit to our Church at this time, to send its messengers into all the world with the Gospel message...."[14] In a subsequent letter from the SPG and the Church Missionary Society (CMS) to all British incumbents, "the Church Assembly in 1960 called for an unprecedented increase in prayer, manpower and money for the Church overseas."[15]

USPG theology has been based on the Trinity and ecclesiology. Dewey states that "it was no longer just 'Christ and his Church' but a fully Trinitarian Theology, God sends His Son and His Spirit, and His Apostles through the Son and by the Spirit. The emphasis shifted from Mission as a function of God's Church to the Church as a function of God's Mission."[16] Ecclesiology and mission were inseparable as far as the USPG was concerned. Dewey states that "on January 1, 1965, after eighteen months of prayer, planning, and litigation, SPG and UMCA died and were reborn as the United Society for the Propagation of the Gospel."[17] All geographical references were dropped. The aim of the unification was to have one British Anglican missionary society in one world. (However, this did not materialize, for the CMS refused to join the USPG.) The United Society existed (as the SPG's 1921 Charter affirmed) to propagate the Gospel anywhere: "We are servants of the Church—overseas and at home."[18]

Soon after the unity of the SPG and UMCA, the new USPG embarked on a massive training program of indigenous leadership in the Church to take over Church leadership. The colonies in Africa had just achieved political independence. The Church gave up most of its schools, hospitals, and farms to the governments. For example, in 1971, the Anglican Church gave the St. Mary's mission farm in Chitungwiza to the Zimbabwe government, which has built on it the Zengeza and Seke residential suburbs for Africans. The USPG emerged at the same time as Vatican II, so it embraced the ideals of Vatican II. For example, USPG became greatly involved in ecumenism, and its missiology, theology, and liturgy changed in favor of Vatican II missiology, theology, and liturgy.

The new USPG also embarked on a policy of accommodation (adaptation), which is a policy of Africanization—indigenization. Helping the heathen overseas gives a reassuring sense of superiority, but the USPG needs to listen, evaluate, and respond appropriately to the requests of the overseas Churches. Braund (quoted in Dewey, 1975) argued that "we are not a Society for the Preservation of the Gospel in a Christian Ghetto, but for its propagation, for making it spread and grow."[19] The second Anglican Consultative Council (ACC) meeting, in Dublin in 1973, stressed that "the responsibility for mission in any place belongs *primarily* to the Church in that place."[20]

The USPG was born during a period of national political liberation movements in Africa and liberation theologies in Africa. Africa has mostly thought of liberation in terms of struggle against colonialism, racial tyranny, and economic and cultural domination by the Europeans and North Americans. A leading African Christian, Burgess Carr, General Secretary of the All Africa Council of Churches (AACC), quoted by John Kingsnorth in *Network*, June 1974,

claimed that "we have yet to reckon with the fact that in the deepest biblical sense of that concept the Christian Church is in itself a movement of liberation."[21] Canon John Kingsnorth, who became the Deputy Secretary of the USPG in 1965, responded by saying that "there is no biblical, historical or contemporary evidence to suggest that all the world will ever be liberated politically.... Yet freedom in Christ is available to all men."[22] The unique salvation offered by Christ, he argued, does not require changing our circumstances. The liberating truth is that nothing can separate us from the love of God.

The USPG was born not to further British colonial interests but to preach the Gospel of Jesus Christ to all nations. However, the USPG took a very active part in some British colonies in the creation and expansion of the British Empire. As Dewey notes, the two aims were inextricable:

> SPG's growth was as *ad hoc* as that of the British Empire. It ought not to disturb us that the propagation of the Gospel in modern times has gone hand in hand with trade and Empire. St. Paul took the Gospel along the trade routes and Roman military roads to the great cosmopolitan commercial cities of the world he knew: proud of his Roman citizenship, he did not hesitate to invoke the protection of an empire many thought cruelly oppressive.[23]

USPG missionaries did not work hand in hand with the British government in its overseas territorial aggrandizement. In the providence of God, the British Empire, despite its world-renowned cruelty, slavery, and economic, political, and social exploitation of the colonies, made possible the spread of the Gospel through a wider world than St. Paul could ever have imagined.

Influenced by the Puritans and the Evangelical Movement, the USPG had two missionary visions: first, "the Prophetic thought of the earth filled with the knowledge of the Lord Jesus Christ as the waters cover the sea. The other vision was evangelical: The sense of God's command to preach the Gospel to all nations and peoples."[24] William Carey, an English Baptist (1761-1834), was fired with the sense of evangelism. His work affected the USPG and the Anglican Church in England, and they also became evangelical in their outlook. The high British imperial and high British missionary era extended from about 1880-1920. Mission and ecclesiology went hand in hand. British missionaries had ecclesiological presuppositions.[25] In Zimbabwe, British mission came together with British colonial rule. In the 1850's, too, mission thinking had often been dominated by a belief in the essential commitment of Christianity to commerce and civilization. Missionary ideology, as a consequence, was integrated with political and economic ideas and with policies related to slave trade abolition. In these cases, USPG missionaries genuinely believed that British rule would be more beneficent than the alternative—another colonial power.

In other cases USPG missionaries argued for British preemption lest French rule should open Catholic doors, the converse in fact of the view of many British administrators that Catholic missionaries would serve French interest. J.D. Hargreaves has propounded the thesis that an imperialist religion developed in the late nineteenth century Britain produced by a consensus of new forms of secular rationalism, evangelical piety and broad based Christian humanism.[26]

USPG missionaries used various means for the conversion of the "heathens" to Jesus Christ. Such intent to convert the heathens to Jesus Christ reached the USPG missionaries because they were touched by the Evangelical Revival. For the first two or three decades of the USPG missionary movement, interest in missions was restricted to the Evangelicals but it soon engulfed the whole of the USPG. When the USPG became evangelical, it saw preaching as calling sinners to God through faith in Christ. The USPG felt that it was its duty to preach the Good News of Jesus Christ to all nations irrespective of race and color because it saw no difference in principle between the "baptized heathen" in Britain and in non-Christian peoples overseas. The USPG went out to preach Christ crucified and nothing else. The Evangelicals have influenced the Anglican Church and hence the general British life. In particular, the idea of Britain as a Christian nation, with Christian responsibilities overseas, took root in the USPG.

The birth of the SPG in 1701 had nothing to do with the protection of British colonial interests overseas. It had nothing to do with British Empire building. Theirs was to preach the Gospel of Jesus Christ. The outcome was victory for evangelism among the indigenous people of the British colonies. Sometimes the factors which influenced British colonialism also influenced the USPG missionaries. For example, both the British government and the USPG missionaries were interested in Christianity, commerce, and civilization for Zimbabwe. There is no evidence of USPG missionaries opposing British colonization of Zimbabwe. But relations between USPG missionaries and successive British colonial governments in Zimbabwe were not always smooth. USPG missionaries, for example Guy Clutton-Brock, Shearly Cripps, and Bishop Kenneth Skelton (1986) of Bulawayo, were often critical of British colonial governments in Zimbabwe. Addressing a heroes' acre gathering in Harare on the 11th August 1995, at the scattering of the ashes of Clutton-Brock, Robert Mugabe, President of Zimbabwe, maintained that Guy Clutton-Brock made the majority black people in Zimbabwe to be aware of their political and social rights through seminars and workshops and was so highly regarded by the majority of the black Zimbabweans that he was invited as one of the key speakers when the Southern Rhodesia African National Congress (An African Political Party) was founded in 1957.[27]

Most Zimbabweans do not see Christian missionaries in general as being part and parcel of British Imperialism. They see them as the people who came to Zimbabwe with David Livingstone's three Cs—Christianity, commerce, and civilization. This can be shown by the opposition which Aeneas Chigwedere, former Member of Parliament for Wedza constituency, Minister of Education, and Governor of Mashonaland East Province, got from his fellow members of parliament.

Chigwedere urged the government to designate under-utilized mission farms. But speaker after Speaker thereafter opposed the motion, arguing the missionaries were good people who had supported Zimbabwe's liberation struggle, set up schools and universities, or simply educated many Zimbabweans including comrade (Cde.) Chigwedere himself.[28]

From 2000 to the present day, the Robert Mugabe government embarked on a very violent and bloody land-grab program. Zimbabwean white commercial farmers were targeted. They were beaten, some were killed, and their land grabbed from then, but no Church mission farm was confiscated. This shows that missionaries are highly regarded even by violent and avowed socialists like Mugabe.

The USPG missionaries proclaimed the Gospel of Christ to the traditional Shona people in Zimbabwe because it is true; it is not only true because the USPG missionaries proclaimed it. The Gospel of Christ justified the proclamation, but the proclamation does not justify the Gospel. This then brings home the point that British colonial expansion was not the aim of USPG missionaries in Zimbabwe. The slogan of USPG missionaries in Zimbabwe was the three Cs—Christianity, commerce and civilization, but for Cecil John Rhodes, the British Empire builder in the hard political sphere, the slogan was "philanthropy plus five percent". Rhodes left a legacy of white domination and superiority while USPG missionaries left the Church of God and the Gospel of Christ.

USPG missions used three models of religious organization: quarantine, vernacular, and education. The quarantine model of religious organization was used in USPG mission schools, farms, and hospitals. Sanneh described the strategy of the quarantine style: "when from timidity, anxiety, expectation or eschatological fear, the believers maintain a close vigilance over their life and conduct in relative seclusion from the world."[29] The USPG missionaries in Zimbabwe used USPG mission schools, farms, and hospitals to separate all Shona USPG Christians from contact with the outside "heathen" world of ATR. Although their goal was adaptation, a term which signifies the same reality as inculturation, Waliggo describes the difficulty:

> But adaptation did not go far enough to express the reality of an indissoluble marriage between Christianity and each local culture. It implies a selection of certain rites and customs, purifying them and inserting them within Christian rituals where there was any apparent similarity. Then comes the term indigenization. It referred to the same process but underlined the necessity of promoting indigenous ministers in every locality.[30]

What difference did adaptation make to the Shona USPG Christians as far as the integration into Christ of USPG Christianity and ATR is concerned? There is no integration of USPG Christianity and Shona ancestors (ATR) through the accommodation process as far as Shona USPG Christians and Shona Anglican bishops and priests are concerned (see chapter 5). Adaptation involves the use of some Shona cultural elements—for example, drums (*ngoma)*, rattles (*hosho*)—for a special purpose, in this case a USPG Christian religious purpose. It also involves the training of an African ministry. Shona Anglican bishops and priests replace USPG missionaries. Adaptation also involves the translating of English hymns into Shona language and the translating of the Scriptures (Holy Bible) from English into Shona. However, the USPG Christocentric and ecclesiocentric soteriologies continue and are perpetuated by Shona bishops. But under cover of darkness for fear of the bishop, Shona Anglican priests venerate their ancestors and practice ATR (see chapter 5). The Christological expectations of the majority of the Shona USPG Christians and Shona Anglican bishops and priests are not taken seriously by the process of adaptation. By and large, adaptation condemns and rejects Shona ancestors and ATR.

Whenever ATR and USPG Christianity meet, there is potential conflict. Spiritual conflicts exist between ATR and Christianity. It is difficult to separate African culture from ATR because religion is embedded in African culture. ATR is part of the African ethos, and an understanding of it should go hand in hand with USPG Christian evangelization. Ignoring these traditional beliefs, attitudes, and practices may lead to a lack of understanding of African behavior and problems. It is, however, recognized that it is impossible to isolate specific elements and customs of any culture and Christianize them. Where this is being done, the encounter between the Gospel and ATR does not take place at a meaningful level. Only when the encounter is inclusive will inculturation be a force animating and transforming ATR from within. Inculturation means "to make Christianity enter the very blood veins of the Africans, to make it answer their aspirations and anxieties, to make African Christians recover their one identity rather than live in dualism, with one foot in Christianity and the other in an African world view".[31] Adaptation has resulted in Shona USPG Christians and Shona Anglican bishops and priests living in religious dualism. In Zimbabwe, USPG missionaries were not involved in inculturation but in accommodation. Inculturation comprises much more than culture. It involves the entire context: social, economic, political, religious, and educational. In Zimbabwe inculturation should include Shona ancestors in ATR. In the Anglican Church in Zimbabwe, I am the first clergyman to use the term inculturation as defined here. The Anglican Church in Zimbabwe advocates accommodation and not inculturation. Bishop Sabastian Bakare is the first Anglican clergyman to plead for inculturation, but he has never used the term as I will define it (see chapters 4 and 5).

Ronald Oliver noted that the overwhelming result of mission was to open the way for African leadership in the Church and in some significant cases for the Africanization process, which conflicted with Western cultural notions. Implicit ATR resistance to SPG cultural and religious superiority began soon after the arrival of SPG Christianity in 1891 when Bishop Knight-Bruce established the diocese of Harare. This was a result of SPG cultural and religious superiority over ATR. That is, while many SPG missionaries remained unconsciously ethnocentric, and white supremacy was taken for granted, it was felt that not only the souls of black heathens could be saved from eternal damnation, but that they could be educated on SPG and white terms to be good citizens of the British Empire. This SPG attitude was also a reflection of the mid-Victorian Christian and British mind-set that had been imported from Britain and the quite extensive contact that had existed between blacks and whites since the colonization of Zimbabwe in 1890 and which had been maintained to facilitate an agricultural and trade base for the colony. The everyday contact (though limited and racist by modern standards) of whites with blacks should not be underestimated as a prerequisite for later resistance to USPG and white religious, cultural, economic, and political oppression. The dilemma for USPG Christianity was that while it tried to improve the status of Africans, it did not challenge the oppressive structures to which it was umbilically tied and, partly as a consequence, it was not in touch with the black experience of living under a white colonial regime. The USPG organized and theologized at a distance, with all the assumptions of cultural superiority and Christian paternalism. USPG missionary ignorance of black experience intensified after November 11, 1965, when Ian Smith declared Unilateral Declaration of Independence (UDI) from Britain, and the economic, social, and political divide between black and white widened with the increasing adoption of segregationist legislation such as the 1969 Land Tenure Act, the 1971 Act which made Rhodesia/Zimbabwe a Republic, and the various anti-terrorist acts which were continuously promulgated soon after the outbreak of the guerrilla war of independence in 1966.

Africanization was a process of adaptation. Oliver provides an accurate description of this process:

It is therefore against the background of ecclesiastical organizations already largely African in personnel and increasingly self supporting in finance that the specific contribution of the European missionary factor has to be examined and assessed. As the indigenous institutions took shape, the pastoral missionary became less an initiator than a caretaker, holding a well defined position until a native of the country should be ready to occupy it.[32]

The USPG missionaries were to train the local indigenous Zimbabwean people for the eventual takeover of the leadership in the indigenous local Church and spearheading the process of adaptation in the indigenous local Church. The process of vernacularization by the USPG missionaries was the process of adaptation which is still the case in the Anglican Church in Zimbabwe today.

## TYPES OF SOTERIOLOGIES USED IN MISSION BY THE USPG MISSIONARIES

The USPG, an Anglican organization, adheres to the Nicene, Apostolic, and St. Anathasius Creeds: belief in the One, Holy, Catholic, and Apostolic Church, in God the Creator and Sustainer of the universe, in Jesus Christ the Son of God and in the Holy Spirit the giver of life. The Lambeth Quadrilateral of 1888 stated that SPG Christianity was based on the Scriptures and the Creeds which plead for Christocentric and ecclesiocentric soteriologies. USPG Christianity believes in the uniqueness and universality of Jesus Christ—Jesus Christ is the only universal savior. USPG missionaries are basically Christocentric and ecclesiocentric. Explicit knowledge of Jesus Christ, the centrality of Jesus Christ, membership in the Church of Jesus Christ: these are the only requirements for salvation. The presence of the Holy Spirit in the Church and among the members of the Church has all-encompassing powers for salvation. The USPG is Christocentric and ecclesiocentric because it was formed to preach the Gospel of Christ to all nations and to plant the Anglican Church in all nations. The USPG planted the Anglican Church in the British overseas colonies and evangelized the heathens. Colonial Churches were to be USPG missionary centers. The USPG declared in the most emphatic way that Jesus Christ is the universal Savior.

Dewey notes that the gradual movement of the more evangelical people to the Church Missionary Society (CMS) left the SPG looking more "High Church" than its members intended. Nevertheless, in 1973, Dewi Morgan (SPG Editorial Secretary 1951-1963) reported his impressions of the humility and servanthood of the Society. From his talk we can infer that the USPG pleaded for Christocentric and ecclesiocentric soteriologies. Morgan said that for SPG, SPG just did not matter. It was a Servant—a *doulos*—of the Church. And I rapidly learned that 'Church' did *not* mean Church of England (something I as a Welshman was readily disposed to accept anyway) but the Church as itself the servant of the King and the Kingdom whose coming Jesus taught us to pray and work for.[33]

The preaching of the Gospel and the building of Churches are both essential to the USPG. The Gospel proclaims what God does through the life, death, resurrection, ascension and second coming of Christ, and the sending of the Holy Spirit, and calls for the human response of repentance and faith. In 1859, Bishop Samuel Wilberforce of Oxford diocese, son of William Wilberforce, had affirmed that "England can never be clear from the guilt of her long continued slave trade till Africa is free, civilized, and Christian."[34] Anglo-Catholicism was rooted in a profoundly evangelical and personal devotion to Christ. USPG's centrality was on Jesus Christ the Church and the Holy Spirit.

Every generation in every land needs to be evangelized so that it can have explicit knowledge of Jesus Christ and be a member of the Church of God. The Holy Spirit is within the Church and among Christians who are members of the Church. Anglicanism was to be transported to Africa and an African Catholic Church was to be built in Africa. USPG missionaries pleaded for a Trinitarian Christianity which believed in God the Father, Jesus Christ the Son of God, and the Holy Spirit from the Father of the Son. Preaching the Gospel of Christ, uplifting of the Church through prayer, and meeting financial and material needs of the Churches' initiatives were some of the responsibilities of the laity within the Anglican Church. The Anglican Church was to be converted to a closer following of Christ. The Church had the final control and direction of the USPG. The life and death of the USPG was in the hands of the Church. This made ecclesiology a very important and central aspect of the USPG Christianity.

## THE SPG AND UMCA ADVOCATED ADAPTATION OF THE CHRISTIAN GOSPEL AS A MEANS OF EVANGELIZATION

The questions to be asked and answered are these: Can the Christocentric and ecclesiocentric soteriologies of the USPG provide us with enough fertile ground to plead for inculturation without causing tensions and separations between USPG Christianity and ATR? And what happens when USPG Christianity is integrated with ATR and Shona ancestors? A brief history of missions will provide us with the materials for an answer. Bishop Robert Gray, a SPG missionary, arrived in Cape Town, South Africa, in 1847. "He, like David Livingstone, a London Missionary Society (LMS) missionary, loved and respected the Africans as persons and appreciated their culture."[35] In Cape Town in 1861, Charles Frederick McKenzie, a Cambridge mathematician, was consecrated bishop of the UMCA mission to the tribes dwelling in the neighborhood of Lake Nyasa (Malawi) and the Shire river. The UMCA missionaries settled at the Yao village of Magomero and learnt the Nyasa language.[36] McKenzie died on 31st January, 1862, and was buried in Malawi among the Malawian people. William Tozer, who succeeded McKenzie, moved the mission headquarters to Zanzibar and trained an African ministry at

Zanzibar.[37] Edward Steere succeeded Tozer. Steere learned the Swahili language after Dr. Krapf, a CMS missionary, pioneered the translation of the Bible into Swahili. Steere, addressing four young missionaries, summarized the UMCA philosophy of mission, which encouraged inculturation: "follow as far as you can the customs of the place and people."[38] In 1875 Steere trekked into the mainland in order to return some freed slaves to their former homes and planted an African Christian village on the way to Lake Malawi. Chuma was part of the trekking group. African Christian villages were established at Masasi and Newala. John Swedi was the UMCA's first African Deacon.[39]

John Hine became Nyasaland's (Malawi's) third bishop. Hine underscored the UMCA's stress on accommodation:

> What this mission has always professed to aim at is the building-up of a Native Church, which does not mean the baptizing of a number of natives attached to the English mission, and working under its wing, but the Church of the people of the land, irrespective of European influence, adapting itself to the special circumstances of the race and country.[40]

In 1883, Charles Alan Smythies succeeded Steere as bishop of the UMCA. In 1884 he opened the long planned theological College at Kiungani in Zanzibar, providing for it a compelling rationale: "it is always better, if possible to educate the native clergy in Africa than in England...where the good of their education is balanced by the loss of touch with their own people...."[41] In Lesotho, Modderpoort became a centre for European and African work, language study, and translation and mission to Lesotho. In South Africa, by 1881, Grahamstown's clergy had increased from 6 to 47, and its bishop could write: "that we have a Native ministry growing up; and that the foundation is laid of a native ministry fund supported entirely by themselves."[42] In 1898, Frank Weston, a UMCA missionary, left England for Zanzibar. Weston, who succeeded Hine as bishop, was greatly concerned for indigenization and local training of priests.[43] Indigenous Christian art was part of the adaptation process. In Zimbabwe the SPG pleaded for an African Church which was not rooted in Shona ancestors and ATR. The African SPG believed that the Church was there to sanctify their home and life. The Church must be the home of an African.[44]

Charles Gore, president of the UMCA, spoke at the blessing of Central Africa House in London in 1929: "We have always maintained that what we were about was not the transporting of Anglicanism into Africa, but the building up of an African Catholic Church. And the Africans caught the fire of that idea."[45] The building of an African Catholic Church was an accommodation process by the USPG. The USPG did not believe that African cultural religiosity contains Christian elements through which one can truly find Christ. The African bishops and African Christians caught the fire of accommodation. African bishops are in the forefront of pleading for Christian accommodation in Africa (see chapters 4 and 5). The Gospel is to put on an African accommodation dress. In the 1950s, the SPG and the Anglican Church "raised a South African Emergency Fund of £40,000 for simple vernacular literature and to finance St. Augustine's Test School for African ordinands."[46] In Westminster Abbey, in May 1958, Bishop Nigel Cornwall of Borneo, formerly a priest in Masasi, reminded those gathered near Livingstone's grave that "the time had come when the mission must give way to the Church, rooted in the soil and with African husband men."[47]

The USPG embarked on the process of adaptation from the beginning of its formation. Addressing the South African parliamentarians in 1960, the then British Prime Minister, Macmillan, coined his famous phrase "the wind of change". That "wind of change" in Africa blew mainly from Ghana in 1957, the first British colony in Africa to win independence. Africanization of the Church in UMCA areas preceded an atmosphere of political revolution.[48] In 1963, the theological ferment exploded into popular view with Bishop Robinson's *Honest to God.* Indigenizations of overseas Churches accelerated with growing emphasis on theological and lay training.[49] Indigenous people in the British colonies and in countries which were not British colonies were to hear the Gospel of Jesus Christ in their own vernacular. Vernacularization is a process of adaptation. By supporting the process of quarantine of African Christians in Christian villages and vernacularization, the USPG was not supporting inculturation among the indigenous people of Zimbabwe. USPG missionaries in Zimbabwe did not involve themselves in the processes of appropriation and inculturation of the Gospel of Christ into ATR. No serious attempt was made to integrate Shona ancestors into the Christian Gospel. USPG missionaries in Zimbabwe were involved in the process of accommodation. That is, they worked out and produced a convenient arrangement of creating "harmony" between USPG Christianity and ATR. That was a process of adaptation not inculturation. There was no attempt to incarnate Christ into ATR. They did not take Shona ancestors seriously. The accommodation process was done by using the local Shona language. USPG missionaries (a very small number) learnt to read and write the local Shona language. They celebrated the Eucharist in Shona. Greetings were done in Shona. They communicated with the Shona people in Shona. The Bible, the English prayer book, and the English hymns were translated into Shona. That was a process of vernacularization that enabled the USPG missionaries in Zimbabwe to communicate Christianity as the USPG missionaries understood it. That was impossible without using the local language to convey the Christian message to the Shona people.

In the process of accommodation, the USPG missionaries developed an African ministry with very low stipends and very poor working conditions incommensurate with the rest of the USPG missionary organization. Shona Anglican priests were trained to carry on the USPG missionary agenda of accommodation unchanged. Shona priests were taught by the USPG missionaries to condemn and reject Shona ancestors and ATR. Quarantines were set up. These were USPG mission schools, hospitals, and farms, where the "unpolluted pure" USPG Shona Christians lived and worked. The "pure" Shona USPG Christians were separated from any contact with Shona ancestors and ATR. Shona and Ndebele Christians were quarantined by the USPG missionaries at Saint Augustine Tsambe, Daramombe Chivhu, Saint

David Bonda, Saint Patrick Chiwundura, Saint Phillip Guruve, Saint Johns Chikwaka in Murehwa, and Saint James Nyamadhlovu. It was not until the 1960's that the USPG accommodation process used local Shona instruments in worship, such as drums *(ngoma)* and rattles (*hoshos*). Accommodation failed to incarnate Jesus Christ into ATR, for Shona USPG Christians and Shona Anglican priests continue to venerate their ancestors under cover of darkness for fear of the bishop.

## ANCESTRAL QUALITIES, DUTIES, AND POWERS OF JESUS CHRIST SEEN FROM THE USPG VIEW OF ANCESTOR

What I would like to stress from the preceding history, as particularly relevant for my *Mudzimu Mukuru* par excellence Christology, are four points. First, I want to use social anthropology to understand the traditional Shona. For a traditional Shona, God is *Mwari* the Creator and Sustainer of the universe. The Church represents a traditional Shona family or ethnic group. Jesus Christ represents a Shona ancestor, and the Holy Spirit represents Shona ancestors as spiritual beings. Second, I want to subordinate such anthropological data to Christian faith. Third, I want to use analogy when ascribing traditional Shona ancestral categories and other traditional elements to Christian mysteries. And fourth, of course, I want to stress the relevance of my *Mudzimu Mukuru* par excellence Christology for human welfare (our ultimate end).

In all these documents, I am made aware that each culture in its traditions, wisdom, customs, teachings, arts and sciences, has elements conducive to glorifying God, thereby hastening the incarnation of Jesus Christ in each and every culture. However, it is a depressing historical fact that except in Western Europe, America, Canada, New Zealand, and Australia, the Anglican Church has not been able to integrate or incorporate and transform any indigenous culture, thus failing to become adequately native.

The Royal Charters, Supplementary Charters, Conferences, Meetings and Statements by bishops and prominent Anglicans have not recognized the legitimacy of pluralism in the Anglican Church and have not made inculturation a policy. For the USPG, after the 1958 Lambeth Conference, it can be rightly deduced that no culture is totally sacred, just as no culture is totally profane or secular. The particular Anglican Church provinces and dioceses were to enjoy their own independence, their own liturgical usage, their own theological and spiritual heritage. But sadly in Zimbabwe inculturation is not promised to the Zimbabwean Church in the manner of proclaiming the Gospel, in the celebration of the liturgy, and in the provision of canon law. The Royal Charters, Supplementary Charters, Conferences, Meetings, and Statements by bishops and prominent Anglicans do not ask us to utilize our cultural values for ecclesiastical purposes. The documents are not emphatic in their demand that Christological investigation be stirred up in each socio-cultural region. The goals to be striven for by the efforts of the Anglican theologians and Christologians all over the world are to produce theologies and Christologies based on the tradition of the Catholic Church using the culture of the local peoples and to maintain Catholic unity both at local and international levels. The Gospel of Christ certainly is not identified with cultures, and transcends them all, but the Kingdom that the Gospel proclaims is lived by human beings deeply tied to a culture. This provides more guidance and support in developing my *Mudzimu Mukuru* par excellence Christology.

The Royal Charter for the formation of the SPG, the Supplementary Charters, Conferences, Meetings, Sermons and Statements by bishops and prominent Anglicans, by supporting the accommodation process, provoke and motivate me to do Christology from a traditional Shona ancestorhood perspective, so as to make Jesus Christ incarnate among the Zimbabweans. In my opinion, the critical scientific, systematic disclosure of our traditional Shona ancestorhood values will help us anchor ourselves in our Christological inculturation.

The analysis of the Royal Charter for the formation of the SPG, the Supplementary Charters, Conferences, Meetings, Sermons, and Statements by bishops and prominent Anglicans does not legitimize, support, or guide me in developing a *Mudzimu Mukuru* par excellence Christology. Nevertheless, I am motivated to inculturate the Gospel message in our time. As I endeavor to scrutinize thoroughly the Gospel message through our traditional Shona philosophy of life, I open myself for mutual enrichment in genuinely holding dialogue with the Church in its different epochs and eras. Moreover, I have learned from the Church teachings that it is required of me to dig deep into our Shona traditional people's philosophy and wisdom for a systematic scientific and critical Christology and to adapt my *Mudzimu Mukuru* par excellence Christology into catechisms, liturgy, ethics, and indeed the whole Christian life, to guard myself from negative syncretism and false particularism, and to make Christianity explicitly the determining factor in separating the good from the evil in traditional Shona culture. Furthermore, I want to make my *Mudzimu Mukuru* par excellence Christology truly Zimbabwean, African, and worldwide.

This chapter has shown that inculturation is not prescribed, supported, nor guided by the Church authority. Inculturation is condemned by both the Anglican Church and the USPG through Church documents. The accommodation within the Anglican Church tradition does not include the efforts to develop a *Mudzimu Mukuru* par excellence Christology. Nowhere in the USPG Formation Charter of 1701, USPG Supplementary Charters, and USPG Conferences, is Jesus Christ explicitly called Ancestor or Greatest Ancestor par excellence (*Mudzimu Mukuru* par excellence). However, the USPG was and still is deeply rooted in Biblical Christologies, ecclesiologies, soteriologies, and the Trinity. I will also make them very important parts of my *Mudzimu Mukuru* par excellence Christology. USPG Biblical Trinity and ecclesiology will help me develop my inculturated, transformative Trinitarian *Mudzimu Mukuru* par excellence Christology.

The USPG was and still is a missionary organization of a colonial national Church of England. The USPG was and still is interested in creating local national Churches and not a universal Church. The Anglican Church in Britain is to this day a national Church, and it wants to maintain that position. The Supreme Governor of the Church of England is a title held by the British Monarch. The title signifies titular leadership over the Church of England. The canon law of the Church of England makes the Monarch the highest power under God in Britain, with supreme authority over all persons in all causes, ecclesiastical as well as civil. In practice this power is often exercised through parliament and the Prime Minister. The fact that the USPG was the colonial master in Zimbabwe increased tensions and conflicts between ATR and USPG Christianity. ATR views USPG Christianity as a colonial tool to subjugate the Zimbabweans religiously, culturally, politically, socially, and economically. Being part of imperial and colonial Britain gave the USPG missionaries a sense of cultural superiority over the Africans and ATR.

The USPG established the Anglican Church in the British colonies. The Anglican Church went to the colonies as a colonial Church, but with time it grew into a universal Church. The Anglican Church has become universal, but still it maintains colonial and British national structures which do not take into consideration the different cultures from other parts of the world. The universal Anglican Church is *headquartered* in London, its leader, the Archbishop of Canterbury is always British. The Archbishop of Canterbury is chosen by the British Christians and politicians but has jurisdiction of the world-wide Anglican Communion. The USPG carried this British cultural superiority to Zimbabwe. The current problems in the universal Anglican Church, such as the ordination of women to the priesthood and bishophood, abortion, euthanasia, same sex marriages and ordinations, have split the Anglican Church in Zimbabwe as a result of cultural superiority and imperialism by USPG missionaries. Two Anglican African bishops in Zimbabwe, Nolbert Kunonga and Elson Jakazi of the dioceses of Harare and Manicaland oppose USPG religious and cultural superiority and imperialism. They were excommunicated from the world-wide Anglican Communion. A former employee of the USPG in London, Chad Gandiya, was elected bishop of Harare in 2009 to replace Kunonga. The bishop of Mutare will be elected soon, but the USPG will still have a lot of influence in the election of the bishop.

In order for the Anglican Church to be united as One, Holy, Catholic, and Apostolic Church, the USPG missionaries should stop the national and cultural superiority agendas. Along with a colonial structure goes a colonial mentality which is instinctively controlling. It should be realized that world-wide Anglicanism has now entered a post-colonial phase. There is an urgent need for ATR and USPG Christianity to be integrated. The USPG, in pleading for Christocentric and ecclesiocentric soteriologies, does advocate the same Jesus Christ viewed by the Zimbabwean Christians as *Mudzimu Mukuru* par excellence, according to their needs, aspirations, existential problems, thought forms, and mentality. The USPG does not stress the essential Christian elements in the light of the Zimbabwean Church situation. In chapter seven, a comparative analysis of Shona traditional ancestorhood and the ancestorhood of Jesus Christ from the USPG and Biblical points-of-view will find out their similarities and differences.

# CHAPTER 3

## *USPG Missionary Attitudes towards African Traditional Religion (ATR)*

This chapter investigates the attitudes of the USPG missionaries in Zimbabwe towards ATR, ancestors in particular. It also investigates my thesis that USPG missionaries in Zimbabwe advocated a Christ against Shona traditional ancestors, pleading instead for a Christ of Western culture. The chapter looks at the various historical and political periods in Zimbabwe and the USPG missionary bishops, Shona bishops and some priests who worked during those particular historical and political periods: the Pioneer period 1875-1923; the British colonial rule period 1924-1952; the Federation period 1953-1963; Rhodesia's (Zimbabwe's) Unilateral Declaration of Independence from Britain period 1965-1979; and, Zimbabwe's post-Independence period 1980-to the present. I will focus on bishops because they are representatives of their dioceses. I will also refer to individual priests and USPG missionaries. In looking at the post-Independence period in Zimbabwe, this chapter investigates especially Bishop Ralph Peter Hatendi, the first Shona Anglican diocesan bishop in Zimbabwe. I will refer to the Anglican missionary organizations SPG and UMCA as USPG because the USPG inherited their histories.

### ATTITUDES OF USPG MISSIONARIES DURING THE PIONEER PERIOD 1875-1923

The Anglican Church in Zimbabwe was a colonial Church, and it was a white man's Church from Britain. During the Pioneer period,

Rhodesia (Zimbabwe) was ruled by the British South African Company (BSA Co.), a commercial mining company interested in mining ventures in Zimbabwe. The first USPG missionary to come into Zimbabwe was the Reverend Greenstock in 1875.The theological thinking of the missionaries in Zimbabwe led inevitably to problems, misunderstandings, and conflicts with the Shona people. Missionaries were involved in a theological debate as to whether ATR beliefs included any idea of a divine being at all. Most missionaries concluded that it did not.[1] USPG missionaries who came to Zimbabwe thought that they were coming to a people who, if they knew of the existence of God at all, had such small glimmerings of Him that they were hardly worth noticing. For example, the USPG missionaries opposed the killing of twins. By opposing the killing of twins, the USPG missionaries were in actual fact opposing traditional Shona culture and religion, which held that the bearing of twins was a very bad omen for the nation and family. If twins were not killed, disasters such as droughts, wars, diseases, and unexplained deaths would occur. Bishop Knight-Bruce wrote that "I do not think that Christianity has gone very far down into the people generally as yet. The bad customs seem to exist still. Quite late some newly born twins were killed by their both being put into a pot and hot ashes heaped over them."[2]

Bishop Knight-Bruce was of the opinion that the traditional Shona people had no religion. He asked, "what is the religion of the Mashona? It is very hard to say that they have any."[3] USPG missionaries ran into serious trouble when their preaching challenged vital indigenous institutions such as polygamy. The uncompromising attitude of the USPG missionaries towards polygamy was a serious hindrance to the advance of USPG Christianity. "If polygamy is morally right for a Christian, there is no valid reason that we should not be polygamists in England today. If it is morally wrong, it should be given up by Africans."[4] For the traditional Shona people, polygamy was good for their society. It had functional purposes: there were no prostitutes in their society and almost everybody got married. G. Bhebhe, an historian of Lutheran missionaries in Zimbabwe, wrote about missionary attitudes towards ATR in western Zimbabwe. What

Bhebhe wrote also applies to the USPG missionaries in Zimbabwe. Polygamy was condemned by the missionaries on religious grounds and also for being "inhumane" and for degrading women to nothing better than slaves.[5] The "degraded" African neither thought it immoral to practice polygamous marriages, nor did he perceive any moral superiority in monogamy.[6] The first Synod of the diocese of Mashonaland (Zimbabwe) was held on the 19th April 1903, and Bishop Gaul in his Charge to the Synod stated that "we believe that polygamy should in every way be discouraged."[7]

USPG missionaries attacked both the paying of the bride price (*lobola/ roora)* and polygamy (*barika/ chipari*). They argued that *lobola* was used by the traditional Shona people to buy wives. *Lobola* was viewed as encouraging polygamy. The missionaries believed that *lobola* was a purchase of a wife by a traditional Shona man for the purposes of begetting children, among whom girls, when marriageable, were disposed of in order to obtain *lobola/roora*, which was used again to obtain other wives, the final object being to acquire position and substance through possession of women and children. Most white settlers expected Bishop Knight-Bruce to look after the spiritual aspects of the white settlers, and a lot of money was supposed to be directed towards the building of Churches for the white settlers. Salvation for the traditional Shona, it was thought, should come through Jesus Christ only.

It was a task of raising these people, as one missionary indicated, 'from unbridled lust, and all pernicious influence of heathen life, to the purity and moral earnestness of Christianity'. The missionaries believed that this could be achieved through a thorough knowledge of the Bible and a deeper grasp of Christian Graces.[8]

Although the USPG missionaries were convinced of the uplifting power of the Scriptures, they also emphasized the role of Western civilization in ensuring the permanence of the Church. In 1895, Bishop Knight-Bruce described the custom of *chisi* day and its appropriation by the missionaries: on Sunday a [British] flag is hung up, and

Mangwende stops all work. The hoisting of this flag was connected with the Shona custom known as *chisi,* a high day or holiday. At that time the people indulged in many holidays, special days appointed by the chief on which no work was done. On a *chisi* day no work was permitted, except the most necessary cores. It was not long before Bernard [Mizeki's] growing influence with the chief, and a little pressure applied in the name of friendship, caused Mangwende to proclaim every Sunday a *chisi,* so that those who wished to do so could attend the services at the mission. Bernard could hoist a flag beside the "Church", proclaiming the Lord's day, and Mangwende would hoist an answering flag at the top of his fortress, proclaiming the *chisi.*[9]

The *chisi* day was in honour of the regional ancestral spirits (*mhondoro/ midzimu mikuru*) who bring rain and who make it possible for crops and animals to grow well. Burials, for example, were performed only on a *chisi* day. Mangwende, therefore, changed the *chisi* day from Thursday to a Sunday to please the USPG missionaries. However, the change of the *chisi* day was opposed by the *n'anga, mhondoro*. Consequently, on the 18th June, 1896, Mangwende's son, Muchemwa, killed Bernard Mizeki, who was an African USPG catechist among the Shona people.

Knight-Bruce believed that the traditional Shona worshipped a heathen idol and not God. Langham Carter reported on Knight-Bruce's journey to the Zambezi River: "On the Zambezi trek the carriers told him on one occasion that their God would not allow them to go on till I had given them a present. Knight-Bruce refused to make an offering to a heathen idol."[10] Langham Carter also explained that "Knight-Bruce was certain that Christianity and western education were producing a much finer African than the raw savage. White rule would also provide the basis for bringing them the benefits of Christianity."[11] W. R. Peaden, a Methodist Church Minister, described events of the Southern Rhodesia Missionary Conferences that are similar to the experiences of USPG missionaries in Zimbabwe. In 1899, chief Mutasa was blunt with the first African black priest in Zimbabwe, H. Mtobi from South Africa, who went to see him about the Christian

God. Mutasa replied that there was no such a person. "Look here, I do not know your God, and here in my country I am the god of every one of you!'"[12] Mutasa's outburst against Mtobi reveals his recognition that the missionaries wished to oust him from ATR leadership of his people as their secular colleagues had ousted him from the political leadership. Bishop Gaul speaking on the training of the Native Africans in Zimbabwe pleads, "let us save him by teaching him self help in agriculture and trades, together with the higher training in worship and self discipline which our holy religion alone can give."[13] The traditional Shona people were to be saved by the USPG missionaries by preaching the Gospel of Jesus Christ to them.

In 1895 Knight-Bruce and Bernard Mizeki visited chief Makoni to persuade him to take a more favorable attitude towards USPG Christianity. Chief Makoni gave what were in his view several moral objections to USPG Christianity. The first objection concerned the USPG mission opposition to the pledging of an unborn daughter in marriage (*kuzvarira).* Chief Makoni asked: "this teaching does it not makes girls disobedient to their parents and husbands? Does it not mean that the boys instead of getting wives for themselves steal their wives?"[14] A further question by chief Makoni concerned the USPG missions ban on the ancestor cult: "this teaching is it not plainly unnatural? Does it not forbid reverence to the dead and the customary sacrificial offerings to the dead?"[15] The legal and compulsory elimination of bride price (*roora*) was a move by the USPG missionaries to eliminate *lobola* among the traditional Shona people. *Roora* was regarded as a heathen practice by the USPG missionaries. At the Diocesan Conference held at St. Augustine, Tsambe, in 1922, the USPG missionaries passed a resolution in regard to the guardianship of Shona USPG Christian orphans left by the deaths of their fathers. "It was asked that in such cases native custom should not be the deciding factor, but that consideration be given to the fact that such children being Christians should not be handed over to non-Christian guardianship. Also the demanding of excessive *lobola* by Christian parents was strongly condemned."[16] This was against Shona traditional and cultural beliefs. Orphans, together with their mother, the widow (*shirikadzi)*, were to be inherited by one of the deceased's brothers. The widow was to be inherited as a wife (*kugarwa nhaka*). The USPG missionaries condemned inheritance of a widow.

The opposition of the USPG missionaries to ATR continued unabated during Bishop Beavan's Episcopacy (1911-1925). At the same time, ATR opposed USPG Christianity. Shona USPG Christians attended Church services for a variety of reasons, such as getting their children into school, getting medical attention, getting jobs at the mission schools, hospitals, and farms, and also out of curiosity to find out what the strange new USPG Christian teaching was all about. Broderick describes a crisis at this time.

> In 1923 almost for the first time in the history of the mission there arose some organized opposition to the Church at St. David, Bonda. The local chief named Chiobvu, a relative of the paramount Chief Mutasa, had been baptized some years before at St. Augustine, Tsambe, but he was always an unsatisfactory man. He suddenly ordered a c*hisi chemwedzi* which was an old native custom of a gathering at the chief's kraal for offering sacrifices to his ancestors. The whole of the Bonda congregation obeyed his summons and a struggle commenced between the first priest the Reverend G. E. P. Broderick and the chief, and the Church services were deserted. The priest had no alternative but to suspend all communicants from the sacraments and declare that it was a choice between what was due to God, and what to Caesar. For a time there was a sullen and arrogant chief.[17]

USPG Christianity and ATR were at loggerheads. Shona USPG Christians came back to Church after venerating and worshipping their ancestors, but the USPG priest, G. E. P. Broderick, suspended all communicants from receiving Holy Communion. He vigorously maintained USPG missiology. ATR was to be destroyed at any cost.

There was a problem of Shona USPG Christians attending funeral ceremonies of both USPG Christian and non-Christian relatives, especially the bringing-back-home (*kurova guva/chenura)* ceremonies. The matter was debated by the Anglicans in their Native missionary Conference in 1918. It was agreed by both USPG missionaries and African delegates that the instances were widespread in the diocese, and many of the Shona Christians were not only attending but actively participating in non-Christian funeral rites.[18] The practice of Shona USPG Christians participating in the *kurova guva* ceremonies, consulting *n'anga*, and practicing witchcraft (*uroyi)* were condemned by the USPG missionaries. USPG missionaries' opinions on bride-price (*roora*) appear to have been totally ignored. Shona Anglican priests, lay Shona Anglicans, Shona Anglican bishops, in the same way as non-Christians, today continue to demand *roora* for their daughters. As time goes on, and the *roora* demands are ever increasing, there is no reason to suppose that Shona USPG Christians are not raising their demands in the same proportion as their non-Christian neighbors. *Roora* has now been greatly commercialized by both Shona USPG Christians and non-Christians in Zimbabwe. Shona USPG Christians are asking for the mother's cow (*mombe yehumai)*, which is offered to ancestors.

The Shona traditional obligation of a male relative to inherit his deceased brother's wife caused a problem among Shona USPG Christian men. This was also debated at the 1918 Native missionary Conference of the Anglican Church. Here it was pointed out that a Christian man became responsible for his relative's widow whether he would or not, unless the widow's father could be induced to return the *lobola*.[19] Many delegates considered this very difficult. The conference also mentioned the illogicality of a man being required to take up the responsibilities of a husband towards a woman and her children without taking up the privilege of cohabitation. A Shona Anglican priest, who was Peaden's colleague, contends that the widow herself would feel deeply slighted if her guardian who inherited her did not cohabit with her.[20] This is very true, for there is no traditional Shona inheritance of the widow (*kugara nhaka*) which does not include cohabitation and the raising of children for the deceased brother. There is no *nhaka* if there is no cohabitation.

## THE USE OF MISSIONARY INSTITUTIONS

The USPG missionaries used their institutions, including schools, farms, and hospitals to force the traditional Shona people to conform to USPG missiology. Although the early USPG missionaries were primarily preachers, Church and school marched closely hand in hand. Education has been used by USPG missionaries not merely as a means of producing an educated USPG Christian Zimbabwean population, but also to bring the Gospel to that intellectual elite which can hardly be reached by any other method. Even medical training was used as a means for proclaiming the Gospel in action. The need to establish a system of elementary schools for the traditional Shona, as one of the first priorities of USPG mission strategy, was expressed in unusually vigorous terms by the USPG missionary Bishop William Gaul (1897-1907) when he asserted that our whole future development under God depends on our training of the choicest of our pupils from the various schools as catechists and school masters. Teachers, teachers, teachers, are what the natives are demanding. Are they to be Christian or heathen teachers? The answer must come from the Church or from secularism. At present the future is with Christianity.[21]

Although initially there were many traditional Shona hearers of the Gospel of Jesus Christ, there were few adults, especially men, who came forward for membership in the Church. The situation has not changed to this day. The Methodist W. R. Peaden stated in the Southern Rhodesia Report (1925) of the Commission of Native Education: "our great object is evangelizing the native. When I first came I walked from kraal to kraal and found it useless until we started schools—start with children."[22]

This same Commission of Native Education (1925) set up by the Southern Rhodesia Legislative Assembly reported that

In order to strengthen the Christian faith of the African converts, it was felt necessary that they should be able to read the Bible and the Church's instruction about its Christian faith. As missionary work expanded, there developed the need to train evangelists and pastors. People who were selected for this work were given more training than the ordinary school pupils.[23]

USPG missionaries said quite frankly that schools were necessary in order to develop the cultural change for the USPG Christian life. But that method violated the deep rooted traditional Shona principle that the father's consent is required as a primary legal requirement for a marriage. To have that consent forced in that way was bound to be injurious to his own and his family's sensibilities, and to affect adversely their views on the whole purpose of USPG missions. It is little wonder that missionaries were accused of encouraging their converts to steal wives instead of properly asking for them.[24]

The USPG missionaries' aim in obtaining farms was to create model Shona USPG Christian communities which would be islands of light in a sea of heathen and superstitious darkness. USPG mission farms also became refuges for unwanted babies and Shona USPG Christian widows who refused to be inherited *(kugarwa nhaka)*, together with their children. All was done for the civilizing and Christianizing of the natives therein.[25] Villages on USPG missionary farms at St. Augustine Penhalonga, St. Faith Rusape, Christ the King Daramombe, St. Phillips Guruve, St. Patrick's Chiwundura, St. David's Bonda, Cyrene Bulawayo, and St. James Nyamadhlohvu were regarded as essentially Shona USPG Christian villages (quarantines), where the USPG missionaries made their own civic laws and social rules. They represented an object lesson to the surrounding heathens. Polygamy was prohibited on USPG mission farms, and those who practiced it were expelled from the farms. This was the rule from the time the USPG missionaries began to occupy the farms, and those who had already contracted such marriages when the farms became mission property were excluded from this rule. The missionaries, however, had plans that such tenants should be given two years in which to embrace Christianity or be expelled from the farm, and this would involve people who were polygamists giving up all but their first wife.[26]

Medical USPG missions were used to destroy ATR. Visits to USPG medical missions by the traditional Shona were slow at first simply because the traditional Shona had confidence in their *n'anga* and their ability to cure, and they were very suspicious of missionary medicine. Bishop Knight-Bruce gave an account of what USPG missionaries expected when he described the response of John Shoniwa Kapuya, one of the first traditional Shona to be converted to USPG Christianity by Bernard Mizeki in 1896 at chief Mangwende's kraal. Bernard Mizeki used amateur doctoring to cure Shoniwa Kapuya. Bishop Knight-Bruce wrote the following account:

> He became ill and his mother sent for the witchdoctor, who declared that a goat must be sacrificed to his dead father who was causing the illness. Kapuya refused to have the goat killed. He was taken to the mission hut and treated using Western medicine by the USPG African Evangelist Bernard Mizeki, where he was nursed well again. The doctor came, thinking that a goat had been sacrificed and demanded payment. The enraged doctor (*muroyi*) was told that his advice had neither been believed nor followed and that God had made him well.[27]

That was a typical USPG missionary attitude, confident that Western medicine would succeed while traditional methods would fail.

Incidentally Bishop Knight-Bruce made a classic USPG missionary mistake of failing to distinguish between a witch or wizard (*muroyi)* and a diviner (*n'anga)* who counteracts the effects of the witch. Most USPG missionaries virtually equated the belief about ancestors with witchcraft. Dr. A. D. Owen, a USPG missionary doctor at Wreningham near Chivhu, thought that medical missions would win converts to USPG Christianity by demonstrating that it was the more powerful religion. When you merely preach to people, he thought, they immediately ask why their religion is insufficient. Then comes the argument of Dr. Owen: "can men of your tribe, do what ours can? We will show you that although your *molimos/mlimo* are powerful, our

God is more so. We are willing to cure diseases—can your *molimos* do as much? And we are willing to prove this if you bring your sick to us."[28] Western medicine was used by USPG missionaries in order to win over the traditional Shona population to USPG Christianity. Dr. Andrew Fleming, a medical doctor, argued the following: the medical treatment of natives is a recognized part of a missionary's work and is one of the methods adopted for attracting natives. The treatment of the sick is in most cases one of the most popular methods by which missionary effort amongst the native races tries to bring the native under their influence and as such is one of the stronger platforms for appeal for funds to further this cause.[29]

Health and medical services at USPG mission farms were used to destroy the effect of *n'anga* among the traditional Shona and also to prove the superiority of the USPG Christian religion against ATR. Mission hospitals were used as agents to convert the traditional Shona people from ATR to USPG Christianity. Before one was admitted to a USPG hospital, one was to produce both baptism and confirmation cards to prove that one was a Christian. During their treatment at the hospital, African patients were forced to attend Church services four times a day—morning prayers, noon prayers, evening prayers, and compline. Failure to produce the required cards and to attend Church services resulted in the patient being refused treatment and sent back home. The traditional Shona people gradually came to see the value of western medicines and to avail themselves of their resources, yet ATR remained undiminished. *N'anga* have continued to exist up to the present day, and there is every evidence that the profession of *n'anga* is flourishing more in Zimbabwe than ever and that *n'anga* are consulted not only by followers of ATR but also by Shona Christians.

## ATTITUDES OF MISSIONARIES DURING COLONIAL RULE 1923-1952

In 1925, a Shona Christian catechist wrote a significant article in which he said that many Shona people were not reaching the full stature of the USPG Christian life because "they still keep many pagan customs and superstitions". This statement prompted an editorial reply in the *Zambezi Mission Record*, 1922-1925.

Many native superstitions are practiced in secret and the missionary has little or no chance of putting a stop to them unless they are brought to his notice by some member of his flock. Be it remarked that to inform the missionary of what is going on often calls for no small courage on the part of the informant.[30]

Similarly, on the visit to Toroquay of Southern Rhodesia (Zimbabwe) Anglican Bishop Edward Paget, who was bishop from 1925-1957, *The Toroquay Directory and South Devon Journal* (Wednesday, June 16, 1926) wrote that "the religion of the natives in Rhodesia (Zimbabwe) was a vague kind of spirit worship, composed mainly of fear."[31]

At this time, the institution of marriage came to the attention of the USPG. The Anglican Church in Zimbabwe was a very active member of the Southern Rhodesia Missionary Conference, and consequently these Conferences reflected a lot of USPG missionary thinking on ATR and traditional Shona culture. At the Proceedings of The Southern Rhodesia (Zimbabwe) Missionary Conference, held at Salisbury (Harare) from the 2nd-5th August 1926, the USPG missionaries were represented by the Reverend Canon E. J. Lloyd, A. S. Cripps, Cotton (CR), Bell, A. C. Knights, and some white lay representatives. On African Christians and ATR, the conference maintained that "it is little use their prating about liberty and at the same time hugging their old pagan claims. They must put away the things that bring them into bondage—sloth, drunkenness, polygamy *lobola*, forced marriage and witchcraft."[32] A conference of Native Commissioners held in April 1926 passed a resolution that "a native must first obtain a certificate from the Native Commissioner of his district to be allowed to have his marriage solemnized according to Christian rites."[33] The resolution passed by the Native Commissioners in 1926 got the full backing of the USPG missionaries. That certificate was known as the Enabling Certificate. The Native Commissioner was first to explain to the traditional Shona people who wished to get married in Church the intent and consequences of such a marriage because so many traditional Shona people who married according to USPG Christian rites tended to fall into polygamy. The Commissioner also ascertained that such traditional Shona people had not previously registered a marriage under the "Native Marriage Ordinance of 1917". At the proceedings of the Southern Rhodesia (Zimbabwe) Missionary Conference, held at Salisbury (Harare) Southern Rhodesia (Zimbabwe) from 26th-29th March 1928, the USPG missionaries were represented by Bishop Paget, Canon E. J. Lloyd, Reverends Shropshire, Baker, A. C. Knights, and a lay representative, Miss W. M. Goodliffe. At the Conference, Bishop Paget cautioned that "candidates for marriage by Christian rites realize that civil obligations are attached to their solemn profession of a monogamous state."[34] The resolution was seconded by Canon E. J. Lloyd and was adopted by the Conference.

The real difficulty began when the USPG sought definite control of Shona culture through the *kaffir* beer legislation. *Kaffir*, a derogatory Afrikaner word for the blacks in South Africa, means unbelievers. The Africans in Zimbabwe were derogatorily called *kaffirs* by the whites. The 1930 Southern Rhodesia Conference declared that "the deluge would come when the native would have no difficulty in obtaining European liquor, and that was the trend of events today."[35] In ATR beer and meat are regarded as some of the most important elements which should be ritually sacrificed and offered to ancestors. Usually at ancestor veneration gatherings a lot of beer and meat are consumed. A lot of people get drunk. Also, a lot of Shona people get drunk at *nhimbe* gatherings (beer party for work).

Shona USPG Christians were suspended from receiving Holy Communion when it was discovered that they were involved in ancestor veneration, consulting *n'anga*, and polygamy.

On the 30th April 1938, the Diocesan Director of Missions, the Reverend S. J. Christelow, acknowledged that he received the names of some Shona USPG Christians who have been suspended from Holy Communion and some indefinite suspensions have been imposed. Some self-suspended themselves for being involved in polygamous marriages, others for ancestor veneration, and others for visiting *n'anga*.[36]

Africans were not allowed to be buried in the same cemetery as whites because, when Africans venerate their ancestors, they carry pots full of beer to the grave and perform their rituals by pouring libations of beer on the grave. That was regarded by USPG missionaries as satanic. The rituals were regarded as heathen rituals which polluted the cemetery.

## ARTHUR SHEARLY CRIPPS 1869-1952

Arthur Shearly Cripps, a USPG missionary who had studied at Oxford University, was a great champion of the African cause in economic, political, and social matters, so much so that when he died in 1952, major roads in Harare and Chivhu were named after him. The roads still bear his name today. But he condemned and rejected ATR. Cripps did not condone either indolence or polygamy. He was not prepared to accept Africans who practiced polygamy as occupants of the farms which he was later to acquire.[37] Cripps considered that traditional Shona people wishing to marry under USPG Christian rites should not be penalized by having to pay a fee for the Enabling Certificate. However, he did not condone ancestor veneration, divorce, inheritance of widows, pledging of unborn daughters in marriage (*kuzvarira*), replacement wife (*chigadzamapfihwa*), and witchcraft.

In 1931 the Chief Native Commissioner noted that it was Cripps's practice to impose fines on Christian Africans whom he found guilty of immorality. The sterner side of his nature is further illustrated by the case of a tenant who wanted to divorce his wife because she had run away to become a prostitute in Harare. Cripps gave him a summary notice to quit the mission and remained deaf to all entreaties. Opposition to divorce was second only to his detestation of witchcraft. Although he treated the "heathen" African element of his followers with Christian tolerance and regularly consulted the headman, he spoke out against wife inheritance and polygamy, and would not allow polygamists to attend Church services.[38]

Cripps, therefore, believed that ATR was to be judged by the USPG Christian moral code which condemned and rejected ATR. However, most Shona Anglican Christians opted for both USPG Christianity and traditional Shona culture and religion. That persistence of African traditional beliefs in orthodox Churches like the Anglican Church is not a peculiarity of Zimbabwe. It is found all over Africa. E. Fashole-Luke, writing on Christianity and Islam in Freetown, demonstrates that the Freetown Christian lives a real double life. He holds firmly to the doctrines of the Church, but holds equally firmly the traditional beliefs of his Fathers. The Church's refusal to accept and integrate African beliefs and practises into its own doctrines, coupled with its impotence to efface these systems from the minds of the Africans, has succeeded in making the majority of her members in Freetown lead a Jekyll and Hyde existence.[39]

## ATTITUDE OF MISSIONARY BISHOPS DURING THE FEDERATION PERIOD 1953-1963

Racial discrimination against the black Zimbabweans was on the increase during Cecil Alderson's episcopacy. One cannot separate racial superiority from cultural superiority. The USPG missionaries were of the opinion that they were racially and culturally superior to the black Zimbabweans. The Shona Anglican priests were so brainwashed that they ended up believing that European culture was superior to Shona traditional culture. That belief is shown at the Diocesan Synod of 3rd May, 1962, when a motion was moved that shows that the Shona priests believed their economic and cultural status was inferior to that of whites. At the Diocese of Mashonaland (Harare), the 32nd session of Synod 3rd May 1962, a resolution on stipends was proposed by the Reverend W. Nechironga and was seconded by the Reverend P. A. Murindagomo (later Suffragan bishop Murindagomo). The resolution stated that this synod, believing that the cultural and economical status of the African people in this country approximates more closely to that of the white people, so the stipends of the African clergy should approximate more closely the stipend of the European clergy, instructs the diocesan secretary of the conference (DSC) to divide the money available for the clergy stipends in the year 1963/64, beginning on the 1st July 1963, in such a way that an African clergyman shall receive two thirds of the amount receivable by a European clergyman of the same marital status.[40]

The motion was passed through both Houses of the clergy and the laity because the Africans were in the majority in both Houses but the motion was defeated in the House of bishops. Bishop Alderson was the only member and voter in the House of bishops. Bishop Alderson voted against the resolution because he believed that the whites were racially and culturally superior to the Africans. That was typical of most USPG missionaries to Africa. His reasons for voting against the resolution were: "that the white clergy must be given immediate notice of the remuneration or variation of their contract. That many of the white clergy would be compelled to resign. That the bishop would be unable to replace them. That in consequence white congregations would steeply decline in consequence of that. Funds would disappear."[41]

## THE UNILATERAL DECLARATION OF INDEPENDENCE (UDI) PERIOD 1965-1980

Vatican II of 1962-1965 and the World Council of Churches (WCC) affected the whole Anglican Church. Vatican II and WCC advocated that there should be co-existence between and tolerance of different world religions and cultures. They also pleaded for a process of inculturation. These ideas were rejected by Bishop Paul Burrough of Mashonaland (Harare), 1968-1981. In The Pastoral Regulations (1978) of the Diocese of Mashonaland (Harare), Bishop Burrough declared that "NO Christian may partake of funeral meats and drinks offered to the spirits, nor take part in any worship offered to the spirits, nor in any funeral dancing. They should not engage in excessive weeping and wailing."[42] Bishop Burrough rejected and condemned the veneration of Shona ancestors, ritually sacrificed meat, food, and beer. He also condemned all traditional Shona funeral rites. On the *kuzvarira* type of marriage, Bishop Burrough condemned it as repugnant to Christianity and asserted that "the practice of taking *mayinini* or any woman or girl as a *mazwarira* is repugnant to Christianity and is unreservedly condemned."[43]

## POST INDEPENDENCE BISHOPS

Zimbabwe became independent from Britain on 18th April, 1980. What difference did Zimbabwe's independence make to Shona Anglican Clergy and Laity? What difference did it make to the political, economic, and social development of the majority of the Zimbabwean people? There was no difference to the majority of Zimbabweans. In fact, the majority of Zimbabweans were politically, economically, and socially better off before independence. A small elite of both black and white Zimbabweans enjoy the benefits which accrued from Zimbabwean Independence. Decolonization involved the disappearance of white faces which were replaced by black faces. The black elites took over the reins of government. They did not develop government for the benefit of the majority of people in Zimbabwe. The British colonial system continues and is perpetuated by the black elite. The political, economic, and social expectations of the majority of the people in Zimbabwe have not been met and are not looked at seriously. The blacks who took power are white men in black skins (*varungu vatema*). The color of the leaders changed but the government policies did not. The white British colonial system of government remains intact. There is a veneer of change, a change of color of the leaders, but no change of policies.

What happened in the Zimbabwean government after independence happened in the Anglican Church in Zimbabwe. There has been no development in the Anglican Church. Zimbabwean Anglicans expected some sweeping changes with the coming of a black African bishop, Bishop Peter Ralph Hatendi (1981-1995), but change did not come. The Church expected some great transformations, but Bishop Hatendi was a great disappointment. Hatendi did not change USPG Christianity and administration. The Anglican Church in Zimbabwe continued to be a British Church in Zimbabwe. Hatendi, like the USPG missionary bishops, pursued a process of accommodation, and he condemned ATR and inculturation.

Hatendi was afraid of change. Anglican bishops are generally conservative: to change is to risk and not to change is to have security. Hatendi pursued a policy of money first and God second. Consequently, he was not favorably received by his black priests. He also favored USPG missionaries, for they brought more money into the diocesan coffers than the black priests. He surrounded himself with USPG missionaries. Hatendi maintained the diocese of Harare based on a federation of parishes rather than a diocese based on a unitary system. He maintained the status quo at Zimbabwe's independence, and he was not in any way different from his political counterparts. In fact, he was co-opted into the ZANU (PF) government when he was appointed by Robert Mugabe chairman of the Election Supervisory Commission during the 1990, 1995, and 2000 general elections. He is in the Commission to serve the poor people of Zimbabwe. He identifies himself with the poor. He believes that no machinery can deliver the material, economic, social, and political goods to the poor except the political machinery, and hence he decided to be a member of the Commission. The color of the bishop changed from white to black, but the administrative structure and policies of the diocese of Harare did not change. USPG missionaries in Zimbabwe today have no power to influence the theological and soteriological thinking in the Anglican

Church, but the spirit of USPG missionary missiology condemning ATR is maintained by Shona bishops.

Although Hatendi was not favorably received and was a failure as far as inculturation was concerned, I still regard him as a pastor. In 1973, when Hatendi wrote *Shona Marriages and the Christian Church*, he was a theologian and an academic, the Deputy Principal (Deputy Warden) of St. John's Theological College (Seminary) in Lusaka, Zambia. In his book, he was expressing his own theological views, which were different than the official Church theology. However, when Hatendi became Diocesan bishop in 1981, he changed his theological views so that he could become a unifying symbol of his diocese. To be a bishop or to be a priest in the Catholic Church, one has to be a pastor. Bishops should have the capacity to unite all segments of their diocese. Bishops and priests should not be radical in their theological views as they are symbols of unity. Hatendi changed his theology in order to unite his diocese, especially after the divisive war of liberation in Zimbabwe, which raged from 1966 to 1980.

Many USPG missionaries went out to Zimbabwe with the best intentions of carrying out the declared intention of the USPG: to preach the pure Gospel without tying it to any form of British organization, culture, or policy. They usually ended up producing a faithful copy, down to the minutest detail, of that form of British Christian faith to which they themselves were accustomed. The USPG missionaries were not entirely to blame for this. Shona USPG Christian converts were imitative, and it was often they who wished to have everything done in the traditional way in British Churches. This led to the production of Shona USPG Christians who were more British than the British themselves, who condemned everything in Shona traditional culture and religion, and who accepted everything British, European, and American. A very good example of such Shona USPG Christians is the fishers-of-human-beings *(wabvuwi)* group in the Anglican Church in Zimbabwe. They believed that only the British man—Western man—was a man in the full sense of the word. He was wise and good, and members of the traditional Shona ethnic group, in so far as they became westernized, might share in that wisdom and goodness. That was warped thinking on the part of "white" Africans in black skins (*varungu vatema*).

Hatendi showed understanding when he was a priest. In 1973, he pleaded for a combination of USPG Christianity and ATR. Polygamy, he argued, is also a solution to a sex imbalance when women outnumber men. Reverend Hatendi reasoned that putting unworthy motives of some polygamists aside, a Shona polygamist is a humanist. He comes to the rescue of widows and orphans at their hour of need in a cultural environment which does not provide adequately for independent widows and orphans. Those who condemn them do not fully appreciate the service they render to society.[44]

He continued, "bride wealth *roora* means as much to a Shona woman as a ring to a Western woman."[45] The USPG missionaries condemned the paying of *lobola* as un-Christian, but the Reverend Hatendi upheld *lobola* as a stabilising factor in traditional Shona marriages. On marriage, Reverend Hatendi stated: "similarly why should Christ absent himself when two Christians marry in prayer according to Shona custom? Is Christ confined to finely devised solemnization of matrimony according to the Western rite? For a marriage to be Christian it is essential that the two persons be Christian."[46] What is important for them is to be seen and accepted as married persons by their family groups and community, for marriage is essentially of the community. There is no doubt that ninety nine per cent of Shona marriages satisfy customary and traditional requirements. The solemnization of marriages in Churches is an extension or duplication.[47]

When he became bishop, Hatendi negatively changed his attitudes towards ATR. In his Diocese of Harare *AD CLERUM ON OFFENCES* to all Licensed Clergymen of the Diocese of Harare of the 6th October 1990, Bishop Hatendi wrote that "there are allegations that the following offenses are being committed by Clergymen with impunity: Publicly and deliberately participating in divination, *kurova guva, nhaka, mudzimu* practice, freemasonry, sorcery, occult practises, witchcraft and drunken behaviour (Dt. 18:10-13)."[48] In the same *AD CLERUM*, Bishop Hatendi stated about marriage, the blessing of a civil marriage refers to the Marriage Act (Chapter 37). The translation in the *Bhuku reMinamato* (Book of Common Prayer) is misleading. Office (*Hofisi*) refers to African Traditional Marriage (Chapter 238). The latter is potentially polygamous and should not be blessed. The blessing or marrying of a divorcee without the diocesan bishop's authority is an offence. [49]

In his *AD CLERUM ON APARTHEID IN THE DIOCESE* of 8th December 1990, sent to all the Clergy of the Diocese of Harare, Bishop Hatendi warned that there are also reports of syncretistic practices by clergymen and subdeacons. Some are Freemasons and others are officiating at the Shona traditional ceremony of inviting the spirit of the dead back home to be united with the spirits of the clan. Both practises are a denial of God's power to defend, heal and sustain the living. Those who are committing these offenses be warned that if they are caught they will be charged and tried in a Church Court for conduct unbecoming a Clergyman or their licences will be revoked.[50]

In his Diocese of Harare Memorandum of 19th December 1990, which was sent to all Incumbents, Clergy, Churchwardens and Chapel wardens, Bishop Hatendi stated that "clergymen and subdeacons must choose between holding the bishop's licence to officiate, teach and preach in the diocese or practising freemasonry and officiating and/or participating at *kurova guva/ chenura* ceremonies (Josh. 24:15)."[51] In his Diocese of Harare Memorandum of the 4th February 1991 which was sent to all Licensed priests, all Chairmen of Fishers-of-Humans (*Vabvuwi*) and Chaplains on the Decade of Evangelisation and *Vabvuwi,* Bishop Hatendi maintained that "obviously those of us who are unfaithful to their wives, drink to excess, smoke to excess and consult sorcerers and diviners will not support what they (*wabvuwi*) stand for."[52]

In his Diocese of Harare Memorandum of the 16th August 1991, which was sent to All Licensed Clergymen and All Heads of Diocesan Institutions on Healing and Deliverance from the Demonic Powers, Bishop Hatendi stated that

Those who indulge in occult practices, *mashave, midzimu* and *ngozi*, are most vulnerable. Some priests and heads of Church institutions for example mission schools, Churches and hospitals are making people fearful by their words and/or actions. They invite or visit *n'anga* at night. This is yet another offence. However, the bishop does not intend to carry out a witch hunt. Allow your conscience to tell you where you stand as a Christian. It is, therefore, an offence to invite *n'anga* to a Parish or mission school by any member of staff including priests and heads of Diocesan Institutions. Those who do not believe in God Almighty should not live at a mission or Diocesan Institution because they invite Satan to take possession of those who are weak in Faith. [53]

Like Arthur Shearly Cripps and other USPG missionaries, Hatendi threatened to expel from the diocesan institutions all Shona USPG Christians who practiced ATR. In *The Church Of The Province Of Central Africa Diocese Of Harare Synod 1992, Agenda And Reports*, Bishop Hatendi moved "that this Synod of the Church of the Province of Central Africa, Diocese of Harare, believes in the uniqueness and universality of Jesus Christ as the only living God and intercessor and condemns the worship of idols and ancestors."[54]

The 1992 Diocese of Harare Synod set up the Idol and Evangelism Commission which was chaired by the Reverend Canon Archdeacon Dr. Sabastian Bakare, who later became Bishop of Manicaland. Before long, the Idol and Evangelism Commission split into two groups because there was no agreement among its members on the question of accommodation or inculturation. A group led by Dr. S. Bakare proposed an inculturation process, and it produced a "major" report. A group led by Archdeacon W. Simbabure produced a "minor" report which did not plead for inculturation but for the continuation of the USPG Christianity (see appendices two and three). The "major" report advocated change, but the "minor" report advocated the status quo. In its recommendation to the 1994 Synod, the "major" report stated that "the commission recommends that the Synod establish a permanent commission on worship which, among other things, will enable Christians in Zimbabwe, to understand their identity in Christ in their own culture and prepare a more fertile ground to sow the seeds of the Gospel." The majority of the commission members concluded that the major ceremonies of the *kurova guva*, such as the blessing of the millet (*kubata mumera)*, the blessing of the beast (*kutaridza n'gombe/ mombe*), the blessing of beer and meat (*kupira doro nenyama kuvadzimu*), and bringing-the-spirit-into-the-home (*kutora mudzimu nokumuisa mumusha*), can be adapted into Church rites. The Commission concluded that "while many elements of the *kurova guva* rite can find places in the rites and litanies of the Church, the consultation of a diviner *(n'anga)* during the rite cannot be accepted by the Church."[55]

Bakare wrote that "the desecration of sacred sites by the settlers in order to destroy the Zimbabwean sense of connection with the ancestors and history was, therefore, an unforgivable act."[56] Again Bakare contended that "Rhodes' prospects of taking possession of the whole country were good. He did not perceive land as sacred but as an economic commodity, a repository of mineral rather than ancestral wealth."[57] Bakare believed that Fredenberger's comments on African attitudes toward land are worth noting: "I came to realize that everything is centred on caring. One's identity, self-esteem, and position within the community depended upon on how well one respected the memory and wisdom of the ancestors, how carefully one used the land for the good of the present and future communities that would depend upon it."[58] Bakare understood that "the traditional healer does not simply go into the bush to look for herbs from any tree, but is directed in a dream by his or her ancestors to a specific tree whose herbs can provide the right substance to heal the particular disease."[59]

The minority group led by Fr. Archdeacon Webster Simbabure condemned ATR. I joined and supported the minority group because I was afraid of being victimized by the bishop. In this case, I was a traitor to the process of inculturation which I strongly support and advocate. The minor" report condemned inculturation. It followed Kato (1975) and Tienou (1982) in its rejection of Shona ancestors. The "minor" report declared that any other world religion, ATR included, is against the teachings of Jesus Christ. Jesus Christ and not the *vadzimu* is the only Way, the Truth and the Life. Christians should repent from worshipping ancestors. The *Kurova guva* and consulting diviners (*n'anga*) are wrong and sinful. *Kurova guva* and divination produce spiritual dwarfs in the Church of God.[60]

The Diocesan Synod of the Diocese of Harare which met at the Anglican Cathedral of St. Mary and All Saints in Harare from the 7th-8th May 1994 rejected the recommendations of the "major" report simply because they openly pleaded for inculturation to be part of the Christian faith in the Anglican Church in Zimbabwe. The same Synod accepted and adopted the recommendations of the "minor" report which condemned Shona ancestors and ATR.

In rejecting the "major" report, the Synod, through the diocesan Vice Chancellor, Advocate G. S. Wernberg, resolved that: "To the extent that Traditional Rites and ceremonies incorporate communion with spirits or religious beliefs which have no origin or harmony with Christianity, such rites and ceremonies are wholly irreconcilable with and therefore repugnant to Christianity, its precepts and teachings."[61] In support of the "minority" report, the Synod passed a resolution to the effect that no Christian should be involved in certain aspects of ATR which are not compatible with the Christian and Biblical teaching, for they are repugnant to Christianity. Bishop Peter Hatendi supported the "minority" report. In his bishop's Charge to the Fifty Fifth Session of the Harare Diocesan Synod on the 7th and 8th May 1994 he stated: "therefore the ceremony of inviting and welcoming the living dead home (*kurova guva)*, with its emphasis on communion with the totemic community both living and dead instead of the Holy Communion with the High God and the Saints in Christ, is clearly a degeneration of pure religion bordering on idolatry."[62] Thus Hatendi, from defending Shona culture and ATR as a priest in 1973, turned to condemning them once he had become a bishop in 1981.

There is still rampant racial discrimination today in the Anglican Diocese of Harare. The predominantly white parishes refused to accept black Rectors and black Priests-in-Charge. Most white Christians up to this day refuse to be baptized, married, or buried by black priests. White Christians refuse pastoral oversight from black Priests. Human encounter is at its deepest level during pastoral visitations. White Christians refuse pastoral visits from black Priests even when they are sick or ill. On the Reverend James Timothy Neill, Vicar General of the Diocese of Harare, *The Herald* stated that "Rev. Neill confirmed that there is racism within the Anglican Church, mainly whites on blacks. Whites are not comfortable with black priests."[63]

After almost twenty years of independence, all the top posts in the Anglican Church, including Vicar General, Diocesan Secretary, and Diocesan Chancellor, are still held by white Zimbabweans. Bishop Hatendi, in his fight against racial discrimination in the Diocese of Harare was frustrated and limited by the Acts and Regulations of the Diocese of Harare. For example, the Act on the duties of Churchwardens states: "To consult with the Bishop on the Bishop's nomination of an incumbent and to accept the Bishop's appointment on behalf of the ecclesiastical division."[64] When the Bishop is making an appointment of an incumbent to a parish, the Churchwardens of that parish should accept the Bishop's nomination or reject it. The Churchwardens in the predominantly white parishes of Borrowdale, Avondale, and Mount Pleasant in Harare, Banket, Chinhoyi, and Mvurwi refuse black Rectors. The Bishop is forced to appoint white Rectors to white parishes.

On inculturation, Bishop Hatendi says that he strongly believes in inculturation which divorces itself from divination, ancestor veneration, and the bringing-back-home ceremony *(chenura/kurova guva)*. He says that certain aspects of ATR are not in conflict with the Christian faith because they are more or less comparable with stories in the Old Testament (OT). For example, paying a bride price (*roora*) is comparable to both Jacob and Isaac paying bride prices for their wives. These aspects of ATR should be continued by Shona USPG Christians. Shona traditional culture is closely related to the culture in the OT. When USPG missionaries came into Zimbabwe, they saw ATR as a religion of all Zimbabweans. Bishop Hatendi regards ATR as a lemon tree and USPG Christianity as an orange tree. He reasons that in order to grow an orange tree on a lemon tree, one cuts off the trunk of the lemon tree and leaves the stump. Then one again cuts off a small twig of an orange tree and grafts it into the stump of the lemon tree. The tree that results from the grafting of the orange twig into the lemon stump is a pure orange tree which produces pure sweet oranges only and not a hybrid of an orange tree and a lemon tree which produces both oranges and lemons. What, therefore, results from the grafting of USPG Christianity into ATR is not a hybrid Christianity but pure Christianity devoid of divination, ancestor veneration, and the bringing-back-home ceremony.

Bishop Hatendi argues that including ancestor veneration, divination, and the *kurova guva* ceremony in Christianity would be syncretism. Christianity is an all or nothing rule. Either one is a Christian or one is not a Christian. There is nothing like a hybrid, or super, or half Christian. He believes that people who combine both USPG Christianity and ATR are in a spiritual confusion. They think they will sail through the existential problems and situations of this transitory life. Bishop Hatendi believes that Jesus Christ is not a coat which you put on when it is cold, and, when it is hot, you remove it from your body. A true committed Christian should put on Jesus Christ always whether it is hot or cold. People who combine both USPG Christianity and ATR are not totally committed to Christ. They are not one with Christ. They are pseudo-Christians because of the material and social benefits which they get from Christianity. Their spiritual home is their ancestors and ATR. They are not filled with the Holy Spirit of Jesus Christ. All they did was undergo the Christian rituals of baptism, Christian marriage, and confirmation, but they are not truly converted to Jesus Christ as their only Lord and Savior. They still belong materially, socially, and spiritually to the kingdom of their ancestors.

## EVALUATION

The USPG missionaries and Shona Anglican bishops, including Bishop Hatendi, were children of their times. Their theological and missiological thinking was affected by the prevailing political, economic, and social environments surrounding them. Some of the USPG missionaries such as Knight-Bruce, Gaul, Powell, Beaven, and Paget lived in a period before scientific study of anthropology had revealed the significance and logical coherence of ATR and African traditional culture. USPG bishops such as Alderson and Paul Burrough lived and worked during a period of a very high tide of African nationalism and a period of a liberation war in Zimbabwe. Alderson and Burrough spent more time on political and economic issues than on the relevance or irrelevance of Shona ancestors and ATR in the Anglican Church in Zimbabwe.

Hatendi was ambivalent because of his financial insecurity. He continued the USPG missionary condemnation of ATR when he became bishop because he wanted money from the rich white Zimbabweans so that he could run the diocese. Without the whites' financial backing, the diocese would have become bankrupt. In 1973 when he was a priest, Hatendi pleaded for inculturation. When he became bishop he condemned and rejected inculturation. Hatendi was a victim of circumstances. Although Hatendi might have wanted some change, he was prevented from effecting that change by the prevailing political, social, and economic environment in Zimbabwe. The Diocesan Acts and Regulations were not changed to suit the new political and social dispensation which was brought by Zimbabwe's independence in 1980. He was afraid of violating the Diocesan Acts and Pastoral Regulations of the British colonial era (1974 and 1978) which still hold to this day. The Anglican Church is governed by Canons, Acts, and Regulations. One cannot just violate them willy nilly without being brought before the Church's court. The Canons, Acts, and Regulations are changed by the Synod, which is the Church's parliament. USPG missionary bishops and Bishop Hatendi were faced with existential situations, problems, and needs, but they understood, presented and interpreted Jesus Christ as they had inherited Him from the Anglican Church in Britain.

Humans have a tendency to despise what is unknown or not understood, and so ATR and Shona traditional culture were and still are despised and regarded as barbaric or uncivilized by USPG missionaries and Shona bishops in Zimbabwe. The USPG missionaries and Shona bishops also believed in the prevalent feeling that a western person was and is still superior to black Zimbabweans. This is true because even today, Shona bishops favor white USPG missionaries and priests. However, there is no justification for regarding Shona traditional culture, ATR, or black Zimbabweans in such a light. In their ignorance, both USPG missionaries and Shona bishops, including Hatendi, adopted hostile postures towards ATR and an attitude of pity towards black Zimbabweans because of what is considered to be their state of servitude. They did and are still doing a great deal of harm to the Christian life of the Zimbabweans. Deep rooted customs could not be uprooted overnight without a feeling of insecurity. In some cases, by failing to see the good in some customs, such as polygamy (*barika*), pledging of an unborn daughter in marriage (*kuzvarira)*, replacement wife (*chigadzamapfihwa)* inheritance of a widow (*nhaka*), consulting *n'anga*, ancestor veneration, and bringing-back-home ceremony **(***kurova guva***)**, by calling them evil and diabolic, USPG missionaries and Shona bishops caused the moral criteria of the Zimbabweans to become blurred. The negative attitudes of USPG missionaries and Shona bishops towards ATR, however, led to the rejection of ATR or to an attempt to hold USPG Christianity and ATR in parallel, separate compartments.

The implication of the total rejection of traditional Shona religion and culture by USPG missionaries is the bafflement of the traditional Shona people, who cease to be strong adherents of USPG Christianity.

That includes some Shona Anglican priests who have become involved in a ritual limping dance between Jesus Christ and Shona ancestors. The traditional Shona embrace the new religion (USPG Christianity) and come to terms with Western culture and technology. They are not fully converted to Jesus Christ because they are motivated mainly by material and monetary gains. Shona USPG Christians become involved in two worlds—the USPG Christian world and the ATR world. The traditional Shona who are converted to USPG Christianity are made people of ambivalent spiritual lives. The ambivalence is that, in times of existential crisis, the average Shona USPG Christian reverts to ATR beliefs and practices. When faced with uncertainties of life, the average Shona USPG Christian approaches *Mwari* through Shona ancestors, and on Sundays and at public gatherings he or she approaches *Mwari* through Jesus Christ.

Underneath the appearance of acceptance and understanding, USPG Christianity for many Shona USPG Christians remains a foreign religion. They have not accepted USPG Christianity completely as the all-sufficient religion that meets all human needs. For religion to be valid, it must pervade the whole human existence. Since a person's self-understanding is tied up with his worldview, it is crucial that a Christian evangelist knows and makes use of that worldview if there is to be any assurance of success in communicating the Christian message. USPG missionary attitudes towards ATR produced a clear separation between ATR and USPG Christianity. Separation of ATR and USPG Christianity was hated by the traditional Shona people, who distrusted the USPG missionaries, whom they regarded as emissaries sent by the British colonial rulers to divorce the traditional Shona people from ATR and their traditional culture. Exclusive knowledge of Jesus Christ (Christocentricism) and membership of the Church (ecclesiocentricism) produced a clear separation between ATR and USPG Christianity.

Shona people believed that to become a Shona USPG Christian was equivalent to giving up, once and for all, the habits and the traditions of their forefathers and putting themselves wholly in the hands of the white settler community that they disliked. The traditional Shona regarded the Shona USPG Christians as traitors who had gone to the side of the enemy. They were called the white men's people (*vanhu vevarungu*) or white men in black skins (*varungu vatema)*. The result of attempting to suppress by force ATR was to drive ATR underground. Even though ATR is strictly forbidden under severe penalties, some Shona Anglican priests and some Shona USPG Christians continue to practice ATR secretly at night for fear of victimization by the Shona bishops who perpetuate the USPG missionary missiology.

Shona USPG Christians are afraid of being caught practicing ATR because they fear being evicted from USPG mission farms, fear being denied medical attention at USPG mission hospitals and clinics, fear being denied a place of study at a USPG mission school, fear being dismissed from work if employed by the USPG at any of its institutions, and fear being suspended from receiving Holy Communion by the USPG missionaries. Western medical facilities at USPG mission stations, schools, hospitals, and farms are promoted by USPG missionaries as weapons against ATR. Traditional Shona do not want to rely solely on Western methods of treating disease. Even a Shona person who has been a USPG Christian for several years often feels impelled in times of sickness or disaster to seek first the help of a *n'anga*. By rejecting ATR, the USPG missionaries and Shona bishops acted in agreement with the general principle of the USPG headquarters in Britain which pleaded for accommodation (adaptation).

The condemnation of Shona traditional ancestors and ATR by the USPG missionaries and Shona bishops in Zimbabwe makes it compulsory for me to try to develop an inculturated form of soteriology. What this soteriology will look like will become clear in chapter 6.

# CHAPTER 4

## *Combining ATR and USPG Christianity Without a Sense of Guilty*

This chapter investigates whether traditional Shona ancestorhood is still relevant to the Shona Anglican bishops, priests, and laity. This chapter also investigates the reactions of Shona Anglican bishops, priests, and laity to the condemnation by USPG missionaries of ATR together with the Shona ancestors. In this chapter, by *combining* I mean that Shona Anglican bishops, priests, and USPG Christians all hold USPG Christianity and ATR in parallel but separate compartments of their lives. That is, they alternate between the practice of ATR and USPG Christianity. USPG Christianity and ATR live side by side in their hearts and minds. Also, by *conversion* I mean that one has changed dominion from Shona ancestors to the dominion of Jesus Christ, a change in allegiance in which Christ is accepted as the only Lord and Center of one's life. Missiologically, Shona Christians seek an alternative to practicing USPG Christianity and ATR in parallel. Shona Anglican bishops, priests, and laity plead for a Christ of Shona culture. They believe everything in Shona culture is compatible with a Christian life. I will argue that inculturation is a synthesis of both USPG Christianity and ATR.

# THE CHALLENGE OF BEING HISTORICALLY ACCURATE, ACADEMICALLY SOUND, AND ETHICALLY RESPONSIBLE

The information presented in this chapter is truthful, for I have collected it from Shona Anglican bishops, priests, and laity whom I personally interviewed. The majority of my interviewees did not want their identities disclosed because disclosure would cause them a lot of embarrassment once it became known that they practice both USPG Christianity and ATR. Also the disclosure of their identities would place bishops and priests in a very awkward situation with their archbishop or diocesan bishop respectively, who would have no option but to dismiss them from bishophood or priesthood respectively for they would be found guilty of violating the pastoral regulations as propounded in the *Canons And Constitutions Of The Church Of The Province Of Central Africa* (Salisbury: December, 1961) and *The Pastoral Regulations of the Diocese of Mashonaland* (Harare: 1978), and also of violating *The Acts of the Diocese of Harare* (1974). The Diocesan books are possessed by every Anglican priest in the Diocese of Harare. The disclosure of the identities of lay people would result in their suspension from receiving Holy Communion and from holding any Church post.

All five Shona Anglican diocesan bishops, 65 Shona Anglican priests, and 600 Shona USPG Christians who agreed to be interviewed acknowledged that they are involved in a ritual of limping dance between Christ and Shona ancestors. They are all quite aware of the fact that what they do is contrary to the pastoral teaching of the Anglican Church in Zimbabwe. However, they acknowledge that by practicing ATR against the teaching of the Anglican Church in Zimbabwe they do not have any sense of guilt. Instead, bishops fear their archbishop, priests fear their bishop, and the Shona USPG Christians fear both the bishop and the priests, and they all fear the Church's pastoral regulations.

# RESULTS OF THE FACE-TO-FACE INTERVIEWS WITH SHONA ANGLICAN BISHOPS, PRIESTS, AND LAITY

From January 1990 to February 2000, I approached Shona Anglican (USPG) Christians for a face-to-face interview based on my questionnaire (Appendix 1). I interviewed these people at their places of work, homes, Churches, Synods, Archdeaconry Meetings, at funerals of some Anglicans, at the Fishers-of-Human-Beings (*Vabvuwi)* all-night meetings (*pungwe*), at Mothers' Union Conferences, at Ordination Services of Anglican deacons and priests, at Clergy Conferences and Annual Retreats, at the Bernard Mizeki Shrine at Thydon near Marondera during the Bernard Mizeki Annual Festivals which are held annually every weekend nearest the 18th June—the date Mizeki was martyred.

The first meeting of clergy and laity of the Anglican diocese of Harare on the topic of *Christ and Culture (Chikirisito Netsika)* was held on the 8th January, 1990, at Peter House Girls' High School, Springvale, Marondera, during the Annual Clergy Retreat. The meeting was chaired by Bishop Peter Ralph Hatendi, led by Canon Oliver O. Mutume, Fr. Philimon Mudzvovera, Fr. Nolbert Kunonga (later bishop of Harare, 2000-2009) and Fr. Chad Gandiya (later Bishop of Harare, 2009-present). It was a very lively debate which produced a lot of disagreements as far as inculturation is concerned. That meeting was part of the launch of the Decade of Evangelism, 1990 to 2000, in the diocese of Harare. As a result of that meeting, there were some Synods and Archdeaconry meetings in the diocese of Harare where the topic *Christ and Culture* was debated. I had a good opportunity to meet and interview Anglicans when I was a member of the *Idol and Evangelism Commission* which was set up by the Diocese of Harare Synod in 1992. The Commission presented its report to the Synod of 1994. That Commission looked into the whole question of inculturation in the Anglican diocese of Harare. I also had a good opportunity to meet and interview people when I was a member of the *Bishop's Selection Conference* (a body within the diocese of Harare which selects men who feel that they are called to the vocation of priesthood) from 1992 to 1996.

I collated and tabulated the statements of bishops, priests, and lay people (see tables in Appendix 4). The evidence is there and anyone can crosscheck it to see whether I have correctly interpreted what the people said. On some issues, such as divination, ancestor veneration, and bringing-back-home ceremony, interviewees preferred to remain anonymous. However, they came out in the open on such issues as paying the bride price (*roora/lobola*), paying the mother's cow (*mombe yehumai*), the use of herbs, and belief in witchcraft, because these are not considered very serious offences in the Anglican Church in Zimbabwe, since almost everybody, Christian or non-Christian, practices them openly. Overall, I found that the *Mudzimu Mukuru* par excellence Christology accurately reflects the views of the majority of bishops, priests, and lay people interviewed. It is a faithful translation of the views of Shona Anglican bishops, priests, and lay people.

## SHONA ANGLICAN BISHOPS IN ZIMBABWE

I interviewed 5 of the 6 Shona Anglican bishops in Zimbabwe. One declined to be interviewed. All those interviewed were married, two are now retired, and one is now dead. The following list summarizes their views:

4 are involved in ancestors and ATR,
1 condemned ancestors and ATR
5 paid the mother's cow which was ritually sacrificed to ancestors,
5 give material and financial support towards the propitiation of ancestors,
5 use herbs,
5 believe in witchcraft,
4 get material and financial benefits from ancestors,
1 gets spiritual benefits from Christ,

4 get spiritual benefits from ancestors,
4 fear Canons and Pastoral Regulations,
4 combine Christianity and ATR, and
4 fear death and suffering believed to be caused by ancestors.

## SHONA ANGLICAN PRIESTS IN ZIMBABWE

I interviewed 65 Shona Anglican priests out of a total of between 100 and 150 priests. Of those interviewed, 92% were married, and 22% were retired. The following list summarizes their views:

80% are involved in ancestors and ATR,
12% reject ancestors and ATR,
100 % paid bride price,
100 % paid the mother's cow which was ritually sacrificed to ancestors,
100% give material and financial support towards the veneration of ancestors,
100% use herbs,
100% believe in witchcraft,
88% get material and financial benefits from ancestors,
88% get spiritual benefits from ancestors,
12% get spiritual benefits from Christ,
88% fear the bishops,
88% fear ancestors and
88% combine Christianity and ATR.

## SHONA ANGLICAN CHRISTIANS IN ZIMBABWE

I interviewed 600 Shona Anglican Christians out of about one million in Zimbabwe. Of the people I approached, 86% agreed to be interviewed. Of those interviewed, 82% were married. The following list summarizes their views:

83% are involved in ancestors and ATR,
11% condemned ancestors and ATR,

82% paid bride price,
82% paid the mother's cow which was ritually sacrificed to ancestors,
100% give material and financial support towards the veneration of ancestors,
100% use herbs,
100% believe in witchcraft,
90% receive material and financial benefits from their ancestors,
90% get social benefits from the Church of Christ,
11% get spiritual benefits from Christ,
90% get spiritual benefits from ancestors,
90% combine Christianity and ATR and
90% fear death and suffering believed to be caused by ancestors.

In general, participation in ATR and propitiation of ancestors among Shona Anglican bishops, priests, and lay people is about the same rate for all academic and professional qualifications, marital status, age, place of residence (rural or urban), and sex (male or female).

Shona Anglican bishops, priests, and lay people who combine both USPG Christianity and ATR are of the opinion that Shona traditional chiefs who are Christians should play their traditional roles as chiefs and should enforce traditional customs such as the observance of the day of rest *(chisi)* on every Zimbabwean whether Christian or not Christian. In this regard they agree with K. A. Busia of Ghana who maintains that

> In a society in which political and religious office are combined, the chiefs regard the request for the recognition of the existence of Christians and for the adaptation of native laws as a request for the surrender of authority. As they see it, the Christian Church requests that they should not have power to legislate on certain things for certain members of the community, because the Church desires the right to legislate on these for those of the chief's subjects who have embraced the Christian Faith. Christianity challenges the traditional position of the chief as the religious as well as the political head of the tribe.[1]

At present the Church undermines the position of chiefs as both ATR leaders and tribal political leaders. Shona Anglican bishops, priests, and lay people who are involved in ancestor veneration and ATR also agree with K. A. Busia who in his authoritative study of Ashanti kingship in Ghana states that

> No one could be an adequate chief who did not perform ritual functions of his office. There have recently been elected as chiefs in different parts of Ashanti men who are both literate and Christian. But they have all felt an obligation to perform the ritual acts of their office. They were installed in the stool house, where they poured libations to the ancestors whom they had succeeded. It is as successors of the ancestors that they are venerated and their authority respected, and they could not keep the office without maintaining contact with the ancestors through the traditional rituals.[2]

All my interviewees believe that Christianity is not the only path to *Mwari*. ATR adherents and believers in the world's other major religions are following their own paths to *Mwari*. There is only one summit, one peak, but people take different tracks to get there. *Mwari* is that Summit or Peak. Therefore, according to some interviewees, there is no need to convert ATR devotees to Christianity, since *Mwari* provides them with their own pathway to eternal life. Christianity should be involved in converting people who have no religion and no faith. This is a theocentric soteriology. Accepting that all world religions lead to one *Mwari* is in the view of interviewees not the same as embracing doctrines of other faiths. What we need to learn is that we have to be committed entirely to the way that *Mwari* has called us, while recognizing that we cannot all believe the same way.

The spiritual element is disappearing among the leaders—bishops and priests in the Anglican Church—because their spiritual source is *Mwari* through the intermediation of ancestors. The Shona people are possessed by ancestral spirits not by the spirit of *Mwari*. Only the High priests at Matonjeni are possessed by the Spirit of *Mwari*. However, material benefits come from the Church. At the official level, Shona Anglican bishops, priests, and laity seek salvation from Christ, but at the practical level they are job seekers, for they seek material, social, and financial benefits from the Church. This is understandable because of the traditional Shona understanding and cosmology: ancestors look after us, protect us, and this is shown through power and material aspects.

## THEN WHY BECOME A USPG CHRISTIAN?

If Shona ancestors are still the way to *Mwari* for most Shona Anglican bishops, priests, and Shona USPG Christians, why have they become USPG Christians? Given the fact that ATR is a religion into which *Mwari* revealed Himself and into which the Holy Spirit (*Mweya Anoyera*) is at work, one would have expected Shona people to have remained ATR adherents only, without being converted to USPG Christianity. Both USPG Christianity and ATR are ways to *Mwari*, ways to salvation. Why then combine USPG Christianity and ATR? Also Shona Anglican bishops, priests, and laity agree with A. F. Walls who observed that "probably no group, perhaps no person, is ever converted from one religion to another. They are more likely to be converted from agnosticism after the old ways have failed."[3]

USPG Christianity and Jesus Christ are used by Shona Anglican priests in order to be better off financially, materially, and socially. The combination of USPG Christianity and ATR by some Shona Anglican priests is due to the fact that these priests are caught up in a dilemma. On the religious side, they are deeply rooted in ATR, and forsaking ATR for any other religion means death and disaster to them and their families. Ancestors will punish them. On the material side, USPG Christianity is more rewarding for them, while advocating ATR publicly means immediate dismissal from priesthood. Dismissal from priesthood results in financial and material problems for them.

## WHY DO ATR BELIEFS AND PRACTICES PERSIST?

Why are Shona Anglican priests and some Shona Anglican Christians still practicing ATR? Are they not involved in change? There are big and fast changes in the cultural, political, economic, social, scientific, and technological fields in Zimbabwe today. These changes affect Shona Anglican priests and some Shona USPG Christians, for they are involved in these changes. But religious change is very slow. ATR is life itself for a traditional Shona person. I liken ATR to two things, to the umbilical cord and to the hub of a wheel.

A traditional Shona baby is "soaked" and "clothed" in ATR before birth because of the rituals which are performed before a woman gives birth. Traditionally, a pregnant Shona woman bathes in ritually blessed water containing herbs. Fire is not to be taken from a hut in which a Shona woman gives birth for at least one month. By the time a Shona baby is born, ATR is already in his or her blood. A Shona baby lives and grows up in ATR. Without ATR, he or she is not a complete Shona person. A traditional Shona person literally eats, drinks, and breathes ATR from before birth. To be radically converted from Shona ancestors to Jesus Christ means death to a traditional Shona person. Conversion to USPG Christianity is like cutting the fetus away from the umbilical cord. This separates the fetus from the mother, and the fetus dies. ATR is like the umbilical cord for traditional Shona people; ATR connects people to their ancestors, who in turn connect them to *Mwari*.

One main result of the failure to destroy ATR is that, in spite of the numerical growth of the Anglican Church in Zimbabwe, commitment to Christ on the part of many Shona Anglican Christians has remained superficial. In times of life crises, they combine USPG Christianity and ATR. Y. A. Obaje was right when he said that "the superficiality of the African Christian's commitment is evidenced by the fact that when he is faced with problems and uncertainties he often reverts to African religious practices."[4] The unfortunate neglect of the traditional Shona world-view in the theological formulations that are meant to aid them in their Christian life has left them in a dangerous state of unhealthy spiritual hunger and thirst. Shona Anglican bishops, priests, and laity who combine USPG Christianity and ATR say that they freely alternate USPG Christianity and ATR doctrines, beliefs, and practices. They say also that baptism into USPG Christianity does not entail giving up all former traditional religious ways, attitudes, customs, and values. USPG Christianity and ATR continue to exist side by side in the minds and the hearts of the Shona USPG Christians.

In another sense the traditional Shona people cannot even think of separating ATR from the normal social and economic aspects of life. ATR is like the hub of a wheel. The hub has spokes. One can take away one or two spokes, but one cannot remove the hub and still believe that one has a wheel. If one removes the hub, one has destroyed the wheel. Likewise, when Shona people "remove" ATR, they have destroyed themselves. Shona Anglican priests do not want to accept the USPG concept of a religion which can be separated from one's political, economic, and social aspects of life. They also do not want to destroy their African traditional religion for it is their very life, without which they cannot live. Without the ancestors, the traditional Shona people die spiritually. I agree with Kwesi Dickson who notes: "in Africa life is seen as a whole, undifferentiated into religion and life, into life in the spirit and life in the 'flesh'. It would be alien to the African to cut up life into water tight compartments, and the Christian Scriptures would give backing to this visualizing of life as one whole."[5]

There is no spiritual growth in the Christian sense which comes from USPG Christianity as far as Shona Anglican bishops, priests, and Shona USPG Christians who combine USPG Christianity and ATR are concerned. They get their spiritual growth from *Mwari* through the mediation of their ancestors. Both *Mwari* and ancestors are spiritual beings. Without the blessings from Shona ancestors, there is no spiritual growth for USPG Christians. Moreover, ATR and Shona ancestors do not separate the material and social aspects of life from the spiritual aspect of life. The ancestors who are the sources of spiritual benefits are also the sources of material and social benefits. Headmasters of USPG Mission Secondary Schools get no spiritual benefit from being members of USPG Christianity. They get all their spiritual benefits from Shona ancestors.

Shona USPG Christians and Shona Anglican priests who combine both USPG Christianity and ATR are not converted to Jesus Christ. USPG Christianity for them is for material and social benefits and not for spiritual benefits. ATR helps them to grow both materially and spiritually. Shona ancestors help them to get more USPG material and social benefits. That is why a Shona person seeks the blessings of ancestors before going to work in a USPG mission hospital, school, or farm. One also seeks the blessings of ancestors before going to a USPG mission hospital for treatment. When the next bishop is to be elected, some Shona USPG priests visit and consult a diviner (*n'anga*), who tells them to venerate/worship their ancestors in order to enhance their chances of being elected the next bishop. Being a bishop is a very prestigious position which carries a lot of material, economic, and social benefits with it. This is the reason one sees quarrellings and in-fightings each time a bishop is elected in Zimbabwe in particular and in Africa in general. Ancestors come first in the spiritual, social, and material aspects of life.

For the Shona USPG Christians and priests there are no spiritual benefits per se which are separated from the material and social benefits which one gets from ancestors. And USPG Christianity does not totally separate the material and social aspects of life from the spiritual aspect, although there is a tradition of separation. Historically, an ascetic life of poverty in the Convents, Friaries, and Monasteries was a life of poverty lived so as to enhance spiritual growth. Mortification of the body through fasting was for spiritual growth and not for material growth. Blessed are the poor in spirit (Mt.5:3). However, USPG Christians pray for material, financial, and spiritual benefits from God through Jesus Christ. They pray for good jobs, promotion at their places of work, good accommodation, transport, rain, good harvests, and good governments. All these are material things which enhance spiritual growth. Even more so, ATR does not separate the material, financial, social, and the spiritual aspects of life. They are one and the same thing. They are all obtained from the same source—the ancestors. When the material or the physical aspect of life suffers, the spiritual aspect of life suffers as well.

The more material benefits one gets from the ancestors, the more one venerates one's ancestors and the more one grows spiritually and morally. It is also true for the traditional Shona people that the fewer material benefits one gets from the ancestors, the less spiritual growth one experiences, and consequently the more one venerates one's ancestors with the hope of getting material and spiritual blessings. Spiritual growth in ATR does not come when one is experiencing some existential problems like death, illness, loss of employment, divorce, car accident, or material poverty. But, in Christianity, material poverty and some existential problems can be a source of spiritual growth. They are regarded as a pruning process for spiritual growth (Jn.15:2) and a testing process for spiritual growth (1Pt. 1: 6-7). In ATR, Shona ancestors are used to get both material and spiritual growth. Life in ATR is seen as a whole. There is no separation of the sacred from the profane. The spirit without the flesh is not life. Also the flesh without the spirit is not life. Ancestors do not divide life into the material and the spiritual. Ancestors bless by giving both the material and spiritual aspects of life. Material poverty is a sign of a curse by ancestors. Once one is cursed materially, one is also equally cursed spiritually by the ancestors. This is also true to some extent with USPG Christianity. The Christian Scriptures give backing to this visualizing of life as one whole. In the Old Testament, Abraham, Isaac, Jacob, David, Solomon and others were blessed by God both materially and spiritually.

The ancestors bless someone who wants to be elected to a top Church position: a diocesan bishop, a dean of a Cathedral, an archdeacon, a principal of a theological college, or a headmaster of a mission primary or secondary school. Traditionally, ancestors used to make one a hunter (*muvhimi*) but now they can make one a bishop in the Church of God. Without the blessings of one's ancestors one cannot become a bishop in the Church of God. Traditionally, Africans used to hunt in the forests, but now there are no forests in which to hunt wild animals. Also, if one is seen hunting wild animals without a license, one is arrested and charged for poaching. Good hunters were possessed by ancestral spirits of hunting (*shave remudzimu rekuvhima*). Today, the very good hunters who are possessed by ancestral hunting spirits get very good and high-paying jobs in the Church, government, commerce, industry, and non-government organizations (NGOs) in Africa, Europe, America, Asia, or Australia. The hunting spirits also help one to have a very good education and profession. Those possessed with very good hunting spirits hunt for jobs all over the world. This is why one sees Africans in almost every country working and sending money home to Africa. The hunting spirit sent them there to work.

In ATR one cannot decide to be materially poor. But in Christianity one can decide to be materially poor without any sense of being spiritually poor or of being cursed by God. Material poverty does not give a Christian a sense of being divorced from God and Jesus Christ. In fact, material poverty leads to spiritual growth and a sense of being very close to God and His Christ. Material poverty brings about spiritual affluence. This is because life in Europe and America is divided into the flesh and into the spirit, into the secular (profane) and the sacred. Separation of life into the flesh and the spirit, the sacred and the secular is the result of a money economy. Money has given people the freedom to buy anything they like. With money, one can decide to live a religious life or an unreligious life. One can decide to do without society, without God, and without His Christ. In Europe and America money has taken the place of God and of society. With money there is a general increase in materialism resulting in a feeling that God and His Christ are irrelevant—one can live a normal life without them. This has resulted in moral decadence and spiritual poverty in Europe and America. This secularization of society caused by money is fast affecting Zimbabwean society today. But even with money Africans cannot decide to live without society and the ancestors. Africans are still rooted in ancestor-centricism.

Nevertheless, Shona USPG Christians and Shona Anglican priests who combine USPG Christianity and ATR are facing a spiritual crisis. They have become "half-believers" in Jesus Christ. This has led them to a spiritual chaos. This is not acceptable in as far as their African

Christian growth is concerned. For USPG Christians, the most important thing is the economic power leading to prosperity and material well being that is brought by USPG Christianity. USPG Christianity is material, to some extent, for it urges Christians to pray for some material benefits from God through Jesus Christ. Admittedly, USPG Christianity does have both material and spiritual well-being fused into one compound which cannot be separated. But for Shona Anglicans, spiritual power is brought by ancestors. The pneumatocentricism of Shona ancestors is very spiritual. Both their material and their spiritual well-being come from the ancestors and not from Jesus Christ. God (*Mwari*) and the ancestors are spiritual beings. Living in Shona ancestors means living in the spirit.

Shona Anglican priests who combine USPG Christianity and ATR believe that there are some Shona Anglican priests who have tried to discard their pre-baptismal world of religious belief (ATR) and embrace the USPG Christianity in its entirety. But these people are very few in number and their success is open to debate. The preponderance of empirical evidence shows, on the contrary, that among the traditional Shona people who have accepted baptism in the Anglican Church in Zimbabwe, the great majority have neither wanted to abandon nor succeeded in abandoning completely many aspects of ATR. The severest USPG Christian theological, doctrinal, and pastoral strictures have not deterred them from reverting to ATR when they think it personally or socially necessary.

Shona Anglican priests and Shona USPG Christians do not want to divorce themselves from traditional Shona society. ATR is a community religion: one is born into ATR. However, USPG Christianity is individualistic to some extent. A person can decide to be a USPG Christian or not. One can decide not to be a USPG Christian without any sense of being divorced from the society and also without any sense of being divorced from *Mwari*. One can still live a "normal" life without being a devotee of USPG Christianity. USPG Christianity is individualistic to some extent, but it is also communal to some extent for it pleads for membership in the Christian Church to all USPG

Christians. The Church is the Body of Christ. Every USPG Christian should be a member of the Body of Christ. However, USPG Christianity, unlike ATR is not totally communal.

Shona Anglican priests and Shona USPG Christians are still deeply rooted in ATR beliefs and practices despite more than 100 years of USPG missionaries' teaching against it because ATR still has a functional value in Shona society. I agree with French sociologist E. Durkheim and Zimbabwean sociologist M. F. C. Bourdillion who argue that religion is a function of society. For Durkheim, "totemism (religion) expresses the forces of unity in a family and ethnic group. It promotes unity and togetherness. Totemism represents quasi divine essence that is very close to divine. It symbolises social power."[6] The member of the clan is subordinate to the genius or informing power of the totem. Thus each person behaves in a prescribed manner towards the totem. Bourdillion states that "in practice, ATR has a unifying function in our Shona society, it is part of our culture."[7]

A good illustration of this point by Bourdillion is the phenomenon of independent Churches growing up rapidly all around Zimbabwe. Wherever there is open space around Harare, we find independent Church members singing their prayers on Sundays and several nights of the week. Independent Churches are publically very antagonistic towards ATR. Whereas established Churches like the Anglican Church are often fairly tolerant towards African traditional practices and traditional spirits, independent Churches seem extremely strict and forbid any ATR. Nevertheless, one sees in independent Churches much in common with ATR perspectives: Church members see the world as controlled or influenced by a variety of spirits. Diseases and misfortunes are interpreted as being caused by such spirits as *ngozi, midzimu,* and alien spirits *(mashave)* or by witchcraft. Healing is carried out by exorcising these spirits and cleansing the witches. The Shona traditional way of understanding the world and responding to it can be seen in the independent Churches, while the members of these Churches adopt many Christian symbols. Zimbabwean Christians are responding to the changes in the traditional world view by finding Christian answers.

The cult of the ancestors is a unifying force in Zimbabwe society. As long as the basic agricultural, social, and economic structures remain, Zimbabweans will not easily throw off ATR. As long as the extended family remains important in Zimbabwe, people will from time to time feel the influence of ancestors. As long as the Zimbabwean people are dependent on rain, they will brew beer for the rain-making spirits (*majukwa*).

There is an intrinsic resistance to religious change on the part of Shona Anglican priests and Shona USPG Christians. Western education, science, and technology have not succeeded in bringing about complete religious change. One still finds very educated Shona people seeking the help of *n'anga* and their ancestors: ATR is in their blood. What happens to ATR when the traditional Shona society changes? Change was brought about by commercial contact with the Europeans, Americans, then by the colonial administration, the money economy, and also by science and technology. Notwithstanding these changes, religious changes are slow. We learn our religious culture from infancy onwards. We cannot change childhood as easily as we can change our physical environment. Hence, some of the old habits of thought are going to remain. And these habits come out especially in crises such as serious illness or death. So change takes place over generations rather than within a single generation. Young people who have been brought up in a different environment think differently from old people. Change is also slow to come because Zimbabwe in particular and Africa in general still live in a culture of magic.

So religious change in Zimbabwe is slow, but we can expect it to take place. In the cities and towns, people still acknowledge extended families, but the family is not so prominent in social life or in economic life. Children associate with school friends and neighbors rather than with kin. Each nuclear family has its own homestead and income. The extended family does not have the same importance for young people brought up in such an environment, and one would expect ancestral spirits to lose some of their power. I do agree with Bourdillion who argues that ATR in urban areas is becoming a private matter while Christianity will be the public religion. He states that it is very clear that even where ATR survives in urban populations in Zimbabwe, it changes its functions. In the rural areas, Shona traditional religious rites are public, community affairs. In the urban areas, public religious rites are performed in the Churches, and Shona traditional rites become private affairs, concerned with personal problems and affairs. Even important ethnic or regional spirits (*mhondoro*) and the national spirit *(Mwari)* cult, which have political and economic significance in the rural areas, are concerned only with personal problems and affairs in the urban areas. When people meet a wide range of people from different backgrounds in urban areas, traditional Shona local cults are no longer adequate to govern their responses. People need religion which can cut across the various social backgrounds. Christianity in Zimbabwe helps to fill the gap left when purely local traditional Shona cults are no longer seen to provide an adequate response to the world. Religion is like a national flag that is an emblem; it is a symbol of unity. It is like a coat of arms of a nation, like a badge of an association. Religion is a social phenomenon. Religion is functional, that is, it enhances the overall working of a social system.[8]

Durkheim and Bourdillion both claim that the purpose of religion lies in social organization. But the purpose of religion, including ATR, is not only function but also salvific. Religion does not have to flourish in society only to unify the society. Human beings can be aware of supernatural powers (*Mwari*) without necessarily having any reference to society. As long as one appeals to the ultimate Being (*Mwari*) or to the supernatural, one is religious but does not have to associate this appeal with society or community. Religion is not only functional but has a value of its own.

## EVALUATION

Shona Anglican bishops, priests, and laity see no reason why Shona people should be converted to USPG Christianity, for they are not British. ATR serves the reality of this earthly life. Shona Anglican priests look into the Bible for what fits them and supports them. In their view, Shona Anglican priests need not be converted to Jesus Christ, for they have Shona ancestors who mediate between them and *Mwari*. They do not need Jesus Christ as a way to *Mwari*. What Rattray, quoting a traditional Ashanti priest, says about the Ghanaians applies equally well to Zimbabwean Christians. Rattray maintains that in religious matters, Africans, including Ghanaians, are very pragmatic. If one religious power does not help, another is tried. We in Ashanti dare not worship the sky god alone, or the earth goddess alone, or any one spirit. We have to protect ourselves against, and use when we can, the spirits of all things in the sky and upon earth.[9]

The Zimbabwean understanding of Christianity fits very well into this framework of thought. Zimbabwean Christians are not worried that Christianity is a foreign religion. What they care about are the economic power for prosperity and the material well being brought by Christianity. Christianity is seen as the religious dimension of the ever-dynamic modern life. USPG missionaries in Zimbabwe saw their USPG Christianity as a new religious faith that would destroy and replace ATR. But Shona Anglican priests and Shona USPG Christians agree with N. Smith who says "but Ghanaians saw it (Christianity) as a new religious power to be added to the totality of existing supernatural powers that they could use."[10]

Zimbabwean Christians, like their Ghanaian counterparts, see Christianity as a religious power which should be added to ATR. The Zimbabweans who became Christians found themselves in an ambivalent position. USPG Christianity offered them access to great economic, political, and social prosperities. At the same time they remained firmly rooted in ATR. Zimbabwean Christians combined ATR and USPG Christianity to gain the protection and blessings from the ancestors and to receive material benefits from USPG Christianity. That was existential dialogue between ATR and USPG Christianity. Zimbabwean Christians still hold both ATR and USPG Christianity in parallel but separate compartments of their lives. This does not mean that Zimbabwean Christians believe in dualism or polarity. They strongly believe in a single religious matrix or complex, as Middleton describes the Akrong people of the Akan tribe of Ghana. He explains that "it means only that many serious Christians are not always able to meet all the demands of the Church. They are heterogeneous, so to speak, in their ecclesiastical status but homogeneous in their desire to make the Gospel normative for their lives."[11]

The case studies seem to point to the fact that for most Shona Christians ATR and ancestors rather than Christ or His Gospel remain normative. There is an existential dialogue between ATR and USPG Christianity, in which ATR seems to remain primary while Christianity is used and experienced more like an addition. Christianity is regarded by most Zimbabweans as a new religious power which should be added to ATR for their use.

## IMPLICATIONS OF THE FINDINGS

The Anglican Church in Zimbabwe is fast growing in numbers, but spiritually it is dying. Jesus Christ is not the only Lord and Savior of most Shona USPG Christians, but Shona ancestors are. What Shona Anglican priests do can be compared with what Harold Lindsell said about the enlightenment period:

> Jesus Christ was dethroned as God, the Bible was declared fallible and subjected to the findings of science, the social Gospel was substituted for blood atonement and naturalism replaced a belief in supernaturalism. In an atmosphere of unbelief like this it is impossible for the person and work of the Holy Spirit to fare any better than Christ fared.[12]

Holding USPG Christianity and ATR in parallel has resulted in a ritual of limping dance between Jesus Christ and Shona ancestors.

Theocentric and pneumatocentric soteriologies have produced a Christ of culture. USPG Christianity found a rich traditional Shona culture in Zimbabwe, and this traditional Shona culture was to receive the Word of *Mwari*, and either become richer because of the Gospel message or be destroyed and replaced by USPG Christianity. Shona Anglican priests added Jesus Christ to ATR. By pleading for pneumatocentric and theocentric soteriologies, Shona Anglican priests believe that ATR is deeply imbedded in the hearts of Shona USPG Christians and also in the hearts of Shona Anglican priests themselves.

Shona Anglican priests advocate theocentric and pneumatocentric soteriologies and, therefore, believe that there are some existential problems which are typically African or Shona problems and such problems should be addressed to *Mwari* through the ancestors and not through Jesus Christ. At the same time they believe that Shona Anglican Christians address some problems which are not typically Shona to *Mwari* through Jesus Christ. They believe that both Jesus Christ and Shona ancestors are different ways to salvation. For them a Shona Anglican Christian is free to practice both USPG Christianity and ATR at different times as ways to salvation—as well as material, economic, and social prosperity—depending on what type of problem occurs. For example, Shona Anglican priests do not want a situation where many Shona USPG Christians would seek a USPG Christian burial but also privately, even secretly, have an ATR burial rite performed. Between a USPG Christian burial and a Shona traditional burial there is an alternative: a Shona Christian burial.

Shona Anglican priests who combine USPG Christianity and ATR are *Mwari*-centred (theocentric) not Christ-centred (Christocentric). *Mwari* is not only truly encountered in Jesus Christ but also in Shona ancestors. Jesus Christ is the centre and norm for USPG missionaries only and Shona ancestors are at the centre and norm for Shona people. For Shona people, *Mwari* alone is the absolute, but in their view both USPG Christianity and ATR are relative—Jesus Christ and Shona ancestors are relative. USPG missionaries should continue to carry out what they feel is their universal mission of witnessing to Christ. They should also be able to recognize that ATR too has its mission in the same pluralistic world of witnessing *Mwari* through Shona ancestors.

If there is something unique and normative in USPG Christianity that ATR needs, there is also something unique and normative in ATR needed by USPG Christianity. This is a symbiotic relationship (see chapter 7). USPG Christianity has to introduce the concept of ancestor, and ATR has to give a new meaning to the concept of ancestor. USPG missionaries are not in a position to simply offer Christ as a means to salvation. They must also acknowledge their own salvific nakedness and stand ready to learn from ATR. Shona Anglican priests say that USPG missionaries should learn from ATR that salvation is communal and that the goodness of creation and the danger of making anything final before *Mwari* are not acceptable to the traditional Shona. USPG missionaries in their approach to traditional Shona, who believe in ATR, need not insist that Jesus Christ brings *Mwari*'s definitive, normative revelation. In order to convert the traditional Shona people to Jesus Christ, the Christ who is presented to them should be better than the Shona ancestors in solving existential Shona problems; otherwise their conversion is unthinkable.

Many Shona Anglican priests and Anglican Shona lay people object to the overly exclusive doctrinal conditions proposed to them by the USPG missionaries. Shona Anglican priests who object to the USPG Christianity have concluded that their own ATR makes more sense to them where it matters than does USPG Christianity. Shona Anglican priests who combine USPG Christianity and ATR believe that if USPG Christianity discards certain jingoisms as regards a particular set of symbols and language about *Mwari*, evil, the USPG Christian community, its priests, ministries, and life beyond the grave, then it might be liberated from its dangerous myopia. Shona Anglican priests argue that, by combining USPG Christianity and ATR, USPG Christianity might be freed to appreciate the Spirit of *Mwari* as He has revealed Himself in ATR prior to, during, and after the time of USPG missionary evangelization. Shona Anglican priests want the USPG missionaries to take seriously the fact that ATR is a legitimate interlocutor of USPG Christianity; they can work to fulfill each other and bring Zimbabwe to a fuller awareness of the greatness and superiority of *Mwari*—the *Mwari* of ATR is the same *Mwari* of Jesus Christ.

## A PROBLEM AND AN OPPORTUNITY

Most Shona Anglican priests believe that Shona USPG Christians approach *Mwari* by combining both USPG Christianity and ATR when faced with existential Shona problems. When things are good and Shona USPG Christians have no existential problems, then they are 'true' USPG Christians. When things go wrong, USPG Shona Christians revert to their Shona traditional religious beliefs and practices and consult with their ancestors. Once a problem is classified as a typically African or traditional Shona problem (*izvi ndezvechivanhu*), it is addressed to *Mwari* through the ancestors. Shona Anglican priests who advocate pneumatocentric and theocentric soteriologies approach *Mwari* through Jesus Christ (applying USPG Christianity) when they are hopeful that a solution to their problems is in sight. But once they become pessimistic about getting an immediate solution to their existential problems, they classify their problems as typically African or traditional Shona problems. They then say: "this is a typical Shona problem. It needs traditional Shona ways of solving it (*Izvi ndezvechivanhu, zvinoda kugadzirwa nenzira yechivanhu).*" In such cases they then seek immediate solutions by approaching *Mwari* through their ancestors and not through Jesus Christ.

The pneumatocentric and theocentric soteriologies which are advocated by Shona Anglican priests have some disadvantages, according to Paul Knitter. Knitter asserts that the theocentric model does not represent an evolutionary advance but an evolutionary dead end. A move to theocentric Christologies violates the understanding of Jesus Christ maintained by the New Testament...and debilitates both personal commitment to Christ and a distinctly Christian contribution to the world. Whereas for ecclesiocentricism and Christocentricism, Jesus Christ was seen working mystically, cosmically, anonymously, within all religions. Jesus Christ and his Church were the centre of the salvific universe. But from the various perspectives of theocentricism—the myth of the incarnation, *Logos* Christology, the relativity of all religions and religious figures, ethical hermeneutics—they are placing God, not the Church of Jesus Christ at the centre of things.[13]

Shona Anglican priests, Knitter believes, embrace pneumatocentric and theocentric soteriologies so uncritically that they feel impelled to reduce the Christian faith to a version which can be communicated within the presupposed scheme of ATR. The result is that what they communicate falls short of the Christian faith. That leaves the Shona USPG Christians in a ritual of limping dance between Jesus Christ and Shona ancestors; they are left in the lurch, unable to meet their deeper spiritual needs.

This chapter has shown that most Shona Anglican priests and Shona USPG Christians hold both USPG Christianity and ATR in parallel but separate compartments of their lives. This chapter also shows the need for an inculturation that is dynamic. It cannot be resisted or prevented. Shona Anglican priests and Shona USPG Christians are pleading for a Christ of Shona culture of which the ancestors form an integral part. They have taken it upon themselves to embark on the processes of appropriation and inculturation. This process of inculturation is not directed and authorized by the bishops; it is not based on a sound missiological assessment; hence, it is haphazard. This chapter, therefore, has shown that inculturation is a must which should be undertaken by the Church community and directed by the top Church authorities.

Shona Anglican priests and some USPG Christians are involved in a process of inculturation under cover of darkness despite fear of the bishops. No Church authority opposes inculturation; no Church authority will stop its rising tide. Shona Anglican priests and Shona USPG Christians involved in inculturation should not be condemned and victimized. They should be asked to come out in the open, and they should be directed and encouraged in the process of inculturation. Victimization of Shona Anglican priests who combine USPG Christianity and ATR has failed to produce the desired results after over one hundred years. Shona Anglican priests who combine USPG

Christianity and ATR should be commended and applauded for what they do, but they should be enlightened and directed by Church authorities in the process of inculturation. This, however, presupposes that these Church leaders are themselves "converted" toward a right understanding of inculturation. The Shona priests are trying to give Christianity deeper roots among the Zimbabwean Christians. Therefore, I put my full weight and support behind the Shona Anglican priests and Shona USPG Christians who combine USPG Christianity and ATR, but I will attempt a contribution towards inculturation by creating a trinitarian transformative (*Mudzimu Mukuru*) par excellence Christology (see chapter 7). This process is a combination of ATR and USPG Christian spiritual powers. The findings of this chapter provide a very fertile ground for creating a *Mudzimu Mukuru* par excellence Christology.

# CHAPTER 5

## *An ATR Perspective on Christianity*

This chapter aims to show that the theological and Christological debate which started in Europe and America has come into Africa and has penetrated African theological and Christological thinking. It also aims to show that African Christian theologians are still in the process of trying to find Christological images (faces) and roles of Jesus Christ in ATR (which is African culture), where the ancestors are the mediators between God and the traditional Africans. The chapter investigates how ecclesiocentric, pneumatocentric, Christocentric, and theocentric soteriologies relate to ancestors and are discernible in African contexts, Zimbabwe in particular. African Christian theologians wish to show that African Christology is closely linked to ancestors. The ancestors are at the centre of ATR. In this chapter I will use H. R. Niebuhr's *Christ and Culture* (1951) to investigate the relationships between African Christology and ancestors. The chapter, therefore, looks briefly at five types of Christ: Christ against ancestors, Christ of ancestors, Christ above ancestors, Christ and ancestors in paradox, and Christ the Transformed Ancestor and the Transformer of ancestors.

In Africa the roots of the Christian faith are shallow because Christianity is not integral to African ancestors and cosmology. The failed combination of Christianity and ATR has resulted in the majority of African Christians being involved in a ritual of limping dance between Jesus Christ and African ancestors. This is unacceptable because it keeps Christianity and ATR in perpetual conflict. This situation calls for inculturation of the Gospel into African thought forms based on African ancestors. In the tradition of Saint Augustine and Calvin, who advocated Christ the transformer of culture, I will argue for Christ the Transformed Ancestor and the Transformer of ancestors.

## CHRISTOLOGY AND SOTERIOLOGY IN THE AFRICAN CONTEXT

The Christological and soteriological debate which has been raging in Europe and America among theologians has penetrated African theology. Present day Africans, both traditional and modern, do not have a problem with who God (*Mwari)* is. The Africans are very clear about the position and function of God in the universe: God is the Creator and Sustainer of the universe. The problem for Africans is with Jesus Christ. Who is this Jesus Christ? What is His role and position in the order of salvation? For centuries the traditional Africans were saved by God through the intermediation of the ancestors. God answered their prayers.

Salvation from God came to the traditional Shona without Jesus Christ. Why then bother about this Jesus Christ? Does Jesus Christ have a part in ATR? African Christian theologians should also answer the following questions: if Africans can get salvation from God through ATR and the ancestors without Jesus Christ, then why become Christians? Does true conversion to Christ become possible only when Christianity is combined with African ancestors? These questions create a Christological problem for the Africans and hence a Christological and soteriological debate. In the process of combining Christianity and African ancestors, African theologians are trying to fit Jesus Christ into African ancestors where traditionally He has had no place and role to play. Jesus Christ is a "grafted foreigner" in ATR. The question is not of theology but of Christology: how is Christology being developed by African Christian theologians? How do African

Christian theologians link Jesus Christ with ancestors? Is Jesus Christ duplicating what the ancestors were doing in the past and are still doing today?

Should Africans have nothing to do with this "intruder" Jesus Christ? By having nothing to do with Jesus Christ, Africans will cease to be Christians. We get that tag *Christian* only when we believe in Jesus Christ. If Africans refuse to believe in Jesus Christ, won't God still save them through the ancestors? Is Jesus Christ the better and more effective Way to God? Has Jesus Christ taken over completely the roles played by the ancestors? If this is so, then where are the ancestors? What is the ancestors' function today? In short, is it really necessary for Africans to be converted from ATR to Christianity?

All these questions are to be honestly answered by African Christian theologians. Africans do not want to destroy ATR. They want a "chemical synthesis" of Christianity and African ancestors. Many Africans want to be Christians. They want to graft Jesus Christ into African ancestors under the guise of inculturation. African Christian theologians want to make ATR part of an international religion, and that international religion is Christianity. In their view, the person of Jesus Christ as God incarnate, not the Bible, takes the central place.[1]

ATR is not a bookish and missionary religion like Christianity and Islam. But African Christian theologians are interested in making ATR part of a religion of the book and also to make it part of a missionary religion. African Christian theologians are like a square peg in a round hole if Christianity is devoid of their culture (ATR) and their ancestral identity. Their Christological debate is an attempt to give Christianity deeper roots among the Africans by giving Christianity an African flavor, which is African ancestors.

Jesus Christ hoped for a transformation of the whole earthly form of existence. Belief in Jesus Christ by human beings in their various cultures always means belief in God. No one can know the Father (God) without acknowledging the Son (Jesus Christ) (Jn.14:9). To be related in devotion and obedience to Jesus Christ is to be related to the One God to whom He undeviatingly points. This applies also when discussing the relationship between African tradition and Christian tradition. It is a translation from one language to another, from a Christian language to an African language. A theologian must speak two languages because Christianity is not a culture. It is not a part of any culture or language exclusively but has to use language or culture as a vehicle of communicating its message. Christology should know the theological language and the cultural language. The theological language must retain some central ideas about God and His salvific ideas. The World Council of Churches (WCC) requires theological language for its membership. One has to accept Jesus Christ as both Lord and Savior of the universe. Language is what people get from their culture. They hold firmly to it because it works for them—witchcraft (*uroyi)* and ancestors (*midzimu*) work for traditional Shona people. This is an African view of nature and human beings and is also the Christian view of nature and human beings. There are relationships between Christ and ancestors. Christ and culture belong together. One can sort out how Christ and culture are related in the following five ways developed by H. Richard Niebuhr in *Christ and Culture (1951).*

## CHRIST AGAINST ANCESTORS

In the view of some African theologians, Christ opposes the ancestors. Jesus Christ opposes the customs and traditions of the society in which the Christian lives. Whatever traditional human achievements ATR conserves, Jesus Christ is opposed to them. Jesus Christ confronts human beings with the challenge of an either/or discussion. The Christ against ancestors uncompromisingly affirms the authority of Jesus Christ over the Christian and resolutely rejects ancestors' claims to loyalty. Jesus Christ rejected divorce and opposed some aspects of Jewish culture (religion) (Mt. 19:9, 15:16-20, Mk. 7:1-9). The Christ who would not worship Satan to gain the world's kingdom (Mt. 4:1-11) is followed by the Christians who will worship only Christ in unity with the God whom He serves. African theologians who hold the Christ against African ancestor's position are Byang Henry Kato (*Theological Pitfalls In Africa,* 1975*)* and Tite Tienou (*The*

*Theological Task of The Church In Africa,* 1982*)*. And this view is intolerable to all defenders of ATR, who are content that African ancestors should be offered worship, prayers, and ritual sacrifices.

## THE CHRIST OF ANCESTORS

In the view of some African theologians, Jesus Christ is the supreme example of universal human goodness and the fulfillment of ATR aspiration. They hold a positive view of ATR achievement, but they believe ATR cannot be true to its best ideals except through obedience to Christ. The Christ of ancestors is supported by Shona Anglican bishops, priests, laity, and African Christian theologians such as G. H. Muzorewa, B. Bujo, E. J. Penoukou, and C. Nyamiti, who hail Jesus as the *Messiah* of their society, the fulfiller of its hopes and aspirations, the perfecter of its true faith, and the source of its holiest spirit. They are believers in Christ, and they also seek to maintain community with all other believers. They are at home in the community of ancestors. Shona Anglican bishops, priests, and laity who support the Christ-of-ancestors view feel no great tension between the Church and "the world", the social laws and the Gospel, the workings of divine grace and human efforts, the ethics of salvation and the ethics of social conservation or progress. They interpret ATR through Jesus Christ, regarding those elements in it as most important which are most accordant with His work and person. On the other hand, they understand Christ through ATR, selecting from His teaching and action as well as from the Christian doctrine about Him such points as seem to agree with what is best in ATR and their culture. So they harmonize Christ and ATR, not without excision of stubbornly discordant features, of course, from the New Testament (NT) and social custom. They do not necessarily seek Christian sanction for the whole of the prevailing ATR, but only for what they regard as real in the actual. In the case of Christ, they try to disentangle the rational and abiding from the historical and accidental.

## CHRIST ABOVE ANCESTORS

Some African theologians see a clear distinction between the Spirit of Christ and that of ancestors, but they do not believe that the difference needs to be one of opposition. When ancestors fulfill their proper roles, the distinction is complementary, and a synthesis between Christ and ancestors is possible. These theologians lay great stress on the importance of African ancestors. They follow H. R. Niebuhr, who wrote: "man is obligated in the nature of his being to be obedient to God—not to a Jesus separate from the Almighty Creator, nor to an author of nature separate from Jesus Christ, but to God-in-Christ and Christ-in-God—and that this obedience must be rendered in the concrete, actual life of natural, cultural man."[2] The Christ-above-ancestors view was common in Europe during the Medieval period. Christ came to raise up all institutions to His level. There is nothing in ATR which cannot be made Christian. The Christian form of culture is the best. It replaces the traditional Shona culture. It is an Imperialistic type of Christianity. It promotes a sense of contempt for African ancestors. It says that Christianity is superior to African ancestors. It also believes that every African ancestor and institution can be redeemed by Christ. Families, schools, and all other institutions can be made Christian by Christ Himself. African theologians who plead for a Christ above ancestors include J. S. Pobee (*Toward An African Theology,* 1979*)*, C. Nyamiti (*African Theologies Today,* 1991), A. Obaje (*Theocentric Christologies,* 1992), A. M. Moyo (*The Quest For African Christian Theology And The Problem Of Relationship Between Faith And Culture,* 1983*)*, G. H. Muzorewa (*African Theology Of Mission, 1990)* and G. H. Muzorewa *(The Origin And Development Of African Theology,* 1985*)*.

## CHRIST AND ANCESTORS IN PARADOX

Some African theologians take a dialectical approach, a way of saying both yes and no. They do not accept nor reject ATR with its ancestors. This view is associated with the Martin Luther tradition. All African ancestors were created by God. They depend on God. God reveals and acts in all ATR and ancestors. This is a yes. There is also a "no" side which says that Africa, America, Asia, Australia, and Europe are not the Kingdom of God. No African ancestors are equivalent to the Kingdom of God. There is no superiority of one ancestor over the other. This approach does not hold that African ancestors are the best and only way to God. It holds that there are many ways to God, and a Christian can live in any culture. All cultures can be Christianized. It maintains a tension between Christ of ancestors and Christ above ancestors. This means that for these people there is nothing like a Christian law. No Christian is needed in order to have a good government. Culture and religion should be ruled by reason, common sense, rule of decency and morality but not necessarily by Christ. A Christian ruler is not necessarily the best. There is a distinction between the rule of God and the rule of human beings. This position is taken by Z. Nthamburi *(Christ As Seen By An African; A Christological Quest,* 1991*)* and Akrong *(Christology From An African Perspective,* 1992*).*

## CHRIST THE TRANSFORMED ANCESTOR AND THE TRANSFORMER OF ANCESTORS

In this fifth view, Christ is seen as the greatest transformed ancestor and the transformer of ancestors. ATR on its own stands opposed to Christ, as part of the fallen world, but Christ gives us power to remove the threat which all ancestors contain and to establish ATR on a different basis through His Lordship. H. R. Niebuhr wrote that

Christ is the transformer of culture for Augustine in the sense that he redirects, reinvigorates, and regenerates that life of man, expressed in all human works, which in present actuality is the perverted and corrupted exercise of a fundamentally good nature; which, moreover, in its depravity lies under the curse of transiency and death, not because an external punishment has been visited upon it, but because it is intrinsically self-contradictory.[3]

There is a radical distinction between God's work in Christ and ancestral work in ATR. Jesus Christ judges ATR. Both ATR and ancestors are transformed by Jesus Christ, not replaced by a new creation, though the transformation is so radical that it amounts to a new birth. Jesus Christ has power to transform all things and this includes Shona people and their ATR by lifting them up to Himself. The movement of life issuing from Jesus Christ is an upward movement, the rising of Shona souls, deeds, and thoughts in a mighty surge of adoration and glorification of the Lord Jesus Christ who draws them to Himself.

There is agreement between this view and the Christ-above-ancestors view. Christ the transformer of ancestors is associated with Calvin and Saint Augustine. Shona Christians have a lot to contribute to transform ATR. Christ is the Lord of ATR, but He exercises it as a servant of human beings so as to transform ATR together with the ancestors. Christ is in cultures that try to overthrow slavery and social, political, and economic exploitation. Christ is there to transform society and religions in society. Any culture, ATR included, can be Christian, but no culture is Christian. African theologians who plead for a Christ the Transformed Ancestor and Transformer of ancestors include A. T. Sanon (*Jesus, Master of Initiation,* 1991).

## IMAGES (FACES) OF JESUS CHRIST IN AFRICA

*Hermeneutics:* Unless one takes the view that the Word of God fell down from heaven in the Hebrew language for some people and in the Greek language for others, one must accept that human minds interpret ideas. One should then accept that Biblical Christology is culture-bound. One should also have a critical view of the NT texts. This is a very difficult task, but only then can one argue for inculturation and an inculturated Christology.

*Language:* The traditional Shona people use language both figuratively (metaphorically) and literally. Figuratively, people are called by their totem—for example, pig (*humba)*, monkey (*soko*), heart (*moyo*), or lion (*shumba*). This does not mean that they are literally pigs, monkeys, hearts, or lions. When a person is referred to as a *shumba,* it is a show of reverence and respect and not a statement that one is a lion. When it comes to religion, both the figurative use of language and the literal use of language are used. One should stretch the literal use of language to the figurative use of language. For example, Shona people can call someone by his or her title—father (*baba)*, mother (*amai*), uncle (*sekuru*), or ancestor (*mudzimu*). In the Bible, some images given to God and Jesus Christ are figurative (metaphorical) and some are literal. Figuratively, Jesus Christ is referred to as the Rock (1 Peter 2:8, Rom. 9:33, 1 Cor. 10:4), the Life, the Way, the Truth (Jn. 14:6), the Vine (Jn. 15:5), the Light (Rev. 21:24, 1 Jn. 1:7), the Shepherd (Jn. 10:11), and the King (Mt. 27:11). However, images like father, wisdom, love, son, and *Logos*, as applied to God and Jesus Christ, are literal. All human terms applied to God and Jesus Christ are analogical (partially similar) and figurative (metaphorical), and some are literal. The term Greatest Ancestor *(Mudzimu Mukuru)* as applied to Jesus Christ is analogical (partially similar) and also literal, but not figurative or metaphorical. Analogically (literally similar) and also literally, Jesus Christ is the Greatest Ancestor *(Mudzimu Mukuru)* par excellence for the Zimbabwean Christians.

*Function:* What is the function of Christology? What difference does Christology make to the Christian believer? Christian faith is not faith unless it is based on Christ. A Christology is an intellectual pattern which Christians use to think about political, economic, and social aspects of life in relation to Christ. A Christology shows people that the Gospel of God is relevant to their lives when they are in Christ.

Christology in Zimbabwe, as elsewhere, cannot exist meaningfully outside its social context. The non-negotiables in any Christological position should be the divinity of Christ, the humanity of Christ, the cross, and the resurrection of Christ. How should the Shona people, out of their store of images and symbols, their cultural expressions, their experiences, their hopes and fears, express the humanity, cross, resurrection, and divinity of Christ in a clear and effective way that will lead the Zimbabweans to worship the mystery which is at once tremendous, awe-inspiring, and yet attractive? What follows is a survey of images (faces) of Jesus Christ from across Africa.

## WEST AFRICA

*Explicit Ancestral Images:* West Africa is ahead of the rest of Africa when it comes to the development of African Christology. J. S. Pobee, of the Akan tribe in Ghana, and an Anglican priest, states that "our approach would be to look on Jesus as the Great and Greatest Ancestor—in Akan language *Nana.*"[4] Pobee argues for a functional Christology as fit for the mentality of the Akan people of Ghana. K. A. Dickson, a Ghanaian Methodist theologian, states that "by His death, Christ merits to be looked upon as Ancestor, the Greatest of ancestors who never ceases to be the living dead."[5] Like Pobee and Dickson, Kwame Bediako, a Ghanaian Presbyterian minister asserts that "since ancestral function, as traditionally understood, is now shown to have no basis, in fact, the way is open for appreciating more fully how Jesus Christ is the only and true Ancestor and source of life for all mankind, fulfilling and transcending the benefits believed to be bestowed by lineage ancestors."[6]

Akrong of Ghana gave Jesus Christ a face of an ancestor for he maintains that "Christ our Ancestor is our Saviour par excellence and the actualization of all the aspirations that our human ancestors represent."[7] Jesus Christ, according to Obaje of Nigeria, has become the Supreme Intermediary, replacing all the go-between divinities (ancestors) known to the African convert in ATR. Jesus Christ has taken absolute control as the only Mediator between God and the African people. Obaje contends that "God is at the centre of African Traditional Religions (ATR) and African ancestors are intermediaries between God and the living Africans. Jesus Christ is Hero-Ancestor who dies saving His people. He is also a Mediator-Ancestor who mediates between God and human beings."[8] Penoukou of the Ivory Coast says that Jesus Christ is at the centre of all human history. Jesus is Mediator between God and the whole of creation. Penoukou argues that "in a like perspective, the tendency would be to make of Christ at once the procreative spirit *(Bomynen)*, the ancestor *Joto,* and the holder of all destinies."[9] For Penoukou, Christ as *Joto*—Ancestor—means that He is the Ancestor who is the source of life and the fulfilment of the *Joto*-cosmo-theandric relationship in the world.

*Non-Ancestral Images:* Sanon of Burkina Faso, a Roman Catholic priest, argues that Jesus Christ is the Head and Master of initiation. He claims that, "on this score to say that Jesus is Chief of initiation is to recognize in Him, in our particular cultural tonality, the eldest sibling, who guides to perfection those who have undergone their initiation."[10] Besides giving Jesus Christ the face of an Ancestor, Pobee also gives Jesus Christ the image of a Chief, and has a royal-priestly Christology. He states that "again Jesus as a Chief is human and shares common humanity with the rest of mankind."[11] However, Sawyerr, from Sierra Leone, rejects the application of the image of a chief to Jesus Christ. He argues that traditional African chiefs have now lost most of their power, authority, and influence. They are despotic. They have never been readily accessible to the ordinary people. Sawyerr calls Jesus Christ an Elder Brother. He reasons that "Jesus Christ is Elder Brother, the first born among many brethren who with Him form the Church in which there is no distinction of race, sex, color or social condition."[12] Bediako, in addition to calling Jesus an Ancestor, also calls Him Elder Brother, for he explains that "our Savior is our Elder Brother who has shared our African experience in every respect, except in our sin and alienation from God."[13]

Healing is a very important ministry in the Church in Africa. African Christians, who carry a rosary in their hands and a fetish under their clothing, experience a bipolarity or an ambivalence of religious loyalties between Jesus Christ and African ancestors, which leads one to ask whether Jesus can honestly be present in Africa as a Healer. Yet Kolie, a Guinean, gives Jesus Christ the image of a Healer in Africa, for he explains that "this Jesus will be Healer, Grand Master of Initiation, Ancestor par excellence or Chief of Chiefs, not because I shall have declared Him to be such, but because He will have wrought cures, presided over initiations and given birth to a free person."[14]

*Rejection of Ancestral Images:* Byang Henry Kato was a Nigerian from the Jaba tribe of the North Central State of Nigeria. He had an unsympathetic and a disdainful attitude to non-Christian religions. Kato was interested in safe guarding Biblical Christianity in Africa, for he suggested that

> ATR as well as others be studied carefully but only secondary to the inductive study of God's Word. The New Testament writers and the early Church evangelists did not consider it worthwhile to spend too much of their energy in the study of non-Christian religions. All non-Christian religions belong to one and the same group, 'the unsaved'."[15]

Tite Tienou is a Malian of the same school of thought and background as Kato. He is pastor and a member of the World Evangelical Fellowship (WEF). Tienou maintains that "many African Christian theologians spend most of their time defending African traditional religious practices that are incompatible with biblical teaching."[16] Tienou, like Kato, rejects ATR and their ancestors.

## EAST AFRICA

*Explicit Ancestral Images:* Charles Nyamiti, a Tanzanian Roman Catholic priest, has a Christological approach similar to that of Penoukou. Nyamiti pleads for an African Christology which is based on the Ancestorship of Jesus Christ. Nyamiti argues that "one is, therefore, led to conclude that African brother ancestorship is a true *praeparatio evangelica* for the true Christian doctrine on Christ as the Unique Ancestor of human beings, and that His Ancestorship is the highest accomplishment of its African counterpart."[17] Mutiso-Mbindi, from Kenya, gives Jesus Christ the image of an Ancestor and argues that "Christ, being our Ancestor par excellence, becomes our mediator who continues to intercede for us. As our ancestor, Christ becomes the new source of human lineage."[18] Bahemuka, Kenya, advocates a Christ of ancestors rooted in ATR, for he asserts, "Christ is our Ancestor because He is our Brother, the spoken Word eternally begotten by God Our Father, Word made flesh, who dwells with us."[19]

*Non-Ancestral Images:* Wachege, a Kenyan Roman Catholic priest, gives Jesus Christ the image of an Ideal Elder. He states that "Jesus Christ is our *Muthamaki* (Ideal Elder) but in a higher and more imminent sense."[20] Magesa, also a Kenyan Roman Catholic priest, gives Jesus Christ the image of a Liberator. He claims that "Christ is Liberator because He is at once the foundation, the inspiration, the basic reason and the guarantor of the ultimate success of the struggle for the liberation of the human person, for development and healing—idealistically through the Church."[21] Nasimiyu-Wasike, from Kenya, advocates a feminist Christology which liberates African women from a male-dominated African society. She rejects an androcentric, male-centered culture; she argues that "the third Christological model for African women that arises in women's reflection is that of Christ the Liberator. Christ is the Cosmological Liberator who reconciles all things to God."[22] Nasimiyu-Wasike also proposes the image of the Healer; she explains, "That is the model of Christ the Healer. Jesus attached great significance to exorcism and healing."[23] Mugambi from Kenya, like Nasimiyu-Wasike, gives Jesus Christ the two faces of Healer and Liberator: "the role of Jesus as Healer is very important in the Gospel." [24]

For Mugambi, Jesus Christ is the Liberator of Africans; he argues, "thus there are two theologies, one for liberation and one for perpetuating oppression. Where would Jesus stand? Would He identify Himself with the struggle against apartheid because, after all He struggled against it in Palestine two thousand years ago?"[25] Waliggo, from Uganda, gives Jesus Christ the two images of Healer and Liberator, for he claims that "they [the people] want Christ who is Liberator in all dimensions of life, Christ who is the Healer par excellence of all their diseases and anxieties."[26] Nthamburi argues for

Jesus Christ who liberates Africans from poverty, diseases, suffering, and all evil forces. He argues that "we should not forget that the only way in which we can understand Christ is through concrete historical experience of God's action which is always a liberating experience."[27] Waruta, from Kenya, gives Jesus Christ the images of Prophet, Priest, and Potentate (Prince). He states that "one thing that is very evident in African Christianity is that Africans have understood Jesus as Prophet, Priest and King. Nevertheless, Jesus as Prophet, Priest and Potentate provides for the African people the most perfect model for them."[28]

## CENTRAL AFRICA

*Explicit Ancestral Images:* Bujo, a Roman Catholic priest from The Democratic Republic of Congo gives Jesus Christ the image of Ancestor. He states, "I would like to suggest that such a new way of speaking would be to give Jesus the title of Ancestor par excellence, that is Proto-Ancestor."[29] Kabasele, from the Democratic Republic of Congo, also gave Jesus Christ the image of Ancestor, for he claims that "Christ fits the category of Ancestor because, finally, He is synthesis of all mediation."[30]

*Non-Ancestral Images:* Kabasele also gives Jesus Christ the non-ancestral images of Elder Brother and Chief. He states that, "in this perspective, Christ is the Elder Brother par excellence: it is to Him alone that offering must be made."[31] Again, Kabasele asserts that "first of all Jesus Christ is called Chief (*Mukalenge*) by virtue of the primary denotation of this general word which designates someone who holds some authority and who governs a part of the people."[32]

## SOUTHERN AFRICA

*Explicit Ancestral Images:* Moyo, a Zimbabwean Lutheran bishop, gives Jesus Christ the image of Ancestor. He claims that "Jesus is called the Supreme Universal Spirit Ancestor through whom all other spirits must get access to God."[33] The late Banana, a minister of the Methodist Church and first black President of Zimbabwe, gives Jesus Christ an image of an ancestor, for he holds that "thus, to make the mediatorship of Jesus more meaningful to the Shona-Ndebele people, it is of paramount importance to compliment Jesus Christ in the context of ancestorship. This kind of ancestorship bears the closest analogy to the role of Christ as our Ancestor and Mediator."[34]

*Non-Ancestral Images:* Banana also gives Jesus Christ the image of a diviner, *(N'anga)*. He explains that "Christ is a Healer, but not just a traditional bone thrower. He himself is *Obuyisway*, that is, the inclusive Lord of life."[35] Banana gives Jesus Christ the image of a Liberator: "the forces of oppression were completely defeated as they collided against the cross of Christ. Good News to the poor is a celebration and enactment of the classic and normative liberation struggle in which Jesus Christ defeated all human and spiritual forces of oppression."[36] Gwinyayi Henry Muzorewa, a Zimbabwean United Methodist minister, believes that there are many ways to God; Jesus Christ is not the only way to God, not the only source of salvation. He explains that "the problem with salvation-through-Christ-alone theology is that it knows God too much—so much that it can afford to attempt to limit what God can do to only what God has done in and through the only begotten Son, Jesus Christ."[37]

Jesus Christ is given the image of a Liberator and a black skin by some black African Christologians. Goba, a South African Christologian, affirms that "the Church should be relevant to the struggle and the process of liberation in South Africa. The black Christian communal praxis as a theology of the oppressed reflects a counter-ethos grounded in the liberating spirit of God in Christ."[38] Boesak, a South African and Evangelical Reformed minister, claims that "for black Christians, we affirm with James Cone, to confess Jesus Christ as the black *Messiah* is the only true confession of our time."[39] Masola and Makhubu, black South African Christian theologians, "advocate a Jesus Christ who is more closely identified with the blacks."[40] Dandala, a black South African theologian, argues that "liberation of black South Africans comes from God through Jesus

Christ."[41] Mothlabe, a South African black theologian, argues that, "Jesus Christ is the answer to the South African quest and hunger for freedom and complete emancipation from the chains of apartheid."[42]

## ANCESTORCENTRICISM

Almost all the African theologians dealt with in this chapter give Jesus Christ the image of Ancestor. Even the so-called non-ancestral images given to Jesus Christ, including Healer, Master of Initiation, Chief, Ideal Brother, Elder Brother, Liberator, Priest, Prophet, and Potentate are rooted in the ancestor concept. No one in ATR can be healer, master of initiation, chief, ideal brother, elder brother, liberator, priest, prophet, and potentate without the blessings of God mediated through the ancestors. Africans only fully realize themselves in society. Ancestors are nearer to God than are living human beings; therefore, they are superior to the living human beings, and, therefore, they are venerated and worshipped. The Ancestors work for economic, political, and social justice in their respective families and ethnic groups.

African Christologians who give Jesus Christ the face of an Ancestor realize that African ancestors are the mediators between God and the Africans. African theologians use the roles and functions of ancestors to illuminate the position and functions of Jesus Christ. Jesus Christ is at the apex of the pyramidal hierarchy of ancestors. No African ancestor is above Jesus Christ. The functions of Jesus Christ are the same as those of African ancestors but Jesus Christ performs these functions in an eminent and superior way. Whereas African ancestors fail in some of their functions, Jesus Christ never fails in all His functions. Ancestors are judges in African society. Ancestors have authority and power. They have the capacity to heal. For Dickson, death does not end life. Witches (*varoyi*) and wizards (*varoyi*) are given permission by the ancestors to cause suffering, illness, and death if ancestors are not propitiated. Ancestors send death as punishment. Jesus Christ is Judge par excellence for the Africans. He is not the source of evil. Bediako, like Pobee, Bujo, Penoukou, Nyamiti, Mutiso-Mbinda, Banana, Moyo and Obaje advocate for a Christ above ancestors in the hierarchy of ancestors. By arguing that Christ is the *Joto* (Ancestor), Penoukou is saying that Jesus Christ in an eminent and superior way is at the centre of human history. He is the co-fecundator of birth. He provides newly born babies with the necessary vital energy for His apparition in them. Jesus Christ is the Agent of family and ethnic unity in Africa. He is therefore an Agent of all human relationships in Africa.

Bujo, Moyo, Banana, Penoukou, Nyamiti, Kabasele, Bahemuka, and Akrong are ancestorcentric. Ancestors have been the model for African moral conduct. Now Jesus Christ is the Guarantor of salvation and the source of life. Jesus Christ is the Guarantor of the future. Christ is people-centered, anthropocentric. Like Bujo, Nyamiti bases his African theology on the African understanding of ancestor. He has a Christological approach similar to that of Penoukou. Nyamiti advocates a Christ above ancestors. For the traditional Africans, ancestors are the only mediators between God and human beings, but for African Christians, Jesus Christ and the ancestors are the mediators between God and human beings. Jesus Christ is God incarnate and has sacred powers. The behavior and morality of Christ and ancestors should be emulated by the whole community. Prayers and ritual sacrifices are offered to God through Jesus Christ and ancestors. African theologians argue that Jesus Christ surpasses all the African ancestors in all these functions. The ancestral image of Jesus Christ deepens and broadens the African Christian faith, for example, in the way the Church finds solidarity as a community of believers. African Christian theologians who give Jesus Christ non-ancestral images such as Healer, Master of Initiation, Chief, Liberator, Ideal Elder, Elder Brother have the same aim as in traditional African thought forms which are deeply rooted in the ancestors.

By giving Jesus Christ the images of Ideal Elder and Elder Brother, Wachege, Bediako, Bahemuka, Sawyerr, and Kabasele are aware of the fact that in Africa elder brothers propitiate ancestors on behalf of their younger siblings. Elder brothers are believed to be nearer to the ancestors by virtue of being elder brothers. The ancestors are the elder brothers, and they are closer to Jesus Christ, the source of life. Among the Shona people, when the father dies, the eldest brother is given the name of his deceased father. He is the deceased father incarnate. The eldest brother takes over all the responsibilities of his deceased father. The younger siblings refer to him as "father". The elder brother is possessed by the spirit of the deceased father. By being the deceased father incarnate, the elder brother has become a representative of the ancestors. He is an ancestor, for his deceased father who possesses him is an ancestor. Jesus Christ is both our Elder and Ideal Brother for He is nearest to God our Heavenly Father. He is the first born of God (Col. 1:15-16). Jesus Christ is possessed by the Holy Spirit of God the Father (Mt. 3:16).

The elder brother inherits the junior wives of his deceased father as his wives, and he cohabits with them. In the case of chieftainship, the elder brother becomes the chief after the death of his father. All prayers and ritual sacrifices to the ancestors are offered through the elder brother. The elder brother represents an example to be emulated in every respect, for he is an ancestor. The elder brother is loved the most by the ancestors because they have given him the guardianship of the family or ethnic group. We offer our prayers and worship to God through Jesus Christ. Jesus Christ takes care of us all, for He is God incarnate.

In traditional Africa, the masters of initiation are the chiefs, elder brother, diviners (*n'anga*), spirit mediums, priests, prophets, and kings. They are in constant touch with ancestors. Jesus Christ is the Initiator and Transformer in all African rites of passage. Sanon advocates a Christ above ancestors and Christ the Transformed Ancestor and the Transformer of ancestors. During the rites of passage, ancestors lift the one who undergoes the rites of passage from a lower status to a higher status. The ancestors give that individual the responsibilities of the society. During the rites of passage, ritual sacrifices and prayers of purification are offered to the ancestors. In all rites of passage, such as birth, puberty, marriage, and death, ancestors are invoked, propitiated, and worshipped. Jesus Christ is the Master of

Initiation in Christian rites of passage such as baptism and confirmation. Sacrifices and prayers are offered to God through Jesus Christ for Jesus Christ is in constant touch and dialogue with God. As Master of Initiation Jesus Christ is an Ancestor.

Traditional African states were theocratic. The chief or king was both a religious and political leader. By saying that Jesus Christ is the Chief or Potentate (King or Prince), Pobee, Waruta, Kolie, and Kabasele are reasoning that Jesus Christ is an Ancestor, for African ancestors are judges, legislators, religious leaders, and heads of the family and ethnic group—thc community. Kings and chiefs receive all power and authority from ancestors. When a king or a chief dies, he becomes a territorial/regional ancestor (*mhondoro/mudzimu mukuru*). The *mhondoro* relate to the traditional Zimbabwean in concrete, experiential, and practical terms rather than in a mystical and spiritual manner. Jesus Christ is concerned with the economic, social, and political affairs of all human beings in their past, present, and future.

Kings and chiefs as ancestors symbolize the identity of the Zimbabwean people. Kingship and chieftainship are passed on through rigid ancestral lineage. Christ, through the diviners (*n'anga*) and spirit mediums (*masvikiro)*, is involved in the choosing and enthronement of kings and chiefs. Kings and chiefs play priestly and prophetic roles on behalf of the Africans. The kings and chiefs, as ancestors, are answerable to Jesus Christ. Kings and chiefs preside over African traditional religious rituals, lead people in worship and prayer at rain-making ceremonies (*mukweverera*), enforce the observance of the day of rest (*chisi*), and lead people in all regional and ethnic rituals. Christ, through kings and chiefs, is the Guardian of the land. Kingship and chieftainship are sacred trusts with codes and procedures religiously sanctioned by Christ. The codes and procedures are not changed without first consulting ancestors through diviners (*n'anga)*. Christ is the defense of the community as a whole.

By reasoning that Jesus is the Ancestor-Healer, Kolie, Banana, Nasimiyu-Wasike, Shorter, Mugambi, and Waliggo are saying that healing is a central feature of the ancestors. Christ as an Ancestor has power to heal. Without the blessing of Christ there is no healing. The *n'anga* are empowered by Christ in order for them to perform their duties of healing. Christ heals an African community of its spiritual, physical, political, and social illnesses. Christ also heals moral decadence in an African society. Christ's healing is integral, directed towards physical life, eternal life, and wholeness. Christ has a healing mission to the whole universe. Christ should be invoked, venerated, and worshipped each time there is an illness in the family and community. There are some illnesses and sicknesses which ancestors fail to heal, but Jesus Christ does not fail to heal any type of infirmity.

By giving Jesus the image of the Liberator, Magesa, Nasimiyu-Wasike, Mugambi, Waliggo, Nthamburi, Banana, Boesak, Goba, Masola, Makhubu, Dandala, Buthelezi, Mothilabe, and Mafokeng are using their Christology to integrate the theme of liberation into ancestors. Ancestors are the liberators and saviors of Africans. Jesus Christ fights against all sorts of evil, be they moral, social, political, or economic. Christ the Ancestor is not only Mediator but also the Liberator, not only of spiritual life but also of the material and physical aspects of life. Christ promotes fullness of life here and now. Christ brings liberation in the African context—the total reality of the African people which encompasses cultural, religious (ATR), and socio-economic realities.

Liberation is achieved when Africans are vitally linked to the ancestors. Traditional Africans are always surrounded by a host of ancestors. Ancestors are liberators. Total liberation, which comes from Christ, involves more than relief from illness, famine, poverty, security from civil strife, and deliverance from economic, political and social corruption and exploitation. Total liberation includes the souls of the Africans, their participation in the fullness of life. Liberation links them to the yet unborn and to Christ as well as to the living community around them. Only in Christ is such liberation fully achieved. Liberation for Christians comes about when they are in Christ, vitally linked to Christ (Gal. 3:26-28, Rom. 6, Col. 3:9ff). Jesus Christ, in a very eminent and superior way, fulfils the function of liberation to the Africans. No African Christology is worth its salt without taking into account the role and function of Jesus Christ, the Ancestor Liberator.

Not every Shona person becomes an ancestor. It is not enough to die. One must have lived a virtuous life. One must have left descendants on earth in order to be an ancestor. Recourse to Christ, whatever its motive or occasion, is always the source of liberation and blessing. All important events in the life of an African Christian become an epiphany, or the activity of Christ, or an occasion of renewing contacts with Him. All acts of liberation and daily life must be steeped once more in the presence of the Christ. If a traditional Shona person sneezes or drops something, he or she will call upon the name of the ancestor, as if asking for a blessing or to be liberated. When surprised, a traditional Shona will utter an ancestor's name. Without the existence of Christ, there would be no liberation of Africans. Africans should understand Jesus Christ as the Liberator Ancestor more than they understand their ancestors as liberators. True, total, and ultimate liberation comes from Jesus Christ alone.

By saying that Jesus is Prophet and Priest, Waruta is implying that Jesus is the Diviner (*N'anga*) or an Ancestral Spirit Medium (*Svikiro*). I do not think that diviners (*N'anga*) and spirit mediums (*masvikiro*) have Jesus Christ as Ancestor in mind, nor that they think their authority is derived from supernatural encounters with Jesus Christ. *N'anga*, who are central in the rain-making (*mukweverera*) ceremony, and *masvikiro* are in constant touch with Christ through the pyramidal hierarchy of ancestors, for Christ is at the apex of that pyramidal hierarchy. They mediate between the world of ancestors (*nyikadzimu)* and living human beings. Christ as Ancestor makes history of the Africans, both sacred and profane. He is the Master of Initiation in all rites of passage. *N'anga* and *masvikiro* are both political and religious leaders. *N'anga*, beneficial *mashave*, and *masvikiro* are ancestral spirit mediums through which the life-giving power of Christ comes to human beings. *N'anga and masvikiro* contain within themselves "life forces" from Christ, which they give to the people. They preside over religious rituals, lead people in worship, and solemnize the rites of passage ceremonies. Jesus Christ is Priest, Potentate, and Prophet. He is possessed by the Holy Spirit (*Mweya Anoyera).*

*N'anga* and *masvikiro* are masters of traditional wisdom, rituals, and ceremonial practices. People go to them with the hope of allaying their fears and suffering. *N'anga* and *masvikiro* lead the people in the communal sacrifices, such as the rain-making ceremonies (*mukweverera*), where Christ's intervention as an Ancestor is sought to meet the needs of the community. It is through *N'anga* and *masvikiro* that Christ's power is employed for the purpose of changing the human condition for the better. *N'anga, masvikiro*, and chiefs (*madzishe*) officiate at ritual sacrifices in order to establish the bond between the people and Jesus Christ the Ancestor and among the people themselves. The ritual sacrifice provides the link between Christ and living human beings through the symbolic actions and works of *n'anga, masvikiro*, and *madzishe*.

Diviners and spirit mediums are the moral analysts, the charismatic leaders, the functionary priests, and prophets of Jesus Christ the Ancestor. Their authority as religious leaders derives from traumatic, supernatural encounters with Jesus Christ the Ancestor in the spirit world (*nyikadzimu*). They stand as salvific mediators between the living and the dead. They know the desires, requests, and demands of the people. *N'anga, masvikiro*, and chiefs are ancestors incarnate. Ezekiel Gwembe, SJ, from Tanzania, concludes that a more profound study of the ancestors would not bring us to a better understanding of the saints, but to a better understanding of the person of Christ. It would not lead us to "saintology" but to a "Christology" in an African form. Christ and not the saints fulfils in an excellent form the characteristics of an African ancestor.[43]

Jesus Christ is God incarnate (Jn.1:1-14). He derives special prophetic, Kingly, and Priestly powers from God. Jesus Christ is a Mediator in an eminent and superior way between God and the Africans.

Where are the African ancestors when Jesus Christ is regarded as the *Mudzimu Mukuru* par excellence? What are the roles and functions of African ancestors when Jesus Christ becomes the *Mudzimu Mukuru* par excellence? Are Africans to discard their ancestors when Jesus Christ becomes the *Mudzimu Mukuru* par excellence? When an African becomes a Christian, he or she will understand in an excellent way the characteristics, roles, and functions of ancestors. Ancestors are not to be discarded. Ancestors become saints. They take the characteristics, roles, and functions of Christian saints such as Mary. Africans should pray to ancestors just as they pray to Christian saints. Ancestors should be venerated, for they are linked to the *Mudzimu Mukuru* par excellence, who is the Savior of all human beings. African Christians should pray to the ancestors, although ancestors are not the end point. Catholics pray to Mary, but Mary is not the end point. Africans who convert to Jesus Christ should continue to pray to their ancestors and venerate their ancestors, bearing in mind that it is Jesus Christ the *Mudzimu Mukuru* par excellence who receives all prayers, sacrifices, and worship. African Christians should accept ancestors because they form part of the foundation in the pyramidal hierarchy of ancestors with Jesus Christ at the apex.

## NO CATEGORIZATION OF AFRICAN CHRISTOLOGIES

Theologically, African Christology has no distinctions among ecclesiocentric, Christocentric, theocentric, and Pneumatocentric Christologies, but practically all such distinctions are there. There are no separations among the ancestors, *mhondoro*, *masvikiro*, and *n'anga*. African Christology also has no such distinctions. Jesus Christ functions through the Holy Spirit because, in the doctrine of the Trinity, God the Father, Jesus Christ the Son of the Father, and the Holy Spirit of the Father through the Son are inseparable. African Christology is Pneumatocentric, for an African world view is full of spirits, some good and some evil. Jesus Christ is full of the Holy Spirit, the giver of life (Mt. 3:16, 4:1). Traditional Africans live in the omnipresence of spiritual realities that represent God, and some spirits who represent the devil. God is represented by His spiritual agents, the ancestors. The devil is represented by his spiritual agents, the evil avenging spirits (*ngozi*) and evil alien spirits (*mashave*). African Christology should produce African Christians who are filled with the Holy Spirit of Jesus Christ. African Christology should have the Holy Spirit of Jesus Christ as its driving force. The Spirit of Christ should result in the destruction of all evil spirits among the African Christians.

African Christology is both Christocentric and theocentric because it is rooted in Jesus Christ, who is Lord God (Jn. 20:28). Jesus Christ is the wellspring of the life and health of the living, since life is recycled through procreation. Because of the life-sharing and life-protecting role of Christ, it is necessary that He be contacted on a regular basis to know His will. Christ symbolizes God's presence among the Africans. Christ deals with the day-to-day existential situations of life. Worship of Christ is understood in a temporal or material sense as well as a religious or supernatural sense. African Christians live in the universe of Christ so that every phenomenon and object is associated with ancestors. Becoming a saint/ancestor should be the ultimate goal of every African Christian.

African Christology is ecclesiocentric because the Church is the Body of Christ (Eph. 5:23). All African Christians are members of the Church of Christ. Jesus Christ and the Shona family ancestors (*midzimu yepamusha*) and regional ancestors (*mhondoro/midzimu mikuru*) should be explicitly named by the Shona Christians in prayers and ritual sacrifices. Jesus Christ is the guardian of public order in His Church. Without Jesus Christ, there is nothing African Christians can achieve in the Church of God. Christ is concerned with the health and welfare of His Church. African Christian babies should be named after their family and territorial ancestors. Christ and African ancestors should always be called on for help and guidance by African Christians. Christ is one with His Church; He is the Head of the Church (Eph. 5:23). Christ without a Church is unthinkable as far as African Christians are concerned. African ecclesiology is rooted in Christ.

African Christology generally advances a Christ of ancestors, Christ above ancestors, Christ and ancestor in paradox, and Christ the Transformed Ancestor and the Transformer of ancestors. African

Christology does not separate among ecclesiocentric, Christocentric, Pneumatocentric and theocentric soteriologies. All these soteriologies are embodied within Jesus Christ. Each Church situation is faced with existential problems, needs, and mentalities. The same Jesus Christ is understood and concretely interpreted in diverse ways and has diverse relationships to African ancestors. Only Kato and Tienou advocate a Christ against African ancestors. African theologians who advocate for ancestral Christology are aware that the Church in Africa is faced with existential problems to which European and American theologies can provide no solutions.

African Christologians are attempting to grapple with African existential problems and to relate the Gospel of Jesus Christ to these problems, whether economic, political, social, spiritual, cultural, or liturgical. They are creating, within the mainstream of the Christian tradition, Christologies that are Biblical and ecumenical. These Christologies overcome conflicts of loyalty between African ancestors on the one hand and western Christianity on the other.

African Christologies are diverse and independent, yet they explicate the one mystery of Jesus Christ. None of them claims to be the best or the only one which brings salvation to human beings. All of them are good when they are related to existential Christian situations. African Christologies make Christianity relevant to African people and their culture, and, in that way, they will also continue to enrich the worldwide Church. All these African Christologies help me to develop an African Christianity which appeals first and foremost to the Zimbabwean Church, secondly to the Church in Africa, but also to other parts of the world.

# CHAPTER 6

## *Integrating the Greatest Ancestor of ATR and USPG Christianity in Zimbabwe*

This chapter aims to make Jesus Christ the Greatest Ancestor (*Mudzimu Mukuru*) par excellence more meaningful to the Zimbabwean Christians. I am developing a Trinitarian, transformative Christology integrating USPG Christianity and ATR into the *Mudzimu Mukuru* par excellence Christology, which is an inculturated African Christianity. I am advocating a *Mudzimu Mukuru* par excellence Christianity in response to Zimbabwean Christians' needs, aspirations, thought forms, and attitudes, thereby hoping to contribute to a Zimbabwean Christianity in particular and to an African and worldwide Christianity in general. The chapter examines the Christian teaching on Jesus Christ, the *Logos*, and the *Messiah* in the light of the traditional Shona understanding of *Mudzimu Mukuru*. Based on the traditional Shona understanding of an ancestor (*mudzimu*), it is justifiable, according to both Old Testament (OT) and New Testament (NT) concepts of ancestorhood, together with the Biblical presentation of Jesus Christ, to call Jesus Christ the *Mudzimu Mukuru* par excellence, an Ancestor in a superior and eminent sense.

This chapter reflects systematically on Jesus Christ's mystery from the perspective of traditional Shona ancestorhood. Christ's Ancestorhood is viewed in the light of other Christian mysteries. I must also integrate the four soteriologies: pneumatocentric, theocentric,

Christocentric, and ecclesiocentric. The Trinitarian Christology that transforms USPG Christianity and ATR should be relevant to Zimbabwe. It will take into account and respond to the existential cultural realities of the Shona people in Zimbabwe. My aims are to remove the antagonisms, tensions, and separations which exist between ATR and USPG Christianity and to stop the dissolution of USPG Christianity into ATR and to remove fear of suffering, death, of Shona ancestors, Church Canons, Pastoral Regulations, the archbishop and the bishop. I will accomplish these aims by integrating ATR and USPG Christianity into Christ, who is understood as the Greatest Ancestor (*Mudzimu Mukuru* par excellence). In order to transform the Zimbabwean Christian people and their culture, USPG Christianity has to introduce the concept of Greatest Ancestor (*Mudzimu Mukuru*) par excellence, while ATR has to give a new meaning to the concept of Greatest Ancestor par excellence, with Christ the *Mudzimu Mukuru* par excellence integrated into the Trinity.

Currently, there is a religious or theological schizophrenia among the Zimbabwean Christians because there is no concrete Christological remedy for existential problems unique to Zimbabwean people. USPG Christianity failed to gain deep roots among the Shona USPG Christians because it did not take the traditional Shona concept of ancestor seriously. ATR must be linked to Christ the *Mudzimu Mukuru* par excellence. Nazir-Ali pleads, "Take not Oh Lord, our literal sense. Lord, in thy great unbroken speech our limping metaphor translate".[1] Shona Anglican bishops, priests, and USPG Shona Christians appropriated USPG Christianity in their own way within ATR. They adopted what is helpful and salvific. Shona traditional religious practices and beliefs were appropriated into the NT Christology. The Christian Church has been appropriating rites and customs of contemporary cultures from the beginning. A Trinitarian *Mudzimu Mukuru* par excellence Christology that transforms USPG Christianity and ATR by way of integrating them into Christ is able to solve all existential problems of the traditional Shona people in Zimbabwe.

Every human culture has valuable elements, and ATR can contribute constructively to Christianity. Wachege observes that "the

Gospel certainly is not identified with cultures and transcends them all. But the Kingdom that the Gospel proclaims is lived by man deeply tied to a culture."[2] An African Christian is challenged to be truly African and at the same time to be truly Christian. An African Christian should understand the root causes of the evils in Africa today and also understand the meaning of African cultural practices and customs so that the positive aspects of that culture are retained to become the core African Christian norms. And the negative customs should bc discarded. At the same time, a *Mudzimu Mukuru* par excellence Christology of integration into Christ of USPG Christianity and ATR should have a transformative effect in Zimbabwe. At this time in Zimbabwe, Christ the Transformer of culture is urgently needed because the economic, social, political, and religious institutions are rife with corruption and mismanagement. The Christian Church has spearheaded the transformation process in Africa. For example, in Malawi a pastoral letter from the Roman Catholic bishops resulted in the downfall of the Hastings Kamuzu Banda regime in 1994. More recently, the Zimbabwean Church's prophetic voice resulted in the defeat of the Robert Mugabe regime in June 2008 by Morgan Tsvangirai's Movement for Democratic Change (MDC). Zimbabwean Christians should not lose their Christian nor their African identity (ATR); instead, the Christian and African identities should transform Zimbabwean culture. Therefore, a dialogue between Christianity and ATR is required. Dialogue is both a necessary preparation and an occasion for the proclamation of the Gospel. The uniqueness and universality of the Gospel allow the Gospel of Christ to be translated not only into every language but also into every culture and world view.

I aim to produce a normative *Mudzimu Mukuru* par excellence Christology which engages the dynamic Zimbabwean culture and which also interacts with it. Some aspects of the dynamic Zimbabwean culture, such as paying of the bride price (*roora/ lobola*), witchcraft (*uroyi*), divination (*kushopera*), venerating beneficial alien spirits (*mashave*), worshipping ancestors (*midzimu*) and bringing-back-home (*kurova guva)* ceremony, will be acceptable but have to be transformed and strengthened by the integration of USPG Christianity and ATR into the Trinitarian Transformative *Mudzimu Mukuru* par excellence Christology.

Can Jesus Christ be understood as the *Mudzimu Mukuru* par excellence according to ATR understanding of ancestorhood? If so how? I introduce the African concept of ancestor because in ATR ancestors play salvific roles. . In ATR, ancestors are junior gods, sons and daughters of human beings, prophets (*masvikiro*), kings and chiefs, (*madzishe*), priests (*n'anga*), teachers, and saviors. What makes a traditional Shona person an ancestor (*mudzimu*)? The bringing-back-home (*kurova guva)* ceremony is the final traditional Shona transformative ritual which makes a traditional Shona an ancestor (*mudzimu)*—a junior god. The concept of *Mudzimu Mukuru* should apply to Jesus Christ in an inculturated and transformed manner. *Mudzimu Mukuru* par excellence must feature the Greek concept of *Kyrios* and the Hebrew concept of *Messiah. Kyrios* is the Greek word for God. *Messiah* is the Hebrew word for Savior (God). According to the NT, Christian saints are not superior to Christ. In ATR, the status of the ancestors is comparable to that of the saints. Shona ancestors are not lords (*kyrios*); they are instead mediators. Appropriation, inculturation, and revelation of Christ, the *Mudzimu Mukuru* par excellence, into ATR mean Jesus Christ is both Lord and Saviour.

The bringing-back-home ceremony (*kurova guva*) should be made part of the liturgy in the Anglican Church in Zimbabwe. The Shona Anglican bishops, priests, and laity should be involved in the Christianization of the *kurova guva* ceremony. The *kurova guva* ceremony should be accepted by the Anglican Church in the light of the communion of saints. The Christianization and the transformation of the *kurova guva* ceremony should follow the suggestions of Gundani (*The Second Vatican Council And Beyond: A Study Of The Transformation Process, Power, Transfer And Sharing In The Roman Catholic Church In Zimbabwe 1965-1985*. Harare: University of Zimbabwe, 1994.) By making the *kurova guva* ceremony part of the Church's liturgy, Zimbabwean Christians will be deeply rooted in the

Christian doctrine of the resurrection. During the *kurova guva* ceremony, the deceased Shona person is resurrected. The deceased Shona person becomes a "living dead"¯an ancestor. At the *kurova guva* ceremony, the traditional Shona people say that a dead person has resurrected (*wamuka*). This is said after giving the eldest son the name of his deceased father. The eldest son is the deceased father incarnate.

Diviners (*n'anga*) and divination (*kushopera*) should be involved in the prophetic and healing ministry of the Church. The status of diviners is comparable to that of prophets and healers in the Old and New Testaments. The beneficial alien spirits (*mashave*) such as the pool doctor or mermaid (*shave renjuzu*), rain-making spirit (*majukwa*), and hunting spirit (*shave rokuvhima*), should be accepted, accommodated, and naturalized into the African Christian Church. Likewise, Jesus Christ should be accommodated and integrated into the apex of the pyramidal hierarchy of African ancestorhood as the Greatest Ancestor (*Mudzimu Mukuru*) par excellence.

Paying the bride price (*roora*), including the mother's cow (*mombe yehumai*), should be offered to Jesus Christ the *Mudzimu Mukuru* par excellence through the pyramidal hierarchy of ancestors. During the prayers for the blessing of the mother's cow, the name of Mary the mother of God (*Theotokos* or *Mater Dei*) should be invoked. Christian family leaders, the bishops, or priests should say prayers and offer the bride price by invoking the known Shona ancestors until the prayers reach Jesus Christ the Greatest Ancestor par excellence. After the service, the bride price should be given to the Christian parents of the bride for their own use.

Other aspects of Zimbabwean culture, such as polygamy (*barika/chipari*), inheritance of widows and co-habiting with them (*nhaka*), killing of twins, killing human beings in order to get parts of their bodies to be prosperous in business (*kuchekeresa*), evil alien spirits (*mashave*) for example thieving alien spirit (*shave rokuba/shave regudo*), killing or murdering alien spirit (*shave rehumhondi* or *shave rekuuraya*) and killing babies who have their upper teeth coming out first, must be condemned. Witchcraft, the influencing of lives of other people in a negative way, is the abuse of the Holy Spirit. Jealousy is the root cause of witchcraft. A full member of the *Mudzimu Mukuru* par excellence should bear the fruits of the Holy Spirit and destroy all jealousy (Gal. 5:16-26).

Integration is a selective process like osmosis. Osmosis is a chemical process whereby particles move through a selectively permeable membrane. The *Mudzimu Mukuru* par excellence is like a selectively permeable membrane for He rejects and accepts some aspects of ATR. Selectivity is the process of judgment (Jn. 15:6, Mt. 25, Jn. 15:2, Rev. 18, 19, 20, 21). Transformation by the *Mudzimu Mukuru* par excellence is a critical engagement. It is not rejection, and it is not a mixing (combining) of USPG Christianity and ATR. USPG Christianity and ATR will not become one until they are integrated into the *Mudzimu Mukuru* par excellence and transformed by the *Mudzimu Mukuru* par excellence.

What comes first, integration or transformation? Integration comes first, then transformation, because transformation is a dynamic process. What results from this integration should be like the chemical combination of, say, sodium hydroxide and hydrochloric acid: sodium hydroxide + hydrochloric acid sodium chloride + water ( $Na^{+}0H + H^{+}cl$ $Na^{+}cl + H_{2}O$). New products—sodium chloride (common table salt) and water—are produced which differ both physically and chemically from the original sodium hydroxide and hydrochloric acid. The sodium hydroxide and hydrochloric acid cannot be separated either physically or chemically from the sodium chloride and water. The water is evaporated and lost into the air and only the sodium chloride remains. This is what should happen when USPG Christianity and ATR are integrated into Christ the *Mudzimu Mukuru* par excellence to produce a totally new Trinitarian Transformative *Mudzimu Mukuru* par excellence Christology. It should be impossible to "chemically" retrieve either USPG Christianity or ATR from the new Trinitarian Transformative *Mudzimu Mukuru* par excellence Christology. To use a biological metaphor, the *Mudzimu Mukuru* par excellence Christology should forge a symbiotic relationship between ATR and

USPG Christianity. Symbiosis is a relationship in which two living organisms derive mutual benefit from their association with one another.

A Trinitarian *Mudzimu Mukuru* par excellence Christology throws light on the traditional Shona concept of suffering, where suffering has no salvific value. Shona cosmology is filled with spirits. There is a great abuse of the spirit. On the other hand, the Anglican Church has structures which can control the abuse of the spirit by the Zimbabwean Christians. The Anglican Church is part of the One, Holy, Catholic, and Apostolic Church. The Trinitarian Transformative Christology of integration of USPG Christianity and ATR into *Mudzimu Mukuru* par excellence should not destroy these structures. The Anglican Church should maintain its structures and ceremonies. *Mwari*, the Father of the Son (*Mudzimu Mukuru* par excellence), is the giver of the Holy Spirit (*Mweya Anoyera/Mudzimu Anoyera*). The *Mweya Anoyera* comes from *Mwari*, the Father of the Son. *Mwari* transforms the Zimbabwean Shona people and their culture through *Mudzimu Mukuru* par excellence, His Son, and the *Mweya Anoyera* which is the giver of life. The structure of the Anglican Church in Zimbabwe should also be transformed by the *Mudzimu Mukuru* par excellence, so that there will be no fear of the archbishop, Church Canons, Pastoral Regulations, bishop, Shona ancestors, or death, and there will be no corruption.

Genuine conversion for the Zimbabwean Shona should be to *Mwari*, through both the *Mudzimu Mukuru* par excellence and Shona ancestors. This makes the Shona true Christians, and, as true and committed Christians, the Shona become ambassadors of the *Mudzimu Mukuru* par excellence to transform their own culture. For Christians, integration is not simply to find some peaceful way to live together. The Christian is committed to evangelism. The heart of Christian theology is mission. It is the Zimbabwean Shona people who need to be saved by the *Mudzimu Mukuru* par excellence. The Shona people should live in accordance with the *Mudzimu Mukuru* par excellence's religious and moral standards.

The Letter to the Hebrews in the New Testament addresses the problem of ancestors. The author of the letter does not say no to

Abraham, to Moses, to Melchizedek, to Old Testament Prophets, to sacrificed animals, to blood of animals, to Jewish high priests, but he pleads for their transformation by Jesus Christ, the Sacrifice par excellence (Heb. 9, 10). Likewise the Zimbabwean Christians should emulate the author of Hebrews who does repudiate Jewish religion, Jewish sacrifices, and Jewish ancestors such as Abraham and Moses. The author of Hebrews states that Abraham was the father of Jewish faith. Abraham had a mission. He represented the longing of the Jewish people for the *Messiah*. The author of Hebrews pleads for the integration of Jewish religion into Christ and for the transformation of Jewish religion by Christ.

ATR is also a religious process used by God in the plan of salvation. ATR should be integrated into the *Mudzimu Mukuru* par excellence and transformed by the *Mudzimu Mukuru* par excellence. The first law of thermodynamics states that energy can neither be created nor destroyed, but one form of energy is transformed to another. For example, electrical energy can be transformed into heat energy. The Indian theologian, Samartha states that "transformation is a radical change of perspective which does not require a rejection or negation of the past nor of previously held values, but nevertheless involves a new perception, recognition of the past—a paradigm shift."[3] The *Mudzimu Mukuru* par excellence does not wish to destroy ATR and create a new culture and religion for Zimbabweans. Instead, He dynamically transforms both ATR and Zimbabwean culture.

Transformation of Zimbabwean Christians by the *Mudzimu Mukuru* par excellence is an all or nothing proposition. This is Mendel's law of inheritance. A Zimbabwean Christian is either a believer of the *Mudzimu Mukuru* par excellence, or he is not. There are no "in-betweens", no half-transformed Zimbabwean Christians in the *Mudzimu Mukuru* par excellence. When you are transformed, you are completely transformed. There is no dancing between the *Mudzimu Mukuru* par excellence and the devil (*muroyi mukuru*). One accepts the *Mudzimu Mukuru* par excellence as one's only Lord and Savior, or one does not become a Christian at all. Physicists state that energy is released in quanta (packets). Quanta of energy from the same energy level have the same amount of joules of energy. Likewise, all Christians who are in the *Mudzimu Mukuru* par excellence have eternal life and have the same destination in the spirit world (*nyikadzimu*). All those who are in the *Mudzimu Mukuru* par excellence are saved. All those who are in the *Mudzimu Mukuru* par excellence have the same amount of the Holy Spirit (*Mweya Anoyera*). One takes the *Mudzimu Mukuru* par excellence into one's life wholly. The *Mudzimu Mukuru* par excellence affects and transforms one's whole life. One puts on the *Mudzimu Mukuru* par excellence until one dies. The *Mudzimu Mukuru* par excellence transforms every aspect of the Shona life.

The traditional Shona understanding of ancestor should be transformed in order to understand Jesus Christ as the Greatest Ancestor par excellence. Shona Christians elevate Jesus Christ to a level higher than any of their ancestors because of the many material and spiritual benefits they get from Christ. As *Mwari,* Jesus Christ speaks from Matonjeni/Njelele/Matopas. He issues oracles from Matonjeni. Christ is not a foreigner (*mutorwa*). He is a family member. He is the Greatest Ancestor par excellence, for He surpasses all Shona ancestors in every respect. But that transformation should not do away with Shona ancestors. Shona ancestors still have a role to play in the pyramidal hierarchy of ancestors (*kukwira gomo kupoterera).* Shona ancestors are functionally similar to the *Mudzimu Mukuru* par excellence in that they are both in the pyramidal hierarchy of ancestors, and they can be considered saints like Mary. The *Mudzimu Mukuru* par excellence is the Creator and Sustainer of the universe, whereas Shona ancestors are not creators and sustainers of the universe. The *Mudzimu Mukuru* par excellence is the giver of life, and it is through Jesus Christ as the *Mudzimu Mukuru* par excellence that Shona ancestors can continue to guarantee fertility among their relatives.

The Trinitarian Transformative Christology of integration of USPG Christianity and ATR into *Mudzimu Mukuru* par excellence should liberate and transform USPG Christianity from its separation tendencies and ATR from dissolving Christianity to the point where no Christianity remains. The God we believe in is both immanent and transcendent; therefore, Christology should be inculturated as well as trans-culturated. The continually transformed Christian culture will assist the Zimbabweans in their progress towards *Mwari*.

## BIBLICAL NOTIONS OF ANCESTOR

Hermeneutics of the NT provide the framework with which to look into Zimbabwean practices and to develop my Trinitarian transformative Christology of integration of USPG Christianity and ATR into the *Mudzimu Mukuru* par excellence. Mugambi states a position I endorse: the Bible is one of the basic sources of Christian instruction. The cultural tradition of those who introduced Christianity to Africa may be irrelevant for the needs of Africa today, but the Bible cannot ever be irrelevant for any Christian. There may be differences of emphasis in the theological interpretation of the Bible by various Christian denominations and theologians, but there can be no difference of opinion with regard to the relevance of this book in the life of a Christian.[4]

I am not going to compromise the humanity, divinity, the cross, and the resurrection of the *Mudzimu Mukuru* par excellence, for these are the four non-negotiables of any authentic Christology.

Nowhere in the Bible is Jesus Christ explicitly called Ancestor or Greatest Ancestor (*Mudzimu Mukuru*) par excellence. My quest for ancestral qualities, ancestral duties, and ancestral powers of Christ is inspired by the traditional Shona view of "ancestor". There are mentions of ancestors in the Bible (Lev. 26:45, Mt. 1:1-17, Lk. 3:23-38, Rom. 5:12-21, I Cor. 15:22) where the term *ancestor* means a long-dead person from whom one is descended. But in ATR *ancestor* means a junior god. Jesus as the new Adam (Rom. 5:12-21, I Cor. 15:22), is the more revealing idea of ancestor. The genealogical narratives (Mt. 1:1-17, Lk. 3:23-38) show that Jesus is at the apex of the hierarchy of Jewish ancestors. One cannot fully understand Christ without having the knowledge that ancestrally Jesus is linked to Adam, Abraham, and

David. Jesus Christ is the Son of all the Jewish ancestors. The purpose of the genealogy is to show that Jesus is the *Messiah* (Mt. 1:1, 16), the term in the history of salvation that was begun with the promises to Abraham. Jesus is the King *Messiah*, Son of David, *Messiah* of Israel and Son of Abraham. Jesus is the new Adam, initiating the new humanity (Rom. 5:12-21, I Cor. 15:22). Adam, the first ancestor, is linked to Christ, the Head of the new humanity.

In the ancient oriental religions, kings were taken to be god's sons. Cyrus was a son of God (Isa. 44:28, 45:1). In Hellenism, anyone who was considered to have divine powers had the term *son of God* attributed to him. Roman emperors also understood themselves to have miraculous powers and a special vocation. Cullman comments that "we notice then that the title in the orient and in Hellenism implies possession of godly powers or peculiar vocation."[5] In the same way, Jesus Christ is the Son of God (Mk. 1:1, Mk. 3:11, 5:7, Mk. 14:61 Mk. 15:39). However, Cullman argues that "as attributed to Jesus the title Son of God signifies the historical and qualitative uniqueness of His relation to His Father. It expresses His Divine Majesty, His absolute union with God, as well as His total obedience to His Father."[6] Peter, Satan, and the evil spirits recognized Jesus as the Son of God (Mt. 4:3, 16:17, Mk. 3:11, 5:7). According to Cullman, "the title, Son of God, is majestic and it expresses uniquely the very essence of Jesus' self-consciousness. Jesus' constant experience of complete unity of will with the Father, the full perception of revelation, which makes itself known to Him as a unique recognition of Himself by the Father."[7] Evil spirits regarded Jesus as the Holy One of God (Mk. 1:24) while the early Church expressed its faith in Jesus as the Son of God.[8]

Jesus as Son of God had divine majesty and was obedient to God. He taught and preached the Good News with authority (Lk. 2:46f, Mk. 1:21-28, Jn. 13:13ff). Wachege, noting Jesus "sitting among the doctors of the Jewish law" (Lk. 2:46), claims that "sitting was a sign of being an acknowledged authoritative teacher."[9] It was through Jesus that the Gospel was fulfilled (Lk. 4:21). He told the people to accept the good teaching of the teachers of the law but to reject their evil deeds (Mt. 23:2-3). Jesus as King was different from earthly kings (Mt. 2:1-

2). The wise men from the east discovered that Herod was not an ideal king for them (Mt. 2:2ff). Hence they moved to the east in search of an ideal king (Mt. 2:9f). Christ had sacerdotal duties par excellence. Christ's Priesthood and sacrifice are superior to those of the Jews of the OT (Heb. 1:3, 7:25-27, 9:12, 26). Cullmann concludes that "having been made perfect through His glorification, He became for all who obey Him the source of eternal salvation, and was acclaimed by God with the title of 'High Priest'."[10]

Christ's Priesthood has no end (Heb. 7:23-24). Jesus Christ is Son of God, High Priest and one of us (Heb. 14, 5:8-10, 7:28, 2:10-23). Such super-eminence arises from the fact that Jesus Christ is not just a human being. He is truly God. The images (faces) given to Jesus, such as Son of God, *Kyrios* (Lord), Son of Man, and Saviour (*Messiah*), lead us to Jesus' divinity. According to D. Dunn, "we can say that on the basis of the designation *Kyrios*, early Christianity does not hesitate to transfer to Jesus everything the Old Testament says about God."[11] Jesus is God (Jn. 1:1, 20:28). Jesus and His Father are one (Jn. 10:30), but at the same time the Father is greater than Jesus (Jn. 14:28). Nels Farre (as reported by W. Barclay) maintained that "you can say that Jesus Is God, but you cannot say that God is Jesus. God was still directing His universe in omniscience, omnipotence and omnipresence, when the Man Jesus was on this earth, but in this Man Jesus we see absolutely, perfectly, completely, uniquely, unrepeatable God as God is in His personal relationship with men."[12]

Also, John contends that God is Love (I Jn. 4:8). We can say God is love, but we cannot say love is God. Although Christ transcends the Shona titles of ancestor, and more so when He is understood as the Greatest Ancestor par excellence (*Mudzimu Mukuru* par excellence), some of the Shona characteristics of ancestorhood are also applicable to Him although in an eminent sense. Therefore, in our perception of the Shona traditional notion of *Mudzimu Mukuru*, it is justifiable, according to both OT and NT concepts of ancestor, to call Jesus Christ *Mudzimu Mukuru* but in a more eminent sense, *Mudzimu Mukuru* par excellence.

## TRINITARIAN ROOTS

There is no concept of the Trinity in ATR. How can the Shona Christians relate the *Mudzimu Mukuru* par excellence to the Trinity, the typically Christian understanding of God? The traditional Shona people totally agree with the concept of God the Father (*Mwari*) and that of the Holy Spirit (*Mudzimu Anoyera/Mweya Anoyera*), but there is no equivalent term for the concept of Son of God. Hence, for the traditional Shona people, the concept of the Trinity does not exist. The Shona USPG Christians feel at home with the Fourth Gospel's high Christology where Jesus is God, because He is in the Father and the Father is in Him and the two are one (Jn.17:20-23). The traditional Shona people are also very accustomed to the whole concept of the incarnation. For example, all Shona spirit mediums (*masvikiro/ mhondoro*) are incarnational. So for the Shona Christians to understand the Christian doctrine of the Trinity, I am referring to Jesus Christ, the *Mudzimu Mukuru* par excellence, as the Son of God incarnate.

Zimbabwean Christians do not find it foreign to call Jesus Christ God. Shona Christians are at home with Thomas when he called Jesus Christ my Lord and my God (Jn. 20:28), for the Shona have a saying that your ancestors are your Gods (*Mwari wako ndiye midzimu yako).* So for Shona Christians, if Jesus Christ is the *Mudzimu Mukuru* par excellence, He is *Mwari.* For the traditional Shona people, the *Mudzimu Mukuru* is the *Mudzimu Anoyera.* Hence the Shona Christians are at home calling Jesus Christ the *Mudzimu Mukuru* par excellence and God *Mwari* and the Holy Spirit (*Mudzimu Anoyera*).

As the *Mudzimu Mukuru* par excellence, Jesus Christ judges all Shona ancestors and all Shona people, rewarding the good and punishing the evil. By defining Jesus Christ the *Mudzimu Mukuru* par excellence this way, I am following a pattern accepted by the early Church. Dunn, for example, notes that "the title Son of God was a term readily understood in Palestine but was a foreign concept elsewhere. For that reason the early Evangelists did not use the term outside Palestine."[13] Likewise, the Fourth Gospel's high Christology transformed the Jewish concept of Son of God into the idea of God the Son, the eternal *Logos*, who from the beginning was one with the Father. This represents how the essential meaning of the incarnation was translated into the Greek culture. I suggest that the same thing must be done among traditional African cultures and religion.

This translation faces a potential challenge from Christian orthodoxy, which, since the fourth century, has defined the Trinity as a fundamental belief of Christian faith. But this definition has not been uniformly interpreted over the centuries and thus is open to re-interpretation in the light of new cultures it enters. Just as the high Christology of the Fourth Evangelist did not mean that the Father and the Son were identical, so it is possible to understand Jesus Christ the Son as the *Mudzimu Mukuru* par excellence (*Mwari*), who becomes incarnate. There exists, therefore, a relationship between *Mwari* and the Shona Christians through the incarnate *Mudzimu Mukuru* par excellence just as the Fourth Gospel describes believers becoming one with the Father through the Son. This interpretation allows one of the orthodox meanings of the Trinity to operate among the Shona Christians without insisting that they use terminology which is foreign to them.

Christ's Ancestorhood is deeply rooted in the Trinity, incarnation, and redemption. Christ's Ancestorhood is not only the property of Him as the Son but also of the Father and the Holy Spirit (*Mweya Anoyera*). All three persons, due to their oneness in the divinity, are involved in Christ's Ancestorhood. Unlike that of the traditional Shona, Christ's Ancestorhood is rooted in the perfect community of the divine Trinity. It is the *Logos* incarnate by virtue of the mission from the Father in the power of the *Mweya Anoyera* that Jesus Christ becomes our *Mudzimu Mukuru* par excellence. Unlike Shona ancestors, Christ's Ancestorhood is intertwined in His divine person as the eternal *Logos*. The concept of Jesus Christ as the *Mudzimu Mukuru* par excellence demands that we integrate it into the Trinity in view of the doctrine of appropriation.

Wachege states that "by appropriation we mean a mode of predication in which the properties or activities of God which are common to the three persons are attributed to an individual person."[14]

The doctrine of appropriation leads us to affirm that, in the Trinity, *Mwari* the Father, *Mwari* the Son of the Father, *Mwari* the Holy Spirit (*Mweya Anoyera*) of the Father, through the Son are involved in the *Mudzimu Mukuru* par excellence's Ancestorhood in accordance with His unique role. The Ancestorhood of Christ has its origin in *Mwari*, the Son and *Mweya Anoyera*. It is in *Mwari* that Christ's Ancestorhood has its ultimate origin since all that the *Mudzimu Mukuru* par excellence has (and is) is from *Mwari* the Father (Jn. 3:16, 4:9-11). When Christ acts as our *Mudzimu Mukuru* par excellence, it is also *Mwari* who is active in Him and through Him. In this way it is an Ancestorhood which belongs to the inner life of the Trinity itself. The *Mudzimu Mukuru* par excellence's ancestral salvific activity is the work of the whole Trinity, but each Person in his own way. So the *Mudzimu Mukuru* par excellence's Ancestorhood and salvific mission are a prolongation of the Trinitarian life in human community.

## JESUS CHRIST THE GREATEST ANCESTOR (*MUDZIMU MUKURU*) PAR EXCELLENCE FOR AFRICANS

The Shona people of Zimbabwe should stay within the realm of the ancestor as the figurative image of Jesus Christ and should not lapse into paganism or rank superstition. The Christian Church is drenched in symbolism (images) since the very incarnation, the Man of God, is in its deepest meaning a symbol (image) of *agape*, God's out-flowing love. The image of Jesus Christ as the Greatest Ancestor par excellence helps both liturgy and worship in the development of Christianity in Zimbabwe, and in Africa as a whole just as bread, wine, and oil are used as vehicles of divine significance in the Christian Church.

The Greatest Ancestor par excellence as the African image of Christ is more than a clever means to convey an idea through external signs. It is a means of sharing in the life of the Savior in such a way that the whole being of the African man, woman, boy, girl, child, and baby is involved. Take the image of Christ as exemplified in the cross. The cross was never a mere illustration of an abstract truth. Winzen observes that "we find the cross long before Christ, all over the world, held in great esteem as a 'sacramental', that represented and caused the wholeness of life because it seemed to gather into itself the entire universe. This sacramental character of the cross remains in the Christian use of the symbol."[15] We make the sign of the cross as a blessing, not for some "magical" reason. The cross represents the life-giving death of Christ, and leads us into "the breadth, the length, the depth, and height" of the love of Christ (cf. Eph. 3:18). The image of Christ as the Greatest Ancestor par excellence for Africans represents the fullness of salvation wrought by Christ. The image of Christ as the Greatest Ancestor par excellence is not limited to one particular aspect of Christ's work. It comprehends the whole history of redemption joining the beginning with the end. Christ as the *Mudzimu Mukuru* par excellence embraces death and life, humility and glory. The symbolic character of the passion and the death of the Lord consists exactly in the fact of His crucifixion and His exaltation as He explained it Himself through the 'sign' of the Brazen Serpent. The image of Christ as the *Mudzimu Mukuru* par excellence points to the mystical identity between Christ and the Africans. Like rays descending from the glorified Savior, the image of Christ as the Greatest Ancestor par excellence joins together the beginning and the end of the history of redemption. The image embraces death and life, it unites Christ, the Head, and the Church with the laity—the Body of Christ. Furthermore, Christ as the Greatest Ancestor par excellence draws the whole African universe into Christ's healing powers. The image of Christ as the Greatest Ancestor par excellence points to His cosmic dimension.

Shona Christians should also accept the images given to Jesus Christ which are not found in the Bible, such as Jesus Christ as the Ancestor, Chief, Diviner, Liberator, Master of Initiation, Head of Initiation, Elder Brother, Ideal Elder, and Healer. What are the differences between the real Christ and the figurative images? The Anglican Church in Zimbabwe objects to the images of Jesus Christ which are outside the Bible. But, figuratively, Biblical images of Jesus Christ are the same as those outside the Bible which are used by African Christian theologians. The functional Christology as propounded in the Bible is the same as the functional roles of Shona ancestors. By virtue of being an Ancestor, Jesus Christ is a Master of Initiation, an Elder Brother, a Diviner, a Liberator, a Chief, a King, a Priest, and a Prophet. The image (face) of ancestor is all embracing. It does not exclude any other image given to Jesus Christ by the Shona people or by African Christian theologians.

Our working hypothesis is that Jesus Christ is the Greatest Ancestor (*Mudzimu Mukuru*) par excellence. Does Jesus Christ possess the Shona traditional ancestorhood qualities? Becoming a Shona ancestor is not an event. It is not a one day or one month or one year affair. To become a Shona ancestor, one has to be morally upright, live to a ripe old age, leave offspring, have a 'good' death, and have fulfilled all the necessary Shona traditional transformative rites from conception to the *kurova guva* ceremony. The birth of a Shona child is accompanied with traditional transformative rituals including the name-giving ceremony. These facts partly parallel what happened to Jesus Christ at his birth. The Jewish community name-giving (Mt. 1:20-23, Lk. 2:21) and circumcision (Lk. 2:21ff) were performed after the birth of Jesus. God gave Jesus a name through an angel (Mt. 1:23-25). Shona traditional children are given the names of their ancestors through the mediation of the spirit mediums (*masvikiro*). Jesus was God incarnate (Jn. 1:14), was an Ancestor, from the moment of His fleshly conception in the womb of the Blessed Virgin Mary. As God and *Messiah*, Jesus eminently possessed in Himself all that was positive in the Shona traditional ancestral qualities. In this way, the child Jesus transcended ATR conceptions and practices of ancestorhood and yet fulfilled them completely.

For the traditional Shona, marriage is one of the preconditions for becoming an ancestor. One has to prove one's fecundity in producing and nurturing life because the traditional Shona are pro-life and pro-community. Although Jesus Christ never married, He accomplished this requirement in a non-procreative manner so that we may have life in abundance. Christ is married to the Church, and Christ and the Church are one body (Eph. 5:21-23). The Church is the Bride of Christ. Christ's marital bond with the Church is through baptism (Jn. 3:5). So Christ fulfilled the matrimonial requisite but in a spiritual and eminent way before one can become a traditional chief, there is an enthronement ceremony where one is made a traditional chief by the spirit mediums (*masvikiro*). There was an enthronement ceremony to make Jesus Christ chief. The cross was Christ's throne (Mt. 27:34). Jesus Christ is superior to Shona diviners (*n'anga*), spirit mediums (*masvikiro*), regional spirit mediums (*mhondoro*), traditional chiefs, and ancestors. Jesus Christ's Chieftainship was not conferred on Him through an appointment by the *masvikiro*, as is the case with a Shona traditional chieftainship. Jesus Christ became a Chief because He addressed people with authority (Mt. 7:29, Lk. 4:32).

How was Jesus Christ incorporated into ancestorhood? Jesus Christ's ancestorhood was founded on His divine Sonship and *Messianic* mission. Ancestorhood was conferred to Jesus Christ by His Heavenly Father at the moment of His fleshly conception through the spiritual anointment of the Holy Spirit (Lk. 1:35). The Holy Spirit came on Jesus at His conception (Lk. 1:35), at His baptism (Lk. 3:22, 4:1) and at His temptation (Lk. 4:18). For the traditional Shona, resurrection occurs when the "'living dead', the Shona ancestors, possess their children and grandchildren. Shona *n'anga* and *masvikiro* are possessed by the spirits of Shona ancestors. Jesus Christ had been possessed by the Holy Spirit to such an extent that Paul could even say that the Lord is the Spirit (II Cor. 2:17). Shona ancestors are also spiritual beings who dwell in the spirit world (*nyikadzimu*). An ancestor among the traditional Shona people is a person who dies in peaceful relationship with all his or her kin. That is why when people know that they are going to die, they call their close relatives and friends (*sahwira*) to them to disclose their hidden property, bless them and divide among them their inheritance (*nhaka)*, to crown their eldest son as their successor and to leave their last will (*mashoko okupedzisira*)—both in justice and love—and their wish to be remembered by all of them.

That is what Jesus did when He knew that the hour of His return to His Father was drawing near (Jn. 13:1, 14:27, 15:15). According to Dufour, this salvific message was really the inexhaustibly rich property or treasure He had received from His Father and now left it to His disciples for their inheritance. He even went as far as to give them His own Body and Blood as their spiritual food and drink and an imperishable memorial of His loving company with them as well as of His ineffable love for them shown especially in His own passion and death on the cross (Mt. 26:26f, Mk.14:22ff, Lk. 22:19-20).[16]

Jesus gave the Holy Spirit to His disciples (Jn. 14:16 ff.). He gave Mary to the care of St. John (Jn. 19:26-27). A. Jones argues that "since the patristic epoch, Catholic tradition has rightly seen this event as the handing over of His Mother to all human beings represented by St. John at the foot of the cross."[17] Jesus Christ's farewell speech also contained His last will (Jn. 13:34-35, 15:12-13, Mt. 18:18-20, Mk. 16:15ff). He blessed them (Lk. 24:50-51, Jn. 14:2-3). So, like Shona traditional people before they die, Jesus Christ, knowing that He was about to die, called His disciples together and disclosed to them His 'hidden properties', divided among them their inheritance, crowned the eldest, Peter, His successor, and left them His last will and His work to be remembered by them.

Jesus Christ, like Shona ancestors, played the role of reconciling and unifying people among themselves and with God. However, Jesus Christ, unlike Shona ancestors, rendered unreserved service indiscriminately. Jesus Christ's liberating mission was beyond family, territorial, local, and geographical confines—His liberating mission is universal (Lk. 4:24-27, Lk. 4:18-19, Mt. 28:18-20). Jesus Christ spoke of liberation within the context of loving one's neighbor as oneself (Mt. 22:34-40) and extending charity to all (Mt. 5:43-48). Jesus Christ thus surpasses Shona ancestors in that He is the Liberator who offers the remedy for the very core of servitude, which is sin. Jesus Christ is the Good Shepherd. He surpasses Shona ancestors in shepherding His followers (Jn. 10:1-21) because Shona ancestors are at times uncaring shepherds.

Shona ancestors are leaders and rulers in their communities. However, they are despotic, for they cause illnesses, deaths, calamities, and misfortunes if they are not venerated. For this reason, Shona people fear their ancestors, who want to be served first before they serve. Jesus Christ is a ruling, leading, and suffering Servant who unites Himself with *Mwari*. Among His disciples He is like a slave. He does not disdain even the most menial slave labor (Lk. 22: 26-27). Jesus Christ is a serving Ruler (Lk. 22:27) who leads by sacrificing His own self (Mk. 10:45). Jesus Christ notices His disciples' ambitions for leadership (Lk. 22:24-27). He is Himself the humble servant (Jn. 13:4-17, Mk. 20:25*ff*). He is not to be feared because He causes no illnesses, deaths, calamities, and misfortunes. He loves and blesses those who hate Him and who are His enemies (Lk. 6:27-36).

Without the presence of the ancestral spirits, Shona diviners (*n'anga*) and *masvikiro* do not perform their duties. ATR is full of spirits. Jesus Christ was filled with the Holy Spirit (Mt. 4:1). He was filled with the Holy Spirit at His bodily conception (Mt. 1:21-22, Lk. 1:35), at His baptism (Lk. 3:21-22, Mk. 1:10-11), and at His resurrection (Jn. 20:21-23). In the words of Congar, "The peculiar roles played by the Holy Spirit at His (Jesus') bodily conception, at His baptism in the Jordan, and at His resurrection, verified the supereminence and fullness of Jesus Christ's Lordship and ruling, making it not only total and absolute but also eschatological and economic."[18] Thus Jesus Christ ruled in service for the common good. He did this perfectly.

Jesus Christ died for His family, the Church. He established His family better than the Shona ancestors do theirs. He became the Savior (Eph. 5:23) who gave hope to His family (Jn. 16:33). He fulfilled His family duties in His conduct, words, parables, (Mt. 5:22*ff*, 22:39, Mk.12:30, Jn. 13:34-35), mutual forgiveness (Mk. 5:38*ff*, 18:21-22,

Lk. 17:4, 6:27*ff*) and by condemning divorce (Mt. 5:31-32, 19:3ff, Mk. 10:1ff, Lk. 16:18). Shona ancestors have a task of developing human relationships by showing people how they are related to one another and to *Mwari*. Some of the taboos among the traditional Shona people are incest, murder, beating one's mother (*kurova amai*), and violating the *chisi* day. Taboos result in the anger of Shona ancestors who then cause droughts, deaths, illness, epidemics, wars, natural calamities, disasters, and natural abnormalities. Shona ancestors develop healthy interpersonal, inter-family and inter-tribal relationships. Beneficial alien spirits such as the mermaid/pool doctor (*njuzu*) and hunting (*kuvhima*) alien spirits (*mashave*) are very good examples of developing good human relationships with foreigners and among foreigners (*vatorwa*). Jesus Christ promotes better relationships than Shona ancestors. Christ loved sinners (Lk. 15:2, Lk. 19:1-10). He had table fellowships where He established healthy relationships between God and people as well as between people with fellow people (Jn. 13:3, Lk. 22:14-23, 19:7-8, 10:38-42, 7:36-50). In this regard, the God-man surpasses immeasurably all the care and benefits that Shona ancestors provide for their family members.

Shona ancestors have the power to effect reconciliation, thereby bringing about unity and harmonious living between and among families and ethnic groups. A *kurova guva* ceremony or ritual sacrifices and prayers (*bira*) cannot be performed when some family members or ethnic group members are not present. Shona ancestors refuse ritual sacrifices and prayers which are offered when there are divisions and in-fighting within the family or ethnic group. Shona ancestors enforce reconciliation among the traditional Shona by causing misfortunes, disasters, and sickness to the members of the warring families or ethnic group. Jesus Christ's power in reconciliation surpasses all the more that of Shona ancestors by destroying the root cause of discord and divisions, which is sin. Unlike the reconciliation of Shona ancestors, which is based on fear of the ancestors, the reconciliation of Jesus Christ is based on justice and mutual love—the love of God and neighbor (Mk.12:29-31). Shona ancestors also have judicial powers, for they can curse and bless. Shona ancestors have power over life and death. Hence, Shona people fear their ancestors. Jesus Christ is the best judge, with supreme judicial powers.

In ATR, gender is not an impediment towards ancestorship. In the pyramidal hierarchy of ancestors, ancestral status is based on seniority and not on sex. Jesus came into this earthly world as male but also as God (*Mwari*). As *Mwari*, He is without gender. God is Spirit, and those who worship Him should worship Him in spirit and in truth (Jn. 4.24). All human beings are equal in Jesus Christ (Gal. 3:28-29). Shona ancestors are teachers of the traditional way of life and its worldview, but Jesus Christ is the best teacher of the way of life, which is the way to God. Jesus Christ Himself is the Way, Truth, and Life (Jn. 14:6).

At the *kurova guva* ceremony, the eldest son is given the name of his deceased father, and he becomes the deceased father incarnate. Peter was chosen the Vicar of Christ (Mt. 16:13-20, Jn. 21:15-17). This choice is connected to Peter's Great Confession (Mk. 8:27-30, Mt. 16:13-20). Jesus Christ made Peter the Rock of His Church, and gave him the two keys and the cross (Jn. 21:18). Just as at the *kurova guva* ceremony, the eldest son is given the name and authority of his deceased father to run his dead father's family, Peter was made the head of the Church (Lk. 22:27, Jn. 13:4-15).

In ATR, Shona ancestors' last will and words have special power: obedience brings blessings, and disregard brings misfortune. That is why, before Shona traditional people die, they want all the close relatives (*hama dzepedyo*) and close friends (*masahwira/shamwari*) to be present so that they can personally tell them their last will. Jesus Christ expressed power in His last will (Mt. 28:18-20). There is a connection between Jesus Christ's last will and the fate of the Church. The Church has always depended and will always depend on how Christians correspond to Jesus Christ's admonitions and commands—the great commission (Mt. 28:19-20). The miseries in the Church and the world at large are in the final analysis due to the disregard of Jesus Christ's last will.

Shona ancestors are remembered through spirit possession of their children and grandchildren, through the naming of their children and grandchildren, and through the propitiation of ancestors. Jesus Christ is remembered and relived in the Eucharist: "Do this in memory of me (1 Cor. 11:24). Pope John Paul II argued that "by means of what we are doing in the Eucharistic service of bread and wine, this memorial makes present all His paschal mystery, from which the Church, the Body of Christ, constantly comes into being, lives and grows."[19] Also the cross reminds Christians about Christ. A traditional Shona pours a libation or a morsel of food (*sadza*) on the ground in remembrance of the ancestors, or puts on ancestral clothes (*machira emidzimu*), or puts on ancestral beads (*zvuma zvemidzimu*) in remembrance of the ancestors. Shona ancestors have sacrificial trees—*mutiusinazita* near Marondera and in Buhera near Birchnough bridge and *muchakata/ muhacha* trees—under which prayers and ritual sacrifices are offered. Jesus Christ's sacrificial tree is the cross. Also, continuous rebirth through Christian baptism, from generation to generation, is a sure way of remembering and reliving Jesus Christ. The name Christian, given for the first time to Christians at Antioch (Acts 11:26), is a sure way of remembering and reliving Him.

The powers of the Shona ancestors are limited because, during their earthly lives, they were sinful human beings, sometimes falling short of expectations. The powers of Jesus Christ are absolute because He never sinned or fell short of His expectations (2 Cor. 5:21, Heb. 4:15). Jesus Christ is the answer to the limitations of the powers of the Shona ancestors. The source of the powers of Shona ancestors is *Mwari*, but Jesus Christ is *Mwari* Himself, hence His absoluteness in relation to Shona ancestors.

Traditional Shona society is theocratic. Shona ancestors are both the religious and the political leaders acting through the traditional Shona chiefs and the territorial spirit mediums (*mhondoro*). Christian society is not theocratic, so to speak: God is the only one in charge. First of all, there is no Christian society, only Christian persons or groups. The belief that a Christian society is theocratic is not only a very dangerous one, but it is also theologically untenable, for this is a totalitarian position, utterly reprehensible and historically ridiculous. Yet all liberation and black Christologies claim that Jesus Christ is both a religious and political leader of the Christians. This is a controversial, if not dangerous, proposition which easily leads to intolerance. But, Jesus Christ surpasses Shona ancestors as both a religious and a theocratic leader, for He rules with righteousness and justice. Christ's Kingdom is not of this world (Jn. 6:15, 17:14, 8:23, 18:36. At any rate Christ, unlike many political leaders, never uses violent means to achieve His goal (Jn. 18:36, Mt. 26:51-53). Jesus Christ manifested total obedience and surrender to *Mwari's* will. Not only did He preach obedience to *Mwari*, but His whole life corresponded to *Mwari's* will (Phil. 2:8, Rom. 5:15).

Christ offered Himself as a sacrifice. His Eucharistic ritual at the Last Supper and His death on the cross were two sacrificial offerings to *Mwari*. In the Eucharist, Jesus Christ played a priestly role similar to those played by traditional Shona elders, *n'anga*, *masvikiro*, *mhondoro*, and ancestors. His sacrifice, like that of Shona ancestors, had a communal dimension, in as much as it was for the benefit of the whole human community. Both Jesus Christ's and Shona ancestors' sacrifices are intended to glorify *Mwari*, to pray to Him, and to appease Him for the offenses committed against Him. Jesus Christ offered Himself as the final and true sacrifice (Eph. 5:2, 1 Cor. 5:7, Rom. 3:25). Shona ancestors offer animal and object sacrifices instead of themselves. By His sacrifice on the cross, Jesus Christ reconciled us with *Mwari* and freed us from the slavery of sin (Mt. 20:28, Mk. 10:45, I Tim. 2:14, Col. 1:13, 2:15, II Tim. 1:10, Col. 1:20). By offering Himself as a sacrifice, Jesus Christ was called by *Mwari* to His eternal priesthood (Heb. 5:5*ff*, 7:23*ff*) in Heaven, interceding for all who come to *Mwari* through Him (Heb. 7:25). More than are Shona ancestors, Jesus Christ is committed to prayer. He referred to God as *Abba* (Mk. 14:36, Rom. 8:15, Gal. 4:6).

Shona ancestors bless their family and ethnic group members when ritual sacrifices and prayers are offered to *Mwari* through them and also curse them when no ritual sacrifices and prayers are offered. A curse from Shona ancestors is revoked when ritual sacrifices and prayers are offered to *Mwari* through them. In contrast, Jesus Christ blesses (Mk.

10:13, 16, Mt. 14:19, Mk. 6:41, 8:7, Lk. 9:6, Lk. 24:30, Mt. 26:26, Lk. 24:50f Acts 3:26, Eph. 1:3, Mt. 25:34) but never cursed anyone. The "woes" of Jesus Christ against the Scribes and the Pharisees (Mt. 23:13, 14, 15, 23, 25, 27, 29) are not equal to Shona ancestor "woes". The punishments of Jesus Christ were meant to bring back to God's fold those who have gone astray. Shona ancestor punishments are basically punitive and ill-willed. Christ blessed His enemies and even prayed for them (Lk. 6:28, Mk.14:46, Mt. 27:39ff, Lk. 23-34). However, Jesus Christ, like Shona ancestors, will punish those who die without repentance (Mt. 25:41). For Jesus, cursing must be replaced by blessing (I Pt. 3:9).

The similarities between Christ's Ancestorhood and Shona ancestorhood show that not everything in traditional Shona understanding of ancestor is evil. Such ATR ancestorhood elements are endorsements indicating that Christ as *Logos* was already among the traditional Shona people before USPG Christianity came to Zimbabwe by way of USPG missionaries. Similar Shona ancestorhood values should be adopted into the Church in Zimbabwe to help develop Christianity. The differences between Christ's Ancestorhood and Shona traditional ancestorhood do not indicate an alienation of Christ's Ancestorhood from that of the Shona traditional people, nor do they annul His Ancestorship in the traditional Shona sense.

The lack of some typically Shona rites of passage ceremonies—for example, the *kurova guva* ceremony—is a sign that Christ's Ancestorhood transcends all family, ethnic group, or social differences. Nor does His Ancestorship lose anything by the absence in Him of superstitious, erroneous or repulsive elements linked with the Shona traditional conception or practice of ancestorhood. Such absence is, in fact, a sign of the purity of Our Lord's Ancestorhood. There are enough parallels to allow us to affirm that Jesus Christ is the true and only *Mudzimu Mukuru* par excellence in the traditional Shona sense.

## DYNAMICALLY TRANSFORMED CHRISTIAN CULTURE IN ZIMBABWE

Cultural transformation is very important and necessary for the modern world because there is so much mobility. According to Nazir-Ali, Gregory's charge to Augustine when he was sent out rather reluctantly to England was "to take the culture of the local people seriously, not needlessly to destroy what he found there, but somehow to transform it by the proclamation of the Gospel."[20] And it is this charge, I believe, that is at the root of the Anglican Church in Zimbabwe's commitment to incarnate the *Mudzimu Mukuru* par excellence among the Zimbabwean Christians. Shona traditional culture and ATR should not be destroyed but should be transformed by the *Mudzimu Mukuru* par excellence. Even Shona traditional shrines should not be destroyed but should be purified and consecrated for Christian use. Some aspects of Shona traditional religion, as previously noted, should be transformed and preserved without compromising the Gospel of the *Mudzimu Mukuru* par excellence. They should be pressed into the service of the Gospel.

Christian faith is not a culture, as such, but it can only find expression and live within a culture. Pope John Paul II, in his Letter to Cardinal Agostino Casaroli, Secretary of State, on the 20th May, 1982, stated that "a faith which does not become a culture is a faith which has not been fully received, nor thoroughly thought through, nor fully lived out."[21] Integration of USPG Christianity and ATR into a trinitarian transformative soteriology with Jesus Christ as the *Mudzimu Mukuru* par excellence will keep the Christian faith growing in Zimbabwe. Pope John Paul II also stated that "evangelization loses much of its force and effectiveness if it does not take into consideration the actual people to whom it is addressed, if it does not use their language, their signs, their symbols, if it does not answer the questions they ask, and if it does not have an impact on their concrete life."[22] Inculturation of the Gospel among the Zimbabweans responds to the very deep desires of the Zimbabwean people and their community to find their own identity. Pope John Paul II, when he spoke in 1980 to African Roman Catholic bishops, clarified this position:

> Inculturation, which you rightly promote, will truly be a reflection of the incarnation of the Word, when a culture, transformed and regenerated by the Gospel, brings forth from its own living tradition original expressions of Christian life, celebration and thought and there is no question of adulterating the Word of God or of emptying the cross of its power (1 Cor. 1:17) but rather of bringing Christ into the very centre of African life and of lifting up all African life into Christ. Thus not only is Christianity relevant to Africa but Christ, in the members of his body, is himself African[23]

Inculturation, therefore, should extend to the totality of Zimbabwean Christian life and doctrine the central ministry of the *Mudzimu Mukuru* par excellence. But the totality should be borne into a dynamic Zimbabwean culture. Inculturation should use Zimbabwean culture as its seed bed, taking from it nutrients and rejecting those aspects which negate Christian growth. Inculturation of Christian life and Gospel in Zimbabwe should be a principle that animates, directs, and unifies the dynamic Zimbabwean culture, transforming it, renewing it, making it so as to bring about a new creation.

Inculturation should destroy the ritual of limping dance between USPG Christianity and ATR which is currently being practiced by most Christians in Zimbabwe. Inculturation should have as its aim: "to make Christianity enter the very blood and veins of the Africans, to make it answer their aspirations and anxieties, to make African Christians recover their one identity rather than live in dualism with one foot in Christianity and the other in a traditional African world view."[24] This process also affects the Church in that the local Church is incarnate in a people, a Church indigenous and inculturated.[25]

The inculturated Church in Zimbabwe should express its particularity without losing its universality. It should be universal by vocation and mission. The process of inculturation involves translating the Gospel into the vernacular language, assimilating the surrounding

Zimbabwean Shona culture, and transforming it. Crollius has articulated these tasks:

The inculturation of the Church is the integration of the Christian experience of the local Church into the culture of its people, in such a way that this experience not only expresses itself in elements of this culture, but becomes a force that animates, orients and innovates this culture so as to create a new unity and communion, not only within the culture in question but also as an enrichment of the Church universal.[26]

The Christian message in Zimbabwe must find its roots in Zimbabwean culture and must also transform this culture. Pope Paul VI, in his 31st July, 1969 address to the African bishops at the closing of the 1st Plenary Assembly of SECAM in Uganda, Kampala, maintained that "You may and you must have an African Christianity."[27]

The local Zimbabwean Church cannot avoid that imperative. It is a challenge to develop suitable catechetical material based on the life experiences of the African Zimbabwean people. A move in this direction would lead to Christianity as a way of life, not as a bookish Christianity where all the answers are contained in a catechism and not in the people's hearts. With our present awareness of cultural pluralism, local Churches can develop worship and teaching materials. Nazir-Ali provides some guidance:

The Church is called to proclaim the Gospel afresh in every age. This means that the Church should be aware of the original contexts in which God spoke and acted among his people and in the wider world. It involved a close study of the languages, cultures and history of the peoples to whom God first revealed himself.... The Church is also called to live out and to share her experience of God as just, powerful and loving in the midst of a variety of cultures, world views and religious beliefs. To be able to do this effectively, the Church needs to understand each of the contexts in which it has been placed.[28]

The Gospel, not the Church, should judge aspects of Zimbabwean culture and ATR. The co-ordination of the Gospel of *Mudzimu Mukuru* par excellence in Zimbabwe should, however, be structured Christologically. The Gospel must remain at all times Good News among the Zimbabweans, helping them to bring forth from their own living tradition original expressions of Christian life, celebration, and thought. The purpose of *Mwari* is to transform and reconcile all people, all cultures, and all world religions to Himself and to one another in His Son, our *Mudzimu Mukuru* par excellence, and it continues in the gift of the *Mweya Anoyera*, in the command to make disciples of all nations (Mt.28:18-20).

## TRINITARIAN *MUDZIMU MUKURU* PAR EXCELLENCE CHRISTOLOGY

There is no theological separation among theocentric, Pneumatocentric, Christocentric and ecclesiocentric soteriological positions because all of them place the *Mudzimu Mukuru* par excellence, who is the Head of the Church (Body), at the center, but practically they are different. Jesus Christ (the Head) without the Church (Body) is incomplete. The Head and the Body belong together. St. Paul sums this up in his teaching about headship. The Church (the Body of the *Mudzimu Mukuru* par excellence), like a tadpole, grows from the Head (the *Mudzimu Mukuru* par excellence). This is a master image. It is a dynamic and organic conception. As the tadpole is already contained in the head and grows from it, so the Church is already contained in Christ and grows from Him. Theologically, theocentric, pneumatocentric, Christocentric and ecclesiocentric soteriologies are one, but practically they are exclusive of each other.

The Christocentricism of Christian traditions is not, in fact, opposed to theocentricism. Dupuis argues that Christocentricism never places Jesus Christ in the place of God; it merely affirms that God has placed him at the centre of his saving plan for mankind, not as the end but as the way, not as the goal of every human quest for God but as a universal mediator of God's saving action towards people. Christian

Theology is Christocentric or Theocentric; it is Theocentric by being Christocentric and vice versa.[29]

This, then, means that the *Mudzimu Mukuru* par excellence is the Sacrament of *Mwari's* encounter with human beings. One suggestion is that of an eschatological paradigm shift. This new paradigm would consist in centering the theology of religions on the *Mudzimu Mukuru* par excellence event, the Reign of *Mwari* which builds through history and is destined to reach its fulfillment in the eschatological time. Is the Reign-of-*Mwari* soteriological position different than the Christocentric soteriological position? No, the two are not different, neither are they exclusive of each other. Dupuis concludes that to affirm it would be to forget that the Reign of God has broken through to history in Jesus Christ and the Christ-event, that it is through the combined action of the risen Christ and his Holy Spirit that the members of the other religious traditions share in the Reign of God historically present, finally, that the eschatological Reign to which the members of all religious traditions are summoned together is at once God's Reign and that of the Lord Jesus Christ.[30]

Once again theocentricism and Christocentricism seem to go theologically hand in hand as two aspects of the same reality. They do not constitute different soteriological positions. Another soteriological paradigm shift is to base the theology of religions on the recognition of the universal presence and action of the Holy Spirit (*Mweya Anoyera/ Mudzimu Anoyera*). Dupuis states that "the Spirit of God has been universally present throughout human history and remains active today outside the boundaries of the Christian fold. He it is who "inspires" in people belonging to other religious traditions the obedience of saving faith, and in the traditions themselves a word spoken by God to their adherents."[31]

What this means is that the *Mweya Anoyera* is *Mwari's* "point of entry" into the life of people, and, hence, the *Mweya Anoyera's* immediate action opens up the way for a distinct soteriological model in the Christian theology of religions, one no longer exclusively

Christocentric but also pneumatocentric. Is a soteriological position based on *Mweya Anoyera* theologically different from a Christocentric soteriological position? No, both the Christocentric and the pneumatological perspectives are theologically inseparable in the Christian mystery, in so far as the cosmic influence of the *Mweya Anoyera* is essentially bound to the universal action of the risen *Mudzimu Mukuru* par excellence. Depuis states that

> Christocentricism and pneumatology must not be set in mutual opposition as two distinct economies of salvation; they are two inseparable aspects of one and the same economy. Nevertheless, the specific role played by the Holy Spirit in salvation both inside and outside the Church, and the immediacy of his action makes it possible to recognize his personal imprint wherever salvation is at work. The influence of the Holy Spirit manifests the operative presence of God's saving action in Jesus Christ.[32]

Christocentricism and pneumatology are inseparable but understood in these diverse ways.

Samartha hesitates to regard the *Mweya Anoyera* apart from the love of *Mwari* and the grace of the Lord the *Mudzimu Mukuru* par excellence. They belong together in the diversified unity of *Mwari's* life. *Mwari* works in the world with two 'hands': *Mudzimu Mukuru* par excellence, the Son of *Mwari* the Father, and the *Mweya Anoyera* of the Father and the Son. Samartha states that Christocentricism and Theocentricism are not alternative. I am Theocentric because I am Christocentric and I am Christocentric because Jesus Christ himself was Theocentric. Neither do I regard pneumatology as another alternative. *Theos* provides the foundation, *Christos*, the anchorage in history, and *Pneuma* the guiding power for Christian life and witness in a pluralistic world.[33]

It is only in the *Mweya Anoyera* of *Mwari* that prayers meet, intentions coalesce, and persons enter into communion. In both Christianity and ATR, *Mwari* is experienced as God the Father

(*Mwari*) and God the Holy Spirit (*Mweya Anoyera*). Both believe in one *Mwari*, who is nevertheless experienced in these diverse ways. Trinitarian transformative Christology integrating USPG Christianity and ATR into the *Mudzimu Mukuru* par excellence helps to transform the use of the *Mweya Anoyera* among the Zimbabweans.

A theocentric perspective is theologically intrinsic in the Christocentric model. The two are theologically one and refer to the same thing. They are not exclusive of each other. But if a Christian theology of religions needs to be Christocentric, it must bring out the full dimension of the mystery of the *Mudzimu Mukuru* par excellence and show its cosmic significance. In particular, a Trinitarian transformative theology of religions shows that the members of the other religious traditions, together with Christians, share in the reign which *Mwari* has established in history through the *Mudzimu Mukuru* par excellence, and that the Spirit of the *Mudzimu Mukuru* par excellence is present among them and operative in them, transforming both the peoples and their cultures.

# CHAPTER 7

## *The Mudzimu Mukuru Par Excellence Christology and Pastoral Relevance*

The aim of this chapter is to explore the spiritual, catechetical, liturgical, and ethical relevance of our *Mudzimu Mukuru* par excellence Christology. I will draw from the Liturgy Lecture Notes (1986-1990) given to me by Bishop Sabastian Bakare and Rev. John Weller when I was a theological student at Bishop Gaul College in Harare.[1]

### THE SPIRITUAL FIELD

Our *Mudzimu Mukuru* par excellence Christology will transform the whole Zimbabwean Church and assist us to live more authentically. We want a new Christian vision: to strive for justice, righteousness, and love among all human beings. We should emulate the *Mudzimu Mukuru* par excellence within our historical, concrete existence despite the difficulty in realizing such a very high ideal. Admittedly, Anglicanism in Zimbabwe is still USPG, and we are still Shona USPG Christians who practice ATR secretly. However, the *Mudzimu Mukuru* par excellence Christology transforms Shona USPG Christians into Zimbabwean Anglicans who, taking Him as their ideal exemplar, will become ancestors. Accepting Jesus Christ as *Mudzimu Mukuru* par excellence involves venturing into His kind of life and living fully according to His will, with Shona ancestorhood values. As a result, we become better assured of moving towards fulfillment in the vitalistic community of the Trinity.

Christ is the *Mudzimu Mukuru* par excellence who restores liberty as He unbinds Zimbabweans from useless superstitious errors and narrow-mindedness of ethnic absolutization. This makes it possible for Zimbabwean Christians to incorporate all people in ethnic inter-communication since all belong to Him as the *Mudzimu Mukuru* par excellence of all human beings. Jesus Christ will release Zimbabwean Christians from today's ethnicism, regionalism, favoritism, corruption, individualism, and selfishness which spoil the unity of all human beings. Belonging together as the family of the self-same *Mwari*, we will strongly guard His kind of human communalism of vitality.

Our *Mudzimu Mukuru* par excellence is our material, social, economic, and spiritual home. Christ will help Zimbabwean Christians establish healthy family lives free from divorce, separations, unemployment, and child abuse. Zimbabwean Christian words, deeds, conduct, and attitudes should correspond to His. Taking Jesus Christ as *Mudzimu Mukuru* par excellence equips Zimbabwean Christians fully for substituting their narrow parochially restrictive concept of family with an all-embracing human family, enabling them to live for one another. The *Mudzimu Mukuru* par excellence Christology will provide a new way of practicing a liberation Christology which is spiritually more enriching. The point of departure must be inculturation. The result will be a genuine Zimbabwean Christian spirituality.

## THE CATECHETICAL FIELD

Our *Mudzimu Mukuru* par excellence Christology is a real attempt to make Jesus Christ more relevant not only to Zimbabweans but to the Church in Africa and the Church in the whole world. It is both apologetically and fundamentally pastoral. Christ the *Mudzimu Mukuru* par excellence becomes our relative, family member, ethnic group member, and model in moral conduct. As such He challenges us to accept Him with traditional Shona generosity. Zimbabwean Christians know that traditional Shona values of ancestorhood provide the ground for their lives and a starting point to create an awareness of human dignity and godliness ecclesiocentrically, pneumatocentrically, Christocentrically, and theocentrically.

The *Mudzimu Mukuru* par excellence Christology will help Zimbabwean Christians explain more meaningfully their Christian faith. Jesus Christ empowers all who accept Him to participate in reigning with Him and in radiating His Ancestorhood to all people. Zimbabwean Christians should take Jesus Christ as their exemplar in talking, speaking, acting, and reacting in interpersonal relationships. He will inspire them to build healthy communities in order to realize His vision of one human family united in the Fatherhood and Motherhood of *Mwari*. Motherhood is expressed as grandmother (*mbuya*) and the great pool of water *(dzivaguru*) meaning sustained fertility. Taking Jesus Christ honestly and decisively as their *Mudzimu Mukuru* par excellence is the surest way for Zimbabwean Christians to enter into the God-head. Such Christocentricism guarantees a fuller life of integrity within the Zimbabwean Christian community. Christ is the zenith of their scale of existential values.

The *Mudzimu Mukuru* par excellence Christology helps Zimbabwean bishops, priests, and pastors learn pastoral techniques from diviners (*n'anga*). A pastoral approach of the *n'anga* has a concern for the people, finding out causes of problems and their solutions. In Jesus Christ as *Mudzimu Mukuru* par excellence, Zimbabwean Christians find a Savior, a Reconciler, a Redeemer, a Liberator, a Master of Initiation, a Chief, a Priest, a King, an Elder Brother, a true Friend, and a possessor of all the good characteristics found in Shona ancestors. Pastors are ever engaged with His obliging mission to let His ancestorhood reign among Christians. Presenting Jesus Christ as *Mudzimu Mukuru* par excellence helps Zimbabwean Christians understand Him in a more intelligible, venerable, and fascinating manner than would be the case with some other images appropriated from European and American Christologies. Christ as

*Mudzimu Mukuru* par excellence is the Zimbabwean Christian joy, hope, and model on which to anchor their lives in the midst of contemporary global confusion and turbulent existential crisis.

Because Christ experienced gradual initiatory rites, Zimbabwean Anglican bishops and priests should introduce effective Christian initiatory rites for young Christians, rites which endorse and accommodate His values. These rites must enhance the youths' solidarity with Christ in such a way that the youth become extensions of His Ancestorhood and perpetuate His Kingdom. The *Mudzimu Mukuru* par excellence should be both the source of attraction for youth and their model of living. For all Christians, His Church, our spiritual and bodily welfare will always depend on the extent to which we heed the admonitions and commands He gave us when He was about to return to *Mwari* His Heavenly Father. In the final analysis, the miseries of the world result from our disregard of Christ's last will.

Seeing Christ as the *Mudzimu Mukuru* par excellence who is fecund in a non-biological sense will help married Zimbabwean Christian couples who cannot father or mother children realize that despite their barrenness or impotence, they can become spiritual parents. The *Mudzimu Mukuru* par excellence brought the good news that He has reconciled us to *Mwari* such that we are all *Mwari*'s adopted children. Such Christian couples can reevaluate the stigma of their fruitless state and consider adopting children.

## THE LITURGICAL FIELD

The *Mudzimu Mukuru* par excellence Christology presents Jesus Christ as the Greatest Ancestor par excellence. Thus the Savior is not a stranger to Zimbabweans. Such catechetical instruction is good preparation for the entry into Zimbabwean Christianized ancestral status through the traditional Shona rituals. First of all, sacraments are different than sacramentals. The Church can neither add to nor subtract from the seven sacraments which were instituted by Christ—the sacraments of Christian initiation (Baptism, confirmation, and Holy

Eucharist), the sacraments of healing (confession and reconciliation and anointing of the sick), and the sacraments of communion (ordination and Christian marriage). On the other hand, the constitutions on Sacred Liturgy explain sacramentals as "sacred signs which bear a resemblance to the sacraments, they signify effects, particularly of a spiritual kind, which are obtained through the Church's intercession. By them men are disposed to receive the chief effect of the sacraments and various occasions in life are rendered holy."[2] Sacramentals owe their institution and legitimacy to the Church. In order to realize the Kingdom of *Mwari*, the Church has power to add new sacramentals for a deeper and more meaningful service of the sacraments.

The Church in Zimbabwe should consider, and, if found worthy, elevate the Shona ancestorhood signs to the level of sacramentals. For instance, thick porridge (*sadza*) and unfermented beer (*mahewu*) should be the elements in the Holy Eucharist. Thick porridge (*sadza*) should be the Bread of Life and unfermented beer (*mahewu*) should be the Blood of Salvation. Jesus Christ is the *Sadza* of life for Zimbabwean Christians. These sacramentals will enable Zimbabwean Christians to celebrate their Christianity with a more serious commitment and with renewed disposition. They would be able to worship *Mwari* in their own Zimbabwean way of life and in accordance with their needs and aspirations. The traditional Shona rituals of passage—the bringing-back-home ceremony (*kurova guva*), divination (*kushopera*), the rain-making ceremony (*mukweverera*), enthronement of a chief, giving the eldest son his deceased father's name and inheritance (*nhaka*) ceremonies—should also be purified, transformed, and Christianized by the Church in Zimbabwe, with the guidance of the *Mudzimu Mukuru* par excellence. This process involves serious study, analysis, evaluation, gradual and continuous catechizing, and evangelizing.

All the Shona transformative rites of passage could become sacramentals. By virtue of the new sacramental rituals, the Zimbabwean Christians, who are candidates to ancestorhood, will get these transformative effects through the Church. There will be no ritual of limping dance between the *Mudzimu Mukuru* par excellence and Shona ancestors. There will be no propitiation of Shona ancestors under cover of darkness for fear of the archbishop, fellow bishops, the bishop, Church Canons and Pastoral Regulations. This form of Christianized entry into Shona ancestorhood will mean participation in the *Mudzimu Mukuru* par excellence's own divine Ancestorhood. To live as a prospective Zimbabwean Christian ancestor will mean to live the *Mudzimu Mukuru* par excellence's own Ancestorhood. In this way, the *Mudzimu Mukuru* par excellence, the Savior, will not only be an exterior model of ancestral life, but through the intercession of the Church in Zimbabwe Through the new sacramentals, Shona ancestors will be vitally linked with the *Mudzimu Mukuru* par excellence so as to allow the Redeemer's Divine Human Ancestorhood to be effective.

The parallels between Shona ancestors and Christian understanding of ancestorhood are indications that the Shona traditional beliefs and customs on ancestorhood are basically good and contain many positive values which are excellent preparatory roads for the Gospel message not only on the mystery of the *Mudzimu Mukuru* par excellence but on the Christian social and ethical life as well. Shona ancestorhood customs deserve to be adopted by the Church. The catechetical, the spiritual, and the liturgical implications which have emanated from the *Mudzimu Mukuru* par excellence Christology are not confined to Zimbabwean Christians but are open to the enrichment of all people of *Mwari*. ATR must be given a Christian dimension. The rituals connected with ATR should be elevated to the level of the sacramentals within the Church in Zimbabwe. This will enable them to signify the social and spiritual effects of the ancestorhood status and functions among the Shona people.

The worship of the Zimbabwean Anglican Christian community, based on the integration of USPG Christianity and traditional Shona religion into the Greatest Ancestor (*Mudzimu Mukuru*) par excellence, leads the Zimbabwean Christian worshippers to act out, in the ever-dynamic Zimbabwean culture, their love of the *Mudzimu Mukuru* par excellence. To worship is to pay homage or reverence to a deity, especially in a formal service. It is adoration or devotion comparable to homage shown towards a person or principle. Charles P. Price states that "worship involves not merely the assigning of worth to what is thought to be worthy, but the assigning of ultimate or absolute worth to what is believed to have ultimate value."[3] However, the question of relative value quickly surfaces. Shona ancestors are of value, as far as the traditional Shona people are concerned, hence the traditional Shona people worship their ancestors because they are of ultimate or absolute value to them. On the other hand, Zimbabwean Christians do not worship Shona ancestors, for they are not of ultimate or absolute value to them. Instead, they worship *Mwari* and the *Mudzimu Mukuru* par excellence for they are of ultimate or absolute value to them. We understand that qualities like beauty are not absolute: beauty is in the eye of the beholder. These qualities are relative, for they depend on the position of the person who makes the judgment. In the same way, the ancestors are of relative value to Zimbabwean Christians because the ancestors are within the Zimbabwean culture. But *Mwari* the Father the Absolute, *Mwari* the *Mudzimu Mukuru* par excellence the Absolute, and *Mwari* the *Mweya Anoyera* the Absolute do not depend on the position of the observer. Worship is our response to *Mwari*. For Zimbabwean Christians, *Mwari*, the *Mudzimu Mukuru* par excellence, is the Absolute, the fixed point to which they are able to refer their morals and decisions.

Zimbabwean Christians should worship *Mwari* as He has given Himself to them in his Son the *Mudzimu Mukuru* par excellence. Zimbabwean Christians believe that the *Mudzimu Mukuru* par excellence is of absolute worth for them, for He has shown them through the Church, through ATR, through sacraments, through sacrifice, through the transformed lives of human beings within their cultures, through His transforming power to forgive sins, and through His power over death itself. In Christian worship, Zimbabwean Christians commit themselves to the *Mudzimu Mukuru* par excellence, for in Him they perceive the ultimate meaning of existence.

## THE ETHICAL FIELD

What does worship require of those who participate in it? What difference does worship make in our attitudes and in the way we live our lives? What is the liturgy after the liturgy?[4] It is the full reality of people and their society, what they do outside the physical Church building. It is what they do from Monday to Saturday as teachers, doctors, farmers, professors, merchants, and politicians when they are doing their daily work. Those who are surrounded and protected by ancestors are in the *Mudzimu Mukuru* par excellence. Christians, who are in the *Mudzimu Mukuru* par excellence, are enabled by Him to lead a new conscious life that should know no sin. There is the renunciation of Satan (*muroyi mukuru*) and the embrace of Christ, the *Mudzimu Mukuru* par excellence.

Paul writes of Christian liberty (Rom. 6:20, 22, 7:3, 8:2, 21; Gal. 2:4, 3:28, 4:22-31, 5:1, 13). Christian liberty is not license, but a service of Christ motivated by love. There is therefore, no condemnation for those who are in the *Mudzimu Mukuru* par excellence (Rom. 8:1). Condemnation clings to unregenerate human beings, who are torn into two because they are flesh dominated by sin but with a mind that recognizes the new order of the *Mudzimu Mukuru* par excellence (Rom. 5:16-18). But Christians no longer live under the dispensation of condemnation (II Cor. 3:9) or of death (II Cor. 3:7). Those baptized in the *Mudzimu Mukuru* par excellence have all clothed themselves in the *Mudzimu Mukuru* par excellence (Gal. 3:27). Baptism is the sacrament whereby Christians achieve union with Christ and publicly manifest their commitment. By putting on Christ, the *Mudzimu Mukuru* par excellence, the baptized Christian adopts Christ's moral dispositions and outlook. Life in the Holy Spirit (*Mudzimu Anoyera*) is life in Jesus Christ. Be renewed in the Spirit of your mind (Eph. 4:23). The First Epistle of Peter exhorts the new Christians to live a moral life worthy of their calling (I Peter 1-4). Those who are in the *Mudzimu Mukuru* par excellence have been crucified with Him who did away with the curse of the law.

The image of slavery is a key part of the Christological basis of Paul's ethics. Paul took up ideas of a cosmic dualism (Gal. 4:3-9). The elements of the world have a demonic aspect and hold human beings in slavery. For Paul, repentance is only the initial act leading up to baptism. The freedom from sinfulness is more than repentance. Paul translates into action the state of having died from the world and risen again within the *Mudzimu Mukuru* par excellence. Christians cannot lead lives of sin while under grace because the new Master—as did the old master, the devil (*muroyi mukuru*)—has a complete claim on their service and holds them in his power. In the new era, Shona Christians stand under one Master, Christ the *Mudzimu Mukuru* par excellence, who commands them and acts through them. Ethics, like the sacraments, is within the sphere of the mystical dying and rising again with the Glorified Christ, the *Mudzimu Mukuru* par excellence. The Spirit bestows upon the baptized a new mind and a new heart. Ethics is the fruit of the *Mudzimu Anoyera* (Gal. 5:22). Instead of the natural mind, Shona Christians possess the mind of the *Mudzimu Mukuru* par excellence (I Cor. 2:16). *Mwari* has bestowed love upon believers through the death and resurrection of the *Mudzimu Mukuru* par excellence and the consequent gift of the *Mudzimu Anoyera*. Where the *Mudzimu Anoyera* of the *Mudzimu Mukuru* par excellence is, there is liberty (2 Cor. 3:17).

Love is the greatest and highest manifestation of 'being in' *Mudzimu Mukuru* par excellence. In Christ, whether one is circumcised or not does not matter, only faith which expresses itself in love (Gal. 5:6). In the most natural way, the mystical dying with Christ and rising with Him is transmitted into a living ethic. Ethics is the necessary outward expression of the translation from the earthly world to the super-earthly, which has already taken place in 'being in' the *Mudzimu Mukuru* par excellence. Christian ethics has to have a bearing on all aspects of justice and love in relation to the concrete lives of people.[5]

An eschatological mysticism of being in the spirit world (*nyikadzimu*) gives Shona Christians an ethic in relation to Jesus Christ the *Mudzimu Mukuru* par excellence. Life in the *Mudzimu Anoyera* creates a Christian ethic valid for all time. Christ the *Mudzimu Mukuru* par excellence proved the truth of His ethic by His way of living it. He became human like us in every respect, but without sin (I Peter 2:22, II Cor. 5:21, Heb. 4:15). So long as the earthly world with all its circumstances still subsists, Christians must live in a spirit of unworldiness in which truth and peace make their influence felt. This is the ideal ethic: to live with the eyes fixed upon eternity while standing firmly upon the solid ground of this world.

# APPENDICES

## *Appendix 1*

### Interview Questionaire: Christ and culture (Chikirisito neTsika)

1. Have you ever listened to the Zimbabwe Broadcasting Corporation (ZBC) Radio Two (2) Programme every Sunday afternoon entitled: *Christ And Culture (ChiKirisito neTsika),* presented by Claudius. G. Mararike of the University of Zimbabwe Sociology Department, Gift Mabhaudhi and Peter Sibanda who is the Secretary General of the Zimbabwe National Traditional Healer's Association (ZINATHA)?

2. What are your views about that programme as far as Christ and culture are concerned?

3. Have you ever read Bishop Ralph Peter Hatendi's memorandum to all licensed clergymen, all diocesan ordinance in training of the 17th January, 1990, entitled *Christ and Culture?* Bishop Hatendi's questionnaire has the following questions which he requested to be answered frankly:

(a) What do you do when a member of your family leaves the hospital uncured of his or her illness?

(b) What do you do in the event of death of a member of a family about divination after the death of a family membe *(gata),* the bringing bach home ceremony of the spirit of a deceased relative *(kurova guva/ chenura)* and inheritance *(nhaka)*?

(c) Is *kurova guva* the same as the USPG Christian memorial service or as the USPG Christian unveiling of the tomb stone?

(d) What do you do about avenging spirits (*ngozi*) in your family? Is a member of your family possesed by ancestral spirits (*midzimu*) or alien spirits (*mashave*)? If possesed what do you do?

(e) Do you take herbs or carry fetishes (*mazango)*?

(f) Do you believe in witchcraft (*uroyi*)? Are you afraid of witchcraft or magic?

(g) Do you observe the Shona traditional day of rest (*chisi*)?

(h) What is that which can be baptised in Shona Traditional Religion (ATR)?

4. Was your home or relative struck by lightning (*mheni)*? If yes what did you do?

5. Are you married? Did you pay the bride price (*roora/lobola*) including the mother's cow (*mombe yehumai*) which is ritually sacrificed to ancestors?

6. Has your wife an unguent (*chinu)* and traditionally and ritually blessed beads (*chuma*) around her waist?

7. Were you given a knobkerrie (*tsvimbo*) after the death of your father?

8 .What do you do when your wife is pregnant or when you are pregnant? Do you visit a traditional midwife (*nyamukuta)* and be given herbs (*mishonga yemasuwo*) and deliver your baby with the help of the *nyamukuta*?

9. Has your baby suffered from fontanell (*nhova*)? What did you do?

10. What do you do when a member of your family is bewitched by *zvishiri/zvivanda/manhepo*?

11. When your wife dies are you prepared to be given a replacement wife (*chigadzamapfihwa*)?

12. When your husband dies are you prepared to be inherited?

13. Do you believe in pledging unborn baby girls in marriage (*kuzvarira*)? Can you pledge your baby girl or your daughter to an avenging spirit (*ngozi*)?

14. Do you have a ritually consecrated bull to the ancestors (*gono remusha*) at your home?

15. Do you believe in witchcraft? What do you do when your daughter is possesed by an alien spirit of witchcraft (*shave rokuroya)*? Do you believe in the *rukawo/runyoka* and goblin (*zvikwambo/ tokoloshis*) types of witchcraft?

16. Do you believe in medicine horns (*makona*)?

17. Do you believe in love portions (*mupfuhwira)*?

18. Do you believe in medicine to harvest more crops (*divise*)?

19. Do you consult diviners (*n'angas*)?

20. Do you believe in alien spirits (*mashave*) such as hunting, thieving, mermaid/pool doctor (*shave renjuzu*) etc? Have you consulted a mermaid/a pool doctor?

21. What is the role of traditional Shona chiefs who are Christians? Should they combine their traditional functions as chiefs for example officiating at the rain-making (*mukweverera*) ceremonies, enforcing the *chisi* day receiving pangolins (*haka/ harakabvuka*) etc with their Christian duties for example being a priest, churchwarden, church councillor, member of the Mother's Union, Fishers of Human Beings ( *Vabvuwi*), and St. Bernard guilds ?

22. Have you experienced barrenness/ infertility (*ngomwa*) in your family? If yes what did you do?

23. Do you have an albino (*musope/murungu dunhu*) as a member of your family? What did you do?

24. Do you have a member of your family who suffers from epileptic fits (*pfari/ zvipusha*)? What did you do?

25. Do you believe in killing human beings and use their body parts in ritual activities (*kuchekeresa*) so as to enhance one's business?

26. Are you afraid of ancestors and death?

27. Are you afraid of the archbishop and the bishop, Church regulations and Canons?

28. Why do you combine Christianity and ATR?

29. Why did you become a Christian?

30. What is your age, academic and professional qualifications, and where do you come from?

# *Appendix 2*

## Report of the Idol and Evangelism Commission which was set up by the Synod of the Diocese of Harare which met in Harare from 12-13 September 1992, Chaired by Fr. Dr. Sabastian Bakare, 1994.

A Report for the Synod of the Anglican Diocese of Harare, 7-8 May 1994, for its consideration. This report was submitted by Fr. Webster Simbabure, Fr. Collis Garikai Machoko and Mr G P Masawi who disagreed with the other report of the same Commission which was submitted by the Chairman, Fr. Dr. Sebastian Bakare and the Secretary, Mr Stephen J Chifunyise. This report was adopted and accepted by the Synod.

### Composition of the Commission

Fr. Dr. Sebastian Bakare (University of Zimbabwe, Ecumenical Senior Chaplain, Mbare Parish) Chairman
Fr. Webster Simbabure (Rimuka Parish)
Fr. Lawrence Mbuwayesango (St. Francis Parish)
Fr. F Fundira (Avondale Parish).
Fr. Dominic Madzimure (Cathedral Parish)
Fr. Justin Samupindi (St. Francis Parish)
Fr. Collis Garikai Machoko (Makonde Parish)
Mrs Venice Sachikonye (Makonde Parish)
Mr E A S Mundangepfupfu (Cathedral Parish)

Ms. Dorothy Makina (Cathedral Parish)
Mr G Masawi (St. Monica Parish Seke)
Mrs Dr. Jane Mutambirwa (Cathedral Parish)
Mrs Sarah Kachingwe (St. Francis Parish)
Mr Stephen J Chifunyise (Mount Pleasant Parish) Secretary

There are doubts about the truth of a majority in the report presented by the other commissioners because the majority of the commissioners did not attend any meetings. Some members submitted their papers on African Traditional Religion (ATR) and then failed to attend any meetings up to the end.

## Disagreements within the Commission

It was clear from the beginning that the commission was divided into two disagreeing groups. The group which had the chairman, Fr. Dr. Sebastian Bakare and Mr. Stephen J Chifunyise the Secretary, was more interested it seemed, in answering the question: How Western and Biblical Christianities (USPG Christianity) can be combined with ATR? They were not interested in condemning some aspects of ATR. They refused to use the Holy Bible as the metre-stick, or as the barometer, or as the thermometer in the work of this Commission. They were of the opinion that the majority of Anglican Christians in Zimbabwe are currently involved in ATR-that is in the bringing back home ceremony (*kurova guva/chenura/kukomba guva*) and in consulting diviners (*n'angas*). Their argument was that, if the Anglican Church teaches against the *kurova guva* ceremony and divination, a lot of Anglicans will leave the Church or a lot of people will still perform the *kurova guva* ceremony and consult diviners in secret under cover of darkness at night. They were more interested it seemed in the quantity of Christians and not in both quantity and quality of Christians.

The other group which comprised of Fr. Webster Simbabure, Fr. Collis G Machoko and Mr G P Masawi, advocated that the *kurova guva* and the consulting of diviners are the works of the devil. And out of step with Biblical teaching. This group was interested in, first answering the question whether ATR and Biblical Christianity should be combined? They were of the opinion that there is no proper or true ATR without the *kurova guva* ceremony and divination. This group was interested in both the quantity and quality of Christians. Hence they refused to compromise quality for the sake of quantity. They used the Holy Bible as the metre-stick.

## Findings of the Commission

The Commission found the following:

1. The *kurova guva/ chenura/kukomba guva* and consulting diviners (*n'angas*) are widely practiced in Zimbabwe by majority of people—87%. A very big percentage of Christians—94%—do participate in divination and *kurova guva.*

The aims of the *kurova guva* are:

i. To make the spirit of the deceased person this is believed to be dangerous and is hovering in the forest, an ancestor (*mudzimu*). No deceased Zimbabwean can be an ancestor without the *kurova guva* ceremony.

ii. To bring the *mudzimu* back home so that he or she can save and protect the members of his or her family from disasters, misfortunes, diseases and deaths.

2. The ancestor or *mudzimu* gives the living members of his/her family good health, harvest, jobs, riches and blessings.
3. If the living members of the family fail to perform the bringing back home ceremony, the dangerous and hovering spirit of the deceased relative will "open doors" *( kuvhura misuwo)* and "unexplainable" illnesses, deaths, disasters and misfortunes will affect the members of that family.
4. The *kurova guva* ceremony ushers the ancestor into the spirit world (*nyikadzimu*).
5. There is no true or proper *kurova guva* without first consulting a diviner.

6. The procedures taken before, during and after the *kurova guva* vary from one region to another in Zimbabwe, but the basic elements are:

i. Consulting a diviner.

ii. Making the dangerous and hovering spirit of the dead an ancestral spirit (*mudzimu*).

iii. Bringing the ancestor back home.

iv. Ushering of the ancestor into the spirit world (*nyikadzimu*). The *kurova guva* ceremony was condemned as the works of the devil by this Commission. The Commission based this finding on the Holy Scriptures.

## The Holy Bible as the Metre-Stick

What does the Holy Bible say about the spirits of the dead and consulting diviners (*n'angas*)? The Holy Bible is totally against ancestor worship, ancestor veneration, ancestor propitiation, appeasing the spirits of the dead and is also totally against the consulting of diviners (*n'angas*). The following verses will make this very clear. (All quotations are from: King James Version).

**Wisdom 3: 1-10 (Deuterocanonical) not part of the Canon):** The spirits of the righteous are in the hands of God and there shall be no torment upon them. In the sight of the unwise they seem to die. And their departure is taken for misery and their going away from us to be utter destruction. But they are in peace.

**Revelation 20:12-13:** And I saw the dead, small and great, stand before God; and the books were opened: and another book was opened, which is the book of life: and the dead were judged out of those things which were written in the books, according to their works. And the sea gave up the dead which were in it; and death and hell delivered up the dead which were in them: and they were judged every man according to their works.

**John 5: 28-29:** Marvel not at this: for the hour is coming, in which all that are in the graves shall hear his voice. And shall come forth; they that have done good, unto the resurrection of life; and they that have done evil, unto the resurrection of damnation.

**Philippians 1:21:** For to me, to live is Christ, and to die is gain. But if I am to live on in the flesh, this will mean fruitful labor for me; and I do not know which to choose. For I am hard-pressed between the two, having a desire to depart and be with Christ, which is far better. (This proves that when the Christian dies he or she goes to be with Jesus Christ and his or her spirit docs not hover in the forest. It is not dangerous).

The Holy Bible is against consulting diviners (*n'angas*). This is indicated by the following verses:

**Leviticus 19:31**: Turn ye not unto them that have familiar spirits, nor unto the wizards; seek them not out, to be defiled by them: I am the LORD your God.

**Leviticus 20:6:** And the soul that turneth unto them that have familiar spirits, and unto the wizards, to go a whoring after them, I will even set my face against that soul, and will cut him off from among his people.

**Leviticus 20:27:** A man also or woman that hath a familiar spirit, or that is a wizard, shall surely be put to death: they shall stone them with stones: their blood shall be upon them.

**Deuteronomy 18:9-13**: When you enter the land the LORD your God is giving you, do not learn to imitate the detestable ways of the nations there. Let no one be found among you who sacrifices his son or daughter in the fire, who practices divination or sorcery, interprets omens, engages in witchcraft, or casts spells, or who is a medium or spiritist or who consults the dead. Anyone who does these things is detestable to the LORD, and because of these detestable practices the LORD your God will drive out those nations before you. You must be blameless before the LORD your God.

**Numbers 23: 23,** There is no divination against Jacob, no evil omens against Israel. It will now be said of Jacob and of Israel, 'See what God has done!'

**2 Kings 21: 6:** And he made his son pass through the fire, and observed times, and used enchantments, and dealt with familiar spirits and wizards: he wrought much wickedness in the sight of the *LORD,* to provoke him to anger.

**Isaiah 8: 19-29**: And when they shall say unto you, Seek unto them that have familiar spirits, and unto wizards that peep, and that mutter: should not a people seek unto their God? For the living to the dead? To the law and to the testimony: if they speak not according to this word, it is because there is no light in them.

**Acts 8:9-13:** But there was a man named Simon, who had previously practiced magic in the city and amazed the people of Samaria, saying that he himself was somebody great. They all paid attention to him, from the least to the greatest, saying, "This man is the power of God that is called Great." And they paid attention to him because for a long time he had amazed them with his magic. But when they believed Philip as he preached good news about the kingdom of God and the name of Jesus Christ, they were baptized, both men and women. Even Simon himself believed, and after being baptized he continued with Philip. And seeing signs and great miracles performed, he was amazed.

**Acts 13:6-12:** When they had gone through the whole island as far as Paphos, they came upon a certain magician, a Jewish false prophet named Bar-Jesus. He was with the proconsul, Sergius Paulus, a man of intelligence, who summoned Barnabas and Saul and sought to hear the word of God. But Elymas the magician (for that is the meaning of his name) opposed them, seeking to turn the proconsul away from the faith. But Saul, who was also called Paul, filled with the Holy Spirit, looked intently at him and said, "You son of the devil, you enemy of all righteousness, full of all deceit and villainy, will you not stop making crooked the straight paths of the Lord? And now, behold, the hand of the Lord is upon you, and you will be blind and unable to see the sun for a time." Immediately mist and darkness fell upon him, and he went about seeking people to lead him by the hand. Then the proconsul believed, when he saw what had occurred, for he was astonished at the teaching of the Lord.

**Acts 16:16-18:** As we were going to the place of prayer, we were met by a slave girl who had a spirit of divination and brought her owners much gain by fortune-telling. She followed Paul and us, crying out, "These men are servants of the Most High God, who proclaim to you the way of salvation." And this she kept doing for many days. Paul, having become greatly annoyed, turned and said to the spirit, "I command you in the name of Jesus Christ to come out of her." And it came out that very hour.

**Acts 19:13-19:** Then some of the itinerant Jewish exorcists undertook to invoke the name of the Lord Jesus over those who had evil spirits, saying, "I adjure you by the Jesus whom Paul proclaims." Seven sons of a Jewish high priest named Sceva were doing this. But the evil spirit answered them, "Jesus I know, and Paul I recognize, but who are you?" And the man in whom was the evil spirit leaped on them, mastered all of them and overpowered them, so that they fled out of that house naked and wounded. And this became known to all the residents of Ephesus, both Jews and Greeks. And fear fell upon them all, and the name of the Lord Jesus was extolled. Also many of those who were now believers came, confessing and divulging their practices. And a number of those who had practiced magic arts brought their books together and burned them in the sight of all. And they counted the value of them and found it came to fifty thousand pieces of silver.

## Recommendations

**Matthew 27: 1-2ff and Mark 14: 53-55ff**

The conflict between Christianity and other world religions and culture is as old as Christianity itself. It is not a new thing. Nor is it unique to Zimbabwe. Every person and every nation which turns to Christ from paganism is faced with this problem. Jesus was a Jew. He grew up in a Jewish religion-Judaism. Jesus Christ rejected some cultural practices, beliefs and teachings of Judaism. Jesus Christ was killed by the Jews because he opposed Judaism. If Jesus opposed and condemned the Jewish religion, it then follows that any other world religion, ATR included, are against the teaching of Jesus Christ . They are heathen religions. Only Biblical Christianity should be taught to Christians in Zimbabwe.

**Acts 26: 1-18ff**

Saint Paul was born in Judaism. He became a Pharisee. He advocated Judaism and killed many Christians, but he was converted from Judaism to Christianity. He, at last opposed significant aspects of the Jewish religion. So like St. Paul, Zimbabwean Christians are born with some cultural trappings of ATR. They grow up in ATR but at their baptism, they convert from ATR to Biblical Christianity. They reject the kingdom of the devil and accept the Kingdom of Christ. As Bible believing Christians, we should have nothing to do with the old dominion of Satan but we should only be concerned about the Kingdom of Christ.

**The First Recommendation:**

Zimbabwean Christians should be aware of the fact that only Jesus Christ and not the ancestors is the Way the Truth and the Life (John. 14:6). Salvation and protection come from God and only through Jesus Christ. Only Jesus Christ and not the ancestors is the Light of the world (John. 8:12). True Christians should repent from all evil and from worshipping ancestors for they are the Light of the world (Matt. 5:14). We are saved by no other name except Jesus Christ's name (Acts 4:12). We should repent from ATR and believe the Gospels (Luke. 3: 8-14).

**The Second Recommendation:**

The Zimbabwean Church should teach that *kurova guva* and divination are the works of the devil. They are sinful. *Kurova guva* and divination should be condemned by bishops, priests and the laity-every Christian. The Church should teach every Christian to follow Joshua's example (Joshua 24: 14-15).

**The Third Recommendation:**

The Church should use the Holy Bible as its metre-stick. The Church should stand on the firm Rock who is Christ and teach the Biblical truth without confusing the people with the so-called "academic theology or universality theology". The Church of God should work to achieve both quantity and quality of Christians but should not compromise Biblical truths or the quality of Christians for the sake of quantity. The Church should teach Biblical truth so as to produce Christian spiritual giants. There is no room for nurturing spiritual dwarfs in the Church of God. *Kurova guva* and divination produce Christian spiritual dwarfs. The Church should be aware of the fact that the battle between Christ and culture is a long, hot and tough battle against sin. The battle was won at the cross. The Old Testament prophets were in a similar difficult battle against both polytheism and culture. It took the Old Testament prophets a very long time to bring about the concept of monotheism (One God) among many Hebrew gods. The Jews accepted the concept of monotheism after thousands of years of teaching. From Moses to Elijah, the battle against polytheism and culture was on and likewise, it will take the Church in Zimbabwe a very long time to destroy ancestor worship and divination. The Church should not give up this battle against sin. The battle will be hot and dangerous but victory through Christ is absolutely certain.

**The Fourth Recommendation:**

The Church should teach that the standards of God are different from the standards of the world. It is the Zimbabwean Christians who should be converted to Jesus Christ and not the other way round. God and Jesus Christ do not need any conversion. It is the Zimbabwean Christians who need Jesus Christ in order to be saved. Jesus Christ does not need to be saved by ATR. If the Zimbabwean Christians need to be saved by Jesus Christ, they should follow Christ and obey His commandments. So Jesus Christ through the Holy Spirit is saying, "Stay away from *kurova guva* and divination". Those who need salvation should follow Christ's instructions. Zimbabwean Christians should be aware of the fact that culture is not static, but is dynamic (ever changing). Cultures are never perfect before God and will never be perfect before Him. Cultures are far short of the glory of God despite their dynamism. The Church should not keep on changing the teaching of Christ as given in the Holy Bible so as to meet and satisfy the needs of a sinful culture and society. Instead the Church should stick to Christ's teachings, no matter what type of changes take place in the scientific, technological, political, cultural, social and economic fields. The Church should be aware of the fact that it is send by Christ as sheep among wolves. "Behold I send you out as sheep in the midst of wolves, so be as wise as serpents and gentle as doves" (Matt. 10:16).

## Inheritance (Nhaka)

1. **The inheritance of property—money, houses, cattle, goats, sheep, farms, clothes, utensils etc**. On this type of property the Commission recommends that, they should be shared two or three days after the burial of the deceased person. This should be done while most of the relatives are still present at the funeral. This reduces a lot of inconveniences. The property of the deceased person should be shared without the *kurova guva* ceremony taking place. No ATR rituals should be done. Only prayers to God through Jesus Christ should be done. If the deceased person had a medicine horn (*gona/ makona*) it should be burned by the Christians present. A medicine horn should not be inherited by a Christian. The Church should encourage every Christian to make a will. The Commission recommends that there should be a "Wills File" at the diocesan offices kept by the diocesan secretary and lawyers.

2. **Inheritance of a widow**. The Commission recommends that, the inheritance of a widow should be done only with the mutual agreement of the two—the widow and the inheritor and only if the inheritor is not married. This should happen when both of them are over twenty one years of age. The widow can opt to be "inherited" by her son, daughter or the sister or aunt of her deceased husband. This does not mean that she is going to cohabitate with anyone of them. It simply means that she is going to remain in the home and she is not going to be remarried or to cohabitate with anybody. There is no incest or homosexuality involved. This is simply a way of telling the world that one is not interested in any sexual relationships. The inheritance of a widow by a married man is adultery. A widow is free to marry anyone after the death of her husband. She is also free to remain single after the death of her husband. The Commission also recommends that, the Church should teach that only by mutual agreement between the two and only when both are over twenty one years of age can male Christians inherit their sister-in-laws (*amainini*) and female

Christiansas replacement wives (*chigadzamapfihwa)*. The pledging of unborn daughters or any girl or woman (*kuzvarira)* is sinful and should be condemned by all Christians. *Kuzvarira* is an evil practice.

Christian relatives of the deceased husband should not chase away the widow from her home simply because she has refused to be inherited as a wife. They should help her materially, financially and spiritually to raise up the children left by their deceased relative. A widow who decides not to be remarried and stays at home should not be secretly involved in love affairs and fornication with any man—deceased husband's relative or non-relative. Involvement in fornication and secrete love affairs with relatives or non-relatives of the deceased husband is the major reason why widows are chased away from their homes. Widows should be true widows and if they decide to remain single, they should be honest to both God and Jesus Christ. They should not be involved in fornication.

**1 Corinthians 7:8-9:** Now to the unmarried and the widows I say: It is good for them to stay unmarried, as I am. But if they have not self-control let them get married; for married life is better than the burning of desire.

**1 Corinthians 7:39-40:** A wife is bound for so long time as her husband liveth; but if the husband be dead, she is free to be married to whom she will; only in the Lord. She is more blessed, though, in my opinion, if she remains as she is, and I think that I too have the Spirit of God.http://www.usccb.org/nab/bible/index.htm

Signed at Harare:

Fr. Webster Simbabure, and Fr. Collis Garikai Machoko

Date: April 14, 1994.

# *Appendix 3*

## Dissenting Report of the Idol and Evangelism Commission which was set up by the Synod of the Diocese of Harare which met in Harare from 12-13 September 1992, Chaired by Fr. Dr. Sabastian Bakare, 1994.

**Composition of the Commission**

Fr. Dr. Sebastian Bakare (University of Zimbabwe Ecumenical Senior Chaplain, Mbare Parish) Chairman
Fr. Webster Simbabure (Rimuka Parish)
Fr. Lawrence Mbuwayesango (St. Francis Parish)
Fr. F Fundira (Avondale Parish).
Fr. Dominic Madzimure (Cathedral Parish)
Fr. Justin Samupindi (St. Francis Parish)
Fr. Collis Garikai Machoko (Makonde Parish)
Mrs Venice Sachikonye (Makonde Parish)
Mr E A S Mundangepfupfu (Cathedral Parish)
Ms. Dorothy Makina (Cathedral Parish)
Mr G Masawi (St. Monica Parish Seke)
Mrs Dr. Jane Mutambirwa (Cathedral Parish)
Mrs Sarah Kachingwe (St. Francis Parish)
Mr Stephen J Chifunyise (Mount Pleasant Parish) Secretary

## Preface

In his letter to one of the commissioners, the Bishop, Peter Hatendi started with a question: "Is ancestor worship idolatrous? Because

Shona speaking people are notoriously religious, most of them will not give up some traditional religious practices." It is for this reason that the Bishop was empowered to set "a commission to study the arguments for and against syncretistic tendencies among members of the Anglican Church."

When the commission began its work, it tried to remind that its task was to find as much information as possible so that the Synod at its next meeting could discuss this issue intelligently. This meant that members have to restrain themselves from being dogmatic and prejudicial. Our aim was not to provide the Synod with answers or even to indicate which direction to take but to put down the facts and views as they came. Being sensitive, the Commission often failed to reach a consensus on what was to be included or not in the final report as its findings. There was diversity of opinion which is reflected in the report as there was no attempt at seeking convergences. It was the view of the Commission that the Synod itself should deal with these diverse opinions as she feels guided by the Holy Spirit into all truths.

The Commission was aware of the fact that the subject at hand was so sensitive that it would inevitably provoke a large number of brothers and sisters to feel strongly one way or the other. The Commission was aware too that there was no such thing as cultural gospel, other than the Good News as revealed to us in Jesus Christ. Members were however, agreed that it would not be wise to simply attack the religious practices of our people as idolatry or primitive and that such an approach would be self-defeating. It was the majority view of the members of the Commission that the persistent practice of traditional rites cannot disappear unless they are encountered with Christ through dialogue (Acts17: 17-28).

The Greeks were fearful of offending any god by failing to give him attention. After dialoguing with them, Paul warns a few followers who became the pillars of the Church in Corinth (Acts 17:34). Therefore, the Commission's findings are expected to lay ground for serious discussion and the future action that should be taken by the Church. Suffice to say that the dialogue between Anglican spirituality and Shona religious views is the beginning of a positive mission.

There is no doubt that the Commission hopes that the Synod will prayerfully look into traditional religious practices of the Shona people and reinterprets anew where there are theologically and Biblically relevant and supportable scriptures. The Commission hopes that the Synod will re-evaluate the Christian Mission in Zimbabwe and by so doing produce Christians who are not promiscuous in faith but faithful to the Lord. The challenge seems to be the need to be a listening and not merely a talking Church. The Church needs to listen, observe and wait for the guidance of the Holy Spirit in the mission.

Through dialogue Nicodemus was made to understand the meaning of re-birth, through dialogue Paul assisted the Athenians from worshipping ignorantly. Evidently, dialogue demands a very high degree of tolerance, it demands taking the people who hold other views seriously. In research and through listening to each other, we could not but feel that every traditional rite of our people needs to be understood, named, unmasked and confronted by Christians.

What the Commission hopes is that through serious discussions the Church may be led to recapture a passion for making Christ known and accepted by everyone and everywhere within our given context. The Commission also hopes that Christians in Zimbabwe will understand their new identity in Christ in their own culture.

The Commission acknowledged a number of unresolved questions: What is the place of Christ in Shona culture? What are the criteria for deciding between the demands of the Gospel and extraneous, culturally relative practices? What structures and practices are needed in the Church to enable sound conversion to be a continuous process?

Authentic confrontation between Christ and traditional religious practices has to begin with the liberation of our minds and lives from control of undeclared captors. The Bible calls for this process of repentance and transfiguration (Rom.12:2, 2Cor. 10: 4-5). Only then will we be in a position to offer pastoral care to those in our Churches who do not know where they belong.

It is the sincere hope of the Commission that the Synod will establish a more permanent Commission on the subject so that the

Church of tomorrow may prepare a more fertile ground to sow the seeds of the Gospel.

....

Rev. Dr. R S Bakare, Chairman

## Summary of Conclusions and Recommendations

1. The Commission recommended that the Synod establishes a permanent Commission on worship which among other things will enable Christians in Zimbabwe to understand their identity in Christ in their own culture and prepare a more fertile ground to sow the seed of the Gospel.

2. The Commission recommended that the Church views seriously her role in state funerals in order to ensure that the Church's place in the high-profiled and well publicized state funerals is not compromised especially in regards to the nature of the funeral rites and the religious status of the people accorded state funerals.

3. The Commission concluded that although a lot may have been written or said about Shona culture, there may be important concepts and practices which have not been adequately documented and analyzed by the Church with a view to understanding the Shona people and for the Church to help them to understand that they are Christ's people too.

4. The majority of the members of the Commission concluded that there were many rites and rituals in the Shona culture which show that the Shona people believed in the existence of the Creator of mankind (*Mwari)* before the advent of Christianity.

5. The Commission recommended that the Church should be more present in the schools and set aside financial and human resources needed in the teaching of the Good News of Jesus Christ in the school system in Zimbabwe.

6. The Commission recommended that the Shona Christian should be enabled so that Christ (The Church) is there to deal with both personal /family concerns and the communal / national concerns of all the people.

7. The majority of the members of the Commission concluded that the major ceremonies in the *kurova guva* such as the blessing of the millet (*kubata mumera*), the blessing of the cow, bull or ox (*kuratidza mombe*) the blessing of beer and meat (*kupira doro nenyama*), the bringing of the spirit back home (*kurova guva*) can be adapted into a Church rite.

8. The Commission concluded that while many elements of the *kurova guva* rite can find place in the rites and litanies of the Church, the consultation of a diviner (*n'anga*) before, during and after the rite cannot be accepted by the Church.

9. The Commission recommended that the Church considers using the attached samples of Church rites of *kurova guva.*

....

Rev. Dr. S R Bakare (Chairman)

# *Appendix 4*

## Table 1 (Part One)

Results Numerical and Percentage Respectively of the Six Zimbabwean Anglican Shona Bishops who Responded to some Face-to-Face Interview Questions During the Decade of Evangelism from 1990 to 2000.

**Key:**
N—Number
A—Age in Years
M—Married
UM-Unmarried
PBP—Paid Bride Price
PMC—Paid Mother's Cow
AI—Agreed Interview
RI—Refused Interview
SCT—Seminary Certificate in Theology
UDT—University Diploma in Theology
UD—University Degree

| N | A | M | UM | PBP | PMC | AI | RI | SCT | UTD | UD |
|---|---|---|---|---|---|---|---|---|---|---|
| 1 | 75 | 1=100 | 0=0 | 1=100 | 1=100 | 1=100 | 0=0 | 0=0 | 1=100 | 0=0 |
| 1 | 71 | 1=100 | 0=0 | 1=100 | 1=100 | 1=100 | 0=0 | 1=100 | 0=0 | 0=0 |
| 1 | 68 | 1=100 | 0=0 | 1=100 | 1=100 | 0=0 | 1=100 | 1=100 | 0=0 | 0=0 |
| 1 | 61 | 1=100 | 0=0 | 0=0 | 1=100 | 1=100 | 0=0 | 1=100 | 0=0 | 1= 100 |
| 1 | 49 | 1=100 | 0=0 | 1=100 | 1=100 | 1=100 | 0=0 | 1=100 | 0=0 | 0=0 |
| 1 | 50 | 1=100 | 0=0 | 1=100 | 1=100 | 1=100 | 0=0 | 0=0 | 0=0 | 0=0 |
| Total 6=100 % | | 6=100 | 0=0 | 5=83 | 5=83 | 5=83 | 1=17 | 4=67 | 1=33 | 1=3 3 |

## Table 1 (Part Two)

**Key:**

IA &ATR—Involved in Ancestors and ATR
GMFS—Give Material and Financial Support
UH—Use Herbs
BW—Believe in Witchcraft
CA& ATR—Condemn Ancestors and African Traditional Religion (ATR)
MFBA—Material and Financial Benefits from Ancestors
SMBCO—Spiritual and Material Benefits from Christianity Only
SBA—Spiritual Benefits from Ancestors
FCPR—Fear of Canons and Pastoral Regulations
FA Fear of Ancestors
CC& ATR Combine Christianity and ATR

| IA& ATR | GM FS | UH | BW | CA& ATR | MF BA | SMB CO | SBA | FC PR | FA | CC& ATR |
|---|---|---|---|---|---|---|---|---|---|---|
| 0=100 | 0=0 | 1=100 | 1=100 | 1=100 | 0=0 | 1=100 | 0=0 | 0=0 | 0=0 | 0=0 |
| 1=100 | 0=0 | 1=100 | 1=100 | 0=100 | 1=100 | 0=0 | 1=100 | 1=100 | 1=100 | 1=100 |
| 0=0 | 0=0 | 1=100 | 1=100 | 0=0 | 1=100 | 0=0 | 1=100 | 1=100 | 1=100 | 1=100 |
| 1=100 | 1=100 | 1=100 | 1=100 | 0=0 | 1=100 | 0=0 | 0=0 | 1=100 | 1=100 | 0=0 |
| 1=100 | 0=0 | 1=100 | 1=100 | 0=0 | 1=100 | 0=0 | 1=100 | 1=100 | 0=0 | 1=100 |
| 1=100 | 0=0 | 1=100 | 1=100 | 0=0 | 1=100 | 0=0 | 1=100 | 1=100 | 1=100 | 1=100 |
| 4=81 | 1=20 | 6=100 | 6=100 | 1=20 | 6=80 | 1=20 | 4=60 | 5=83 | 4=67 | 4=60 |

## Table 2

Results Numerical and Percentage Respectively of the Eighty-Five Zimbabwean Anglican Shona Priests who Responded to some Face-to-Face Interview Questions During the Decade of Evangelism from 1990 to 2000.

**Key:**

N—Number
AI—Agreed Interview
RI—Refused Interview
A—Age in Years
M—Married
UM-Unmarried
PBP—Paid Bride Price
PMC—Paid Mother's Cow
R—Retired
Not—Not Retired
S—Stipendiary
NS—Not Stipendiary
SCT—Seminary Certificate in Theology
UDT—University Diploma in Theology
UDTS—University Degree in Theological Studies
NTT—No Theological Training

| N | AI | RI | A | M | UM | PBP | PMC |
|---|---|---|---|---|---|---|---|
| 8=100 | 7=88 | 1=13 | 80-90 | 7=100 | 0=0 | 7=100 | 7=100 |
| 7=100 | 5=71 | 2=29 | 70-80 | 5=100 | 0=0 | 5=100 | 5=100 |
| 12=100 | 10=83 | 2=17 | 60-70 | 10=100 | 0=0 | 10=100 | 10=100 |
| 18=100 | 13=72 | 5=28 | 50-60 | 13=100 | 0=0 | 13=100 | 13=100 |
| 14=100 | 11=79 | 3=21 | 40-50 | 11=100 | 0=0 | 11=100 | 11=100 |
| 17=100 | 13=76 | 4=24 | 30-40 | 11=85 | 2=15 | 11=100 | 11=100 |
| 9=100 | 6=67 | 3=33 | 20-30 | 3=50 | 3=50 | 3=100 | 3=100 |
| Total=85 | 20=24 | 20=24 | | 60=92 | 5=8 | 60=100 | 60=100 |

| R | NR | S | NS | SCT | UDT | UDTS | NTT |
|---|---|---|---|---|---|---|---|
| 7=100 | 0=0 | 0=0 | 7=100 | 4=57 | 0=0 | 0=0 | 3=43 |
| 5=100 | 0=0 | 0=0 | 5=100 | 4=80 | 0=0 | 0=0 | 1=2= |
| 2=2= | 8=80 | 7=70 | 3=30 | 3=30 | 3=3= | 2=20 | 2=20 |
| 0=0 | 13=100 | 11=85 | 2=15 | 8=62 | 1=8 | 0=0 | 4=31 |
| 0=0 | 11=100 | 8=73 | 3=27 | 3=27 | 6=55 | 0=0 | 2=18 |
| 0=0 | 13=100 | 13=100 | 0=0 | 1=8 | 4=31 | 4=31 | 4=31 |
| 0=0 | 6=100 | 6=100 | 0=0 | 2=33 | 2=33 | 1=17 | 1=17 |
| 14=22 | 51=78 | 45=69 | 20=21 | 25=38 | 16=25 | 7=11 | 17=26 |

## Table 3

Results Numerical and Percentage Respectively of the Sixty-Five Zimbabwean Anglican Shona Priests who Responded to some Face-to-Face Interview Questions During the Decade of Evangelism from 1990 to 2000.

N—Number
TT—Theological Training
IA &ATR—Involved in Ancestors and ATR
GMFS—Give Material and Financial Support
UH—Use Herbs
BW—Believe in Witchcraft
CA& ATR—Condemn Ancestors and African Traditional Religion (ATR)
SCT—Seminary Certificate in Theology
NTT—No Theological Training
UDT—University Diploma in Theology
MFBAC—Material and Financial Benefits from both Ancestors and Christ
SBA—Spiritual Benefits from Ancestors
SMBCO—Spiritual and Material Benefits from Christianity Only
FB-Fear of Bishops
FA Fear of Ancestors
SBAC—Spiritual Benefits from both Ancestors and Jesus Christ
CC& ATR—Combine Christianity and ATR

| N | TT | IA&ATR | GMFS | UH | BW | CA&ATR |
| --- | --- | --- | --- | --- | --- | --- |
| 25 | TT | 18=72 | 3=12 | 25=100 | 25=100 | 4=16 |
| 17 | SCT | 14=82 | 1=6 | 17=100 | 17=100 | 2=12 |
| 16 | NTT | 13=81 | 1=6 | 16=100 | 16=100 | 2=13 |
| 7 | UDT | 7=100 | 0=0 | 7=100 | 7=100 | 0=0 |
| T= 65= 100% | | 52=80 | 5=8 | 65=100 | 65=100 | 8=12 |

| MFBA | SBA | SMBCO | FB | FA | CC&ATR |
| --- | --- | --- | --- | --- | --- |
| 21=84 | 21=84 | 4=16 | 21=84 | 21=84 | 21=84 |
| 15=88 | 15=88 | 2=12 | 15=88 | 15=88 | 15=88 |
| 18=88 | 18=88 | 2=13 | 18=88 | 18=88 | 18=88 |
| 7=100 | 7=100 | 0=0 | 7=100 | 7=100 | 7=100 |
| 57=88 | 57=88 | 8=12 | 57=88 | 57=88 | 57=88 |

## Table 4 (Part One)

Results Numerical and Percentage Respectively of the Six Hundred Zimbabwean Shona Anglican Christians who Responded to some Face-to-Face Interview Questions During the Decade of Evangelism from 1990 to 2000.

**Key:**
N—Number
M—Married
UM-Unmarried
PBP—Paid Bride Price
PMC—Paid Mother's Cow
AI—Agreed Interview
RI—Refused Interview
IA&ATR—Involved in Ancestors and ATR

|  | N | M | UM | PBP | PMC | AI | RI | IA& ATR |
|---|---|---|---|---|---|---|---|---|
| Rural Lay Male | 150 | 116 | 10 | 116 | 116 | 126 | 24 | 105 |
| Rural Lay Female | 150 | 106 | 6 | 106 | 106 | 112 | 38 | 85 |
| Urban Lay Female | 150 | 129 | 3 | 129 | 129 | 132 | 18 | 111 |
| Urban Lay Male | 150 | 141 | 3 | 141 | 141 | 144 | 6 | 127 |
| Total | 600=100 | 492=82 | 22=4 | 492=82 | 492=82 | 514=86 | 86=14 | 428=83 |

## Table 4 (Part Two)

**Key:**

GMFS—Give Material and Financial Support
UH—Use Herbs
BW—Believe in Witchcraft
CA& ATR—Condemn Ancestors and African Traditional Religion (ATR)
MFBAC—Material and Financial Benefits from both Ancestors and Christ
SMBCO—Spiritual and Material Benefits from Christianity only
SBAC—Spiritual Benefits from both Ancestors and Christ
CC& ATR Combine Christianity and ATR
FA Fear of Ancestors
SMBCC—Social and Material Benefits from Church of Christ

| GMFS | UH | BW | CA& ATR | MFBAC | SMBCO | SBAC | CC&ATR | FA |
|---|---|---|---|---|---|---|---|---|
| 9 | 126 | 126 | 12 | 114 | 12 | 114 | 114 | 114 |
| 8 | 112 | 112 | 19 | 93 | 19 | 93 | 93 | 93 |
| 8 | 132 | 132 | 13 | 119 | 13 | 119 | 119 | 119 |
| 7 | 144 | 144 | 10 | 134 | 10 | 134 | 134 | 134 |
| 32=6 | 514= 100 | 514= 100 | 54=11 | 460=90 | 54=11 | 460=90 | 460=90 | 460= 90 |

# *Appendix 5*

## Glossary

| | |
|---|---|
| *Barika/chipari* | polygamy |
| *Chigadzamapfihwa* | replacement wife |
| *Chisi* | day of rest |
| *dziva* | pool |
| *dziva guru* | big pool |
| *gono* | consecrated bull |
| *Guruuswa* | Savanna Grasslands |
| *ishe/ mambo* | chief |
| *karuva* | fruits |
| *kurova guva/ chenura/kukomba guva* | bring back home ceremony |
| *kuruma gore* | feast of the first fruits |
| *kuzvarira* | pledging of an unborn daughter in marriage |
| *mahewu* | sweet beer from unfermented finger |
| *millet* | |
| *mahwe adziva* | rocky place with water |
| *majukwa* | rain making alien spirit |
| *mhandara* | unmarried young woman |
| *mhondoro/ midzimu mikuru* | territorial/regional ancestors |
| *mhuri* | family |
| *midzimu* | ancestors |
| *midzimu yepamusha* | family ancestors |
| *Mitupo* | totems |

| | |
|---|---|
| *mudzimu* | ancestor |
| *Mudzimu Anoyera/Mweya Anoyera* | Holy Spirit |
| *mukuru* | older |
| *mukweverera* | rain making ceremony |
| *munda* | field |
| *Mwari* | God |
| *n'anga* | diviner/traditional healer |
| *ngozi* | avenging spirit |
| *nhaka* | inheritance |
| *njuzu* | mermaid/pool doctor |
| *nyikadzimu* | spirit world |
| *roora/lobola* | bride price |
| *sadza* | thick porridge |
| *shave* | alien spirit |
| *shave rekuvhima* | hunting alien spirit |
| *shave rokushanda nesimba* | working hard alien spirit |
| *shirikadzi* | widow |
| *svikiro* | spirit medium |
| *uroyi* | witchcraft |
| U*sahwira* | friendship |
| *vabvuwi* | fishers of human beings |
| *varoyi* | witches |
| *Vatorwa* | foreigners |
| *vatumwa or manyusa* | messengers |
| *vuhwa* | grass |
| *zviyo/rukweza/rapoko* | finger millet |

# BIBLIOGRAPHY

## List of Abbreviations

AACC—All Africa Council of Churches
ACC—Anglican Consultative Council
ATR—African Traditional Religion
BSACo—British South Africa Company
CBMS—Conference of British Missionary Societies
CMS—Church Missionary Society
CR—Community of the Resurrection
ESC—Electoral Supervisory Commission
LMS—London Missionary Society
MDC—Movement for Democratic Change
NADA—Native Affairs Development Annual
NT—New Testament
OT—Old Testament
RF—Rhodesian Front
SRMC—Southern Rhodesia Missionary Conferences
SPG—United Society for the Propagation of the Gospel in Foreign Parts
UDI—Unilateral Declaration of Independence
UMCA—Universities Mission to Central Africa
USPG—United Society for the Propagation of the Gospel
WCC—World Council of Churches
WEF—World Evangelical Fellowship
ZANU(PF)—Zimbabwe African National Union ( Patriotic Front)

## Primary Sources

### Interviews

Six Shona Anglican Bishops, Eighty-Five Shona Anglican Priests, and Six Hundred Shona Anglican Laity in Zimbabwe were interviewed using my Interview Questionaire: Christ and Culture *(Chikirisito neTsika)*, Face-To-Face Interview Questions during the Decade of Evangelism in the Worldwide Anglican Communion in both Urban and Rural Zimbabwe: 1990-2000 (Appendix 1).

***Note:*** The names of the Shona Anglican bishops, priests and laity who agreed to be interviewed are not disclosed in this book except Bishop Ralph Peter Hatendi. Most bishops, priests, and laity agreed to be interviewed by me and to give me very sensitive information provided I promised to keep their identities anonymous. They feared for their job security, suits in a law court, and their welfare within the Church.

### Archival Sources

Christelow, C. Diocese of Southern Rhodesia: A Circular to the Bishop and all Licensed Clergy from the Director of Missions. National Archives of Zimbabwe, Harare, ANG 16/12/1/1-18, (Anglican Church) 30th April, 1938.

Gibbon, R. G. The Diocese of Southern Rhodesia: *The Link* Magazine. National Archives of Zimbabwe, Harare, ANG/29/4/1, ANG/29/5/2, (Anglican Church) 30th June, 1950. Historical Manuscripts Collection. National Archives of Zimbabwe, Harare. ANG 1/4/5 Sections III and XII (Anglican Church) Missionary Conferences, 1914-1960. The Second Native Missionary Conference in the Diocese of Southern Rhodesia (Zimbabwe) 1918.

Lloyd, E. J. Saint Faith's Newsletter. National Archives of Zimbabwe, Harare, ANG/16/13/1-11, (Anglican Church), Rusape: 16th September, 1928.National Archives of Zimbabwe, Harare, Section XII ANG 1/4/5.Historical Manuscripts Collection, Anglican Church, Missionary Conferences, 1914-1930. The Second Native Missionary Conference in the Diocese of Southern Rhodesia (Zimbabwe), 1918.

National Archives of Zimbabwe, Harare, N3/5/1/1, Fr. Fleischer-Native Commissioner. Inyanga (Nyanga), 29X, 1911.

Paget, E. F. Diocese of Southern Rhodesia Circular: The Relations of the Anglican Communion with other Christian Bodies. National Archives of Zimbabwe, Harare, ANG/1/4/7/14-64, AL/7/1/1/2/3/4/5/6/7, (Anglican Church), 23 rd October 1937.

. *The Toroquay-Directory and South Devon Journal*. (Containing Paget's visit to Britain). National Archives of Zimbabwe, Harare, ANG/1/1/1-66, (Anglican Church), Toroquay: Wednesday, June 16th, 1926.

. A Private Letter to the Society for the Propagation of the Gospel in Foreign Parts (SPG). Missionary Priest at Selukwe (Shurugwi). National Archives of Zimbabwe, Harare, AL/7/4-29, (Anglican Church), 18 th June 1936.

. A Sermon at the Consecration of the Bernard Mizeki Shrine at Thydon.

Marandellas (Marondera), National Archives of Zimbabwe, Harare, ANG/1/4/44/64, (Anglican Church), 18th June 1936.

Proceedings of the Southern Rhodesia Missionary Conference. National Archives of Zimbabwe, Harare, ANG 1/4/5 (Southern Rhodesia Missionary Conferences 1914-1960). The Argus Printing and Publishing Company Limited, 1926.

Proceedings of the Southern Rhodesia Missionary Conference. National Archives of Zimbabwe, Harare, ANG 1/4/5 (Southern Rhodesia Missionary Conferences 1914-1960). The Argus Printing And Publishing Company Limited, 1928.

Proceedings of the Southern Rhodesia Missionary Conference. National Archives of Zimbabwe, Harare, BR/3/3/1-23 (Southern Rhodesia Missionary Conference). Bulawayo: Chronicle, 26-28th June 1930.

## Official Church/USPG Publications and Reports

*1921 Second Supplementary Charter from King George V.*

Dublin Report, *Partners in Mission*. London: SPCK, 1973, p. 53.

*Forward from Fifty-One: 1952 Report.* London: SPG, 1952, pp. 26-28.

Final Statement of the FABC Assembly, No. 12. *His Gospel to Our Peoples, Vol. II.* Manila, 1976.

IMBISA Secretariat. *Inculturation: The Faith that Takes Root in African Cultures. IMBISA Study Document. The Seed is the Word of God.* Zimbabwe, Gweru: Mambo Press, 1993, p. 47.

Kingsnorth, J. quoted by Wyld, P. in: *What on Earth? The USPG 1969 Report.*

*A Letter from SPG in 1959 to all English Incumbents.*

*Network.* January 1974.

*A Remarkable Letter from a Native Catechist, the Zambezi Missionary Report, 1922-1925, 7, 494, 492-493.*

*Southern Rhodesia Report of the Commission of Native Education,* Paragraph 232.

*The Restless Ones, SPG 1957-1958 Report.* London: SPG, 1957-1958, p. 37.

*Wesleyan Methodist Missionary Society S/M South Africa 1906-1911, Stanlake's Report of the Bulawayo and Tegwani Circuits, 31st December 1907.*

*Zimbabwe Catholic Bishops Conference (ZCBC), Responsibilities-Honesty-Solidarity.* A Joint Pastoral Statement No. 4/97 by the ZCBC. Harare: Social Communications Department of the ZCBC, 16th April 1997, pp. 7-8.

**Secondary Sources**

**Books**

Abraham, D. P. "The Role of *Chaminuka* and the *Mhondoro* Cults in Shona Political History" in Stokes and Brown (eds.), *The Zambezian Past—Studies in Central African History.* Manchester, 1966.

Akrong, A. "Christology from an African Perspective" in J. S. Pobee, (ed.), *Exploring Afro-Christology.* Frankfurt am Main, Bern, New York, Paris: Peter Lang, 1992.

Anderson-Morshead, M. *History of the Universities Mission to Central Africa, 1859-1909.* London: UMCA 1897, revised in 1956.

Aplers, E. *Aspects of Central African History.* T. O. Ranger, (ed.), London: Heinemann, 1979.

Askari, H., Hick, J. *The Experience of Religious Diversity.* Aldershot: Avebery, 1985. (Reprint 1987).

Atkinson, N. D. "The Missionary Contribution to Early Education in Rhodesia". J. A. Dachs, (ed.), *Christianity South of the Zambezi. Vol. I.* Gweru: Mambo Press, 1973.

Bahemuka, J. M. "The Hidden Christ in African Traditional Religion". J. N. K. Mugambi, L. Magesa, (eds.), *Jesus in African Christianity. Experimentation and Diversity in African Christology.* Nairobi: Initiative Publishers, 1989.

Bakare, S. *My Right to Land in the Bible and in Zimbabwe: A Theology of Land in Zimbabwe.* Harare: Zimbabwe Council of Churches, 1993.

*The Drumbeat of Life: Jubilee in an African Context. Risk Book Series.* Geneva: World Council of Churches (WCC) Publications. 1997.

Banana, C. S. "The Case for a New Bible" in I. Mukonyora, J. L. Cox, F. J. Verstraelen, (eds.), *Rewriting the Bible: The Real Issues: Perspectives from within Biblical and Religious Studies in Zimbabwe.* Gweru: Mambo Press, 1993.

*"Come and Share": An Introduction to Christian Theology.* Gweru: Mambo Press, 1991.

*The Church and the Struggle for Zimbabw: From the Programme to Combat Racism to Combat Theology.* Gweru: Mambo Press, 1996.

*Gospel According to the Ghetto*. Gweru: Mambo Press, 1980.

Barclay, W. *Jesus as they saw Him.* London: SCM Press, 1962.

Barth, K. (*Einfuhrung in die evangelische Theologie). Evangelical Theology: An Introduction.* (Translated by G. Foley) New York: Holt, 1963.

Beach, D. N. D. *Zimbabwe Before 1900.* Gweru: Mambo Press, 1984.

*The Shona and Zimbabwe 900-1850. An Outline of Shona History.* Gweru: Mambo Press, 1984.

Bediako, K. *Jesus in African Culture: A Ghanaian Perspective.* Accra: Asempa Publishers, 1990.

Beker, J.C. "Colossians" in J. L. Mays, (ed.) J. Blenkinsopp, J. D. Levenson, W. A. Meeks, C. A. Newsom, D. L. Petersen, (eds.) *Harper's Bible Commentary.* San Francisco, New York, Washington: 1988. pp. 1226—1229.

Bhebe, N. *Christianity and Traditional Religion in Western Zimbabwe 1859-1923.* London: Longman, 1977.

"Missionary Activity among the Ndebele and Kalanga—A Survey". J. A. Dachs, (ed.). *Christianity South of the Zambezi. Vol. I.* Gweru: Mambo Press, 1973.

Blood, A. G. *History of the Universities Mission to Central Africa, 1859-1901.* Vol. II, London: UMCA, 1897, revised in 1956.

Bosch, D. J. *Translating Mission: Paradigm Shift in Theology of Mission.* American Society of Mission No. 16. Maryknoll, New York: Orbis Books, 1991.

Bourdillion, M. F. C. *Where are the Ancestors? Changing Culture in Zimbabwe.* Harare: University of Zimbabwe Publications, 1993.

. *The Shona Peoples: An Ethnography of the Contemporary Shona, with special Reference to their Religion (Revised Edition).* Gweru: Mambo Press, 1987.

Bria, I. *The Liturgy after the Liturgy.Mission and Witness from an Orthodox Perspective.* Geneva: World Council of Churches Publications (WCC), 1996.

Bujo, B. *African Theology in its Social Context.* Translated by John O'Donahue. Nairobi: St. Paul Publications Africa, 1992.

Burrough, J. P. *Diocese of Mashonaland, Pastoral Regulations, Instructions and Counsel, issued by the Bishop of Mashonaland (Harare) for the Guidance of the Clergy in their Pastoral Responsibilities and Priestly Obligations.* Salisbury (Harare): Cannon Press, May 1976.

Busia, A. K. *The Political Position of the Chief in the Modern Political System of Ashant: A Study of the Influence of Contemporary*

*Social Changes on the Ashanti Political Institutions*. London: Frank Cass, 1968.

Carey, W. *Enquiry into the Obligations of Christians to use Means for the Conversion of the Heathens.* London: Baptist Missionary Society, 1792.

Cassidy, R. J. *Jesus, Politics and Society: A Study of Luke's Gospel*. New York, Maryknoll: Orbis Books, 1978.

Chigwedere, A. S. *From Mutapa to Rhodes 1000 to 1890 AD.* London: Basingstoke and Harare: Macmillan Publishers Ltd, 1980.

Cobb, J. B. *Living Options in Protestant Theology*. Philadelphia: Westminister Press, 1962.

*Christ in a Pluralistic Age.* Philadelphia: Westminster Press, 1975.

Cobb Jr., J. B. "The Religions." R. King, P. Hodgson, (eds.) (Forward by S. Sykes), *Christian Theology. An Introduction to its Traditions and Tasks.* London: SPCK, 1983.

Cone, J.H. *A Black Theology of Liberation.* 2nd. ed. Maryknoll, New York: Orbis Books, 1986.

*Black Theology and Black Power.* New York: Seabury, 1969.

Congar, Y. M. J. *I Believe in the Holy Spirit*. London: Geoffrey Chapman, 1983.

Crollius, A. R. (S.J.) "Inculturation: Newness and On-going Process" in J. M. Waliggo, A. R. Crollius, (S.J.) T. Nkeramihigo, (S.J.) J. Mutiso-Mbinda, (eds.), *Inculturation: Its Meaning and Urgency.* Kampala, Uganda: St. Paul Publication, Africa, 1986.

Cullman, O. *The Christology of the New Testament*. London: SCM Press, 1959.

Daneel, M. L. *God of the Matopo Hills: An Essay on the Mwari Cult in Rhodesia*. The Hague, Paris: Mounton & Co, 1970.

Dewey, M. *The Messengers: A Concise History of the United Society for the Propagation of the Gospel.* London and Oxford: A. R. Mowbray & Co. Ltd, 1975.

Dickson, K. *Theology in Africa*. London: Darton, Longman and Todd, New York, Maryknoll: Orbis Books, 1984.

Dunn, J. D. G. *Unity and Diversity in the New Testament.* An Inquiry into the Character of Earliest Christianity. London: SCM Press Ltd, 1977.

*Christology in Making*. London: SCM Press, 1980.

Durkheim, E. *The Elementary Forms of Religious Life*. London: George Allen & Unwin Ltd, 1976.

Evans, J. T. *The Church in Southern Rhodesia.* London: SPG, SPCK, 1945.

Farrant, J. *Mashonaland Martyr—Bernard Mizeki and the Pioneer Church.* Oxford: Oxford University Press, 1974.

Freudenberger, C.D. *Global Dust Bowl.* Minneapolis: Fortress Press, 1990.

Fiorenza, E.S. *In Memory of Her: A Feminist Theological Reconstruction of Christian Origins.* London: SCM Press, 1983.

Fitzmyer (S.J), J.A. "Pauline Theology." R.E. Brown, S.S., J.A. Fitzmyer, S.J., R.E. Murphy, O, Carm, (eds.), *The Jerome Biblical Commentary. Volume 1 the Old Testament. Volume 2 the New Testament and Topical Articles.* London: Chapman Publishers, 1968. pp. 800-827.

Gelfand, M. "Medicine and the Christian Missions in Rhodesia 1857-1930". J. A. Dachs, (ed.). *Christianity South of the Zambezi*. Vol. I. Gweru: Mambo Press, 1973.

Gibbon, G. *Paget of Rhodesia: A Memoir of Edward, fifth Bishop of Mashonaland*. Bulawayo: Books of Rhodesia, 1973.

Goodsell, F. F. *You shall be Witness: American Board of Commissioners for Foreign Missions.* Boston (Massachussets), 1959.

Gutierrez, G. *(Theologia de la liberacion, Perspectivas). A Theology of Liberation: History, Politics and Salvation.* (Translated and edited by Sister Caridad Inda and John Eagleson). London: SCM Press, 1974.

Hatendi, R. P. "Shona Marriage and the Christian Church." J. A. Dachs (ed.), *Christianity South of the Zambezi. Vol 1.* Gweru: Mambo Press, 1973.

Hick, J. *Problems of Religious Pluralism.* London: Macmillan, 1985.

Imasogie, O. *Guidelines for Christian Theology in Africa.* Achimota: Africa Christian Press, 1983.

John Paul II. "*African Addresses.*" Bologna: Editrice Missionaria Italiana. 1981, pp. 164-182.

Jones, J.I. "The Epistle to the Colossians." F. Davidson (ed.), A.M. Stibbs, E.F. Kevan (Assistant eds.), *The New Bible Commentary.* London: The Inter-Varsity Fellowship, 1968. pp. 1043-1051.

Jones, A. (ed.), *The Gospel According to Saint John, The Jerusalem Bible.* London: Darton, Longman & Todd, 1966.

Kabasele, F. "Christ as Chief". in R. J. Schreiter, (ed.), *Faces Of Jesus Christ in Africa. Faith and Cultures Series.* New York, Maryknoll: Orbis Books, 1991.

"Christ as Ancestor and Elder Brother" in R. J. Schreiter, (ed.), *Faces Of Jesus Christ in Africa. Faith and Cultures Series.* New York, Maryknoll: Orbis Books, 1991.

Kasper, W. *An Introduction to Christian Faith.* New York: Paulist, 1980.

*Jesus the Christ.* Exeter: Burns & Oates, 1976.

Kato, B. H. *Theological Pitfalls in Africa.* Kenya, Kisumu: Evangelical Publishing House, 1975.

Kirwen, M. C. *The Missionary and Diviner: Contending Theologies of Christian and African Religions.* New York, Maryknoll: Orbis Books, 1987.

Kittel, G. "*Logos*" in Kittel, G. (ed.), *(Theologisches Wortherbuch zum). Theological Dictionary of the New Testament.* (Translator and editor G.W. Bromily), Vol.4, Grand Rapids, Michigan: Eerdmans, 1964-1976, pp, 69-143. 10 Volumes. Volumes 1-4 edited by G. Kittel, Volumes 5-9 edited by G. Friedrick, Volume 10 compiled by R.E. Pitkin.

Knight-Bruce, G. W. H. *Memories of Mashonaland.* New York, London: Edward Arnold Publisher to the India Office, 1895.

*Memoirs of Mashonaland.* Rhodesiana Reprint Library. Vol. 13, Fascimile Reproduction of the 1895 Edition. Bulawayo: Books of Rhodesia Publishing Co. (Pvt) Ltd. 1953.

Knitter, P.F. *No Other Name? A Critical Survey of Christian Attitudes toward the World Religions.* Maryknoll, New York: Orbis Books, 1985.

Kolie, C. "Jesus as Healer" in R. J. Schreiter, (ed.), *Faces of Jesus Christ in Africa. Faith and Cultures Series.* New York, Maryknoll: Orbis Books, 1991.

Krieger, D.J. *The New Universalism: Foundations for a Global Theology*. Faith Meet Faith Series. Maryknoll, New York: Orbis Books, 1991.

Langham-Carter, R. R. *Knight-Bruce-First Bishop and Founder of the Anglican Church in Rhodesia.* Salisbury (Harare): Christchurch, Borrowdale, 1975.

Lepsley, M. *Neutrality or Co-Option? Anglican Church and State from 1964 until the Independence of Zimbabwe.* Gweru: Mambo Press, 1986.

Lindsell, H. *A Christian Philosophy of Missions.* Wheaton, Illinois: Van Kampen Press, 1949.

Macquarrie, J. *Principles of Christian Theology.* (Revised Edition). London: SCM Press Ltd, 1966.

McGarry, C. (S.J.). *Preface.* Hekima College, Jesuit School of Theology. Nairobi, 1982, pp. 7-13.

Magesa, L. "Christ the Liberator in Africa Today" in Mugambi, J. N. K. Magesa, L. (eds.), *Jesus in African Christianity: Experimentation and Diversity in African Christology.* Nairobi Initiative Publishers, 1989.

Maimela, S. S. "Jesus Christ: The Liberator and Hope of Oppressed Africa" in J. S. Pobee, (ed.), *Exploring Afro-Christology.* Frankfurt am Main, Bern, New York, Paris: Peter Lang, 1992.

Maspero, I. M. *The Church of the Province of Central Africa (Anglican), Diocese of Mashonaland (Harare). The Acts of the Diocese of Mashonaland (Harare ) Including the Diocesan Regulations.* Harare: 1st August 1974.

McBrien, R. *Catholicism.* Minneapolis: Winston Press, 1981.

Mofekeng, T. A. *The Crucified among the Cross Bearers: Towards a Black Christology.* Kampen: Uitgeversmaatseheppy, 1983.

Moltmann, J. *Theology Today: Two Contributions Towards Making Theology Present.* London: SCM Press, 1988; Philadelphia: Trinity Press International, 1988.

Mothlabe, M. (ed.), *Essays on Black Theology.* Johannesburg: SCM Press, 1972.

Mugambi, J. N. K. "Christological Paradigms in African Christianity" in J. N. K. Mugambi, L. Magesa, (eds.), *African*

*Christian Theology, an Introduction.* Nairobi: Heinemann, Kenya Ltd, 1989.

Muguez Bonino, J. *Doing Theology in a Revolutionary Situation.* Philadelphia: Fortress Press, 1975. (1980 Reprint).

Mukonyora, I. J. L. Cox, F. J. Verstraelen, (eds.), *"Rewriting" the Bible: The Real Issues: Perspectives from within Biblical and Religious Studies in Zimbabwe.* Gweru: Mambo Press, 1993.

Mutiso-Mbinda, J. "Inculturation: Challenge to the African Local Church," in J. M. Waliggo, A. R. Crollius, (S.J.) T. Nkeramihigo, (S.J.) J. Mutiso-Mbinda, (eds.*), Inculturation: Its Meaning and Urgency.* Kampala: St. Paul Publications, 1986.

. "Anthropology and the Paschal Mystery," *Spearhead,* No. 59. Eldoret, Kenya: Gaba Publications, 1979.

Mutswairo, S. M. *Mapondera: Soldier of Zimbabwe*. Harare: Longman Zimbabwe (Pvt.) Ltd, 1983.

Muzorewa, G. H. *An African Theology of Mission. Studies in the History of Missions.* Vol. 5. New York: Lewiston, Edwin Mellen Press, 1990.

Nasimuyu-Wasike, A. "Christology and an African Woman's Experience" in J. N. K. Mugambi, L. Magesa, (eds.), *Jesus in African Christianity. Experimentation and Diversity in African Christology.* Nairobi: Initiative Publishers, 1989.

Nazir-Ali, M. *Mission and Dialogue Proclaiming the Gospel Afresh in Every Age.* London: SPCK, 1995.

Niebuhr, H. R. *Christ and Culture.* New York, Evanston and London: Harper & Row Publishers, 1951.

Nthamburi, Z. "Christ as seen by an African: A Christological Quest," in J. N. K. Mugambi, L. Magesa, (eds.*), Jesus in African Christianity: Experimentation and Diversity in African Christology.* Nairobi: Initiative Publishers, 1989.

Nyamiti, C. *Christ as Our Ancestor. Christology from an African Perspective: Mambo Occasional Papers, Missio-Pastoral Series No. 11.* Gweru: Mambo Press, 1984.

"African Christologies Today" in J. N. K. Mugambi, L. Magesa, (eds.), *Jesus in African Christianity: Experimentation and Diversity in African Christology.* Nairobi: Initiative Publishers, 1989.

"African Christologies Today" in R. J. Schreiter, (ed.), *Faces of Jesus Christ in Africa: Faith and Cultures Series.* New York, Maryknoll: Orbis Books, 1991.

Obaje, Y. A. "Theocentric Christologies" in J. S. Pobee, (ed.), *Exploring Afro-Christology.* Frankfurt Am Main, Bern, New York, Paris: Peter Lang, 1992.

Oepke, A. "Dia" in Kittel, G. (ed.), G.W. Bromily (Translator and editor), 10 Volumes. Volumes 1-4 edited by G. Kittle, Volumes 5-9 edited by G. Friedrick, Volume 10 compiled by R.E. Pitkin. *(Theologisches Wortherbuch zum ). Theological Dictionary of the New Testament.* Vol.2, Grand Rapids, Michigan: Eerdman, 1964-1976, pp, 65-70.

Oliver, R. *The Missionary Factor in East Africa.* London: Longman, 1970.

*An Outline History of the United Society for the Propagation of the Gospel in CMC/USPG Consultation.* 8-10 February, 1973.

Pannenberg, W. *(Grundfragen Systematischer Theologie). Basic Questions in Theology.* (Translated by G. H. Kehm) London: SCM Press, 1970, 1971.

. *The Theology of Wolfhart Pannenberg.* Postcript by Wolfhart Pannenberg. London: SCM Press, 1974.

Pannikar, R. *The Unknown Christ of Hinduism. Towards an Ecumenical Christophany.* (Revised and Enlarged Edition). Maryknoll, New York: Orbis Books, 1981.

Parrinder, E.G. *African Traditional Religion.* London: Sheldon Press, 1976.

Pascoe, C. F. *Two Hundred Years of the SPG: An Historical Account of the Society for the Propagation of the Gospel to Foreign Parts 1701-1900.* London: SPG, 1901.

Peaden, W. R. *The Development of Missionary Attitudes to the Shona Culture 1890-1923.* R. S. Roberts, (ed.), Central African Historical Association, Local Series 27. Salisbury (Harare): A. W. Bardwell & Co. (Pvt) Ltd, 1970.

Penoukou, E. J. "Christology in the Village" in R. J. Schreiter, (ed.), *Faces of Jesus Christ in Africa. Faith and Cultures Series.* New York, Maryknoll: Orbis Books, 1991.

Pobee, J. S. *Toward an African Theology.* Abingdon/Nashville, Tennessee: Parthenon Press, 1979.

Price, C.P., Weil, L. *Liturgy for Living. The Church's Teaching Series. With the Assistance of a Group of Editorial Advisors under the Direction of the Church's Teaching Series Committee.* New York: The Seabury Press, 1979.

Quinn, J. R. Sacramental in T. C. O'Brien, et al, (eds). *New Catholic Encyclopedia* Vol. 12. (Supplement 17). Washington D.C: Catholic University of America Press, 1981, pp. 790-92.

Rahner, K. *Theologians Today: An Introductory Selection from the Writings of one of Today's Leading Roman Catholic Theologians.* M.Redfern (ed.) London, New York: Sheed & Ward Ltd, 1972.

Rahner, K. *(Schriften Zur Theologie).Theological Investigations.* London: Darton, Longman & Todd, 1974.

Rattray, R. S. *Ashanti.* London, 1923.

Richardson, A. *The Political Christ.* London SCM Press, 1973.

Robinson, J. A. T. *Truth is Two-Eyed.* London: SCM Press, 1979.

Sanneh, L. *Translating the Message: The Missionary Impact on Culture. American Society of Missiology. Series No 13.* New York, Maryknoll: Orbis Books, 1991.

Sanon, A. T. "Jesus, Master of Initiation" in R. J. Schreiter, (ed.), *Faces of Jesus Christ in Africa. Faith and Cultures Series.* Maryknoll, New York: Orbis Books, 1991.

Sawyerr, H. *Creative Evangelism: Toward a New Christian Encounter with Africa.* London: 1968.

Schleiermacher, F.S.D. *(Der Christliche Glaube nach den Grundsazen der evangelischen Kirche). The Christian Faith.* Berlin: Gruyter, 1960.

Schillebeeckx, E.C.F. *(Jezus: het verhaal van een levende). Jesus: An Experiment in Christology.* London: Collins, 1983.

*Christ: The Christian Experience in the Modern World.* London: SCM Press Ltd, 1977.

*God among us: The Gospel Proclaimed.* London: SCM Press Ltd, 1983.

Segundo, J.L. *(Liberation de la teologia). Liberation Theology.* (Translated by J. Drury). Maryknoll, New York: Orbis Books, 1976.

Schreiter, R. J. (ed.), *Faces of Jesus Christ in Africa: Faith and Cultures Series.* New York, Maryknoll: Orbis Books, 1991.

Shorter, A. *African Culture and the Christian Church: An Introduction to Social and Pastoral Anthropology.* New York, Maryknoll: Orbis Books, 1977.

Skelton, K. A. *Bishop of Ian Smith's Rhodesia.* Gweru: Mambo Press, 1986.

Smith, N. *The Presbyterian Church of Ghana, 1835-1960. A Young Church in a Changing Society.* Accra, 1966.

Smith, E. W. (ed.), *African Ideas of God.* London: Edinburgh House, 1950.

Snook, L.E. *The Anonymous Christ: Jesus as Saviour in Modern Theology.* Minneapolis: Augsbury Publishing House, 1986.

Sobrino, J. *(Christologia desde America latina: Esbozo a partir del seguimiento del Jesus historico). Christology at the Crossroads: A Latin American Approach.* (Translated by (J. Drury). London: SCM Press, 1978. (Reprint 1987).

Stauffer, E. "Ego" in Kittel, G. (ed.), (*Theologisches Wortherbuch zum). Theological Dictionary of the New Testament.* Translator and editor G.W. Bromily, Vol.2, Grand Rapids, Michigan: Eerdmans, 1964-1976, pp. 343-362.

Steel, M. "With Hope Unconquered and Unconquerable: Arthur Shearley Cripps, 1869-1952" in O. T. Ranger, J. C. Weller, (eds.). *Themes in the Christian History of Central Africa.* London, Nairobi, Ibadan, Lusaka: Heinemann, 1975.

Steere, D. V. *God's Irregular-Arthur Shearley Cripps.* London: SPCK, 1973.

Thompson, H. P. *Into all Lands: The History for the Propagation of the Gospel in Foreign Parts, 1701-1950.* London: SPCK, 1951.

Tienou, T. *The Theological Task of the Church in Africa.* Nigeria, Iobaja: Africa Christian Press, 1982.

Tillich, P. *Systematic Theology.* London: Nisbert, 1953.

Verstraelen, F. J. (General Editor), A. Camps, L. A. Hoedemaker, M. R. Spindler, (eds.), *Missiology: An Ecumenical Introduction. Text and Contexts of Global Christianity.* Grand Rapids, Michigan: William B. Eerdmans Publishing Company, 1995.

"The Christian Bible and African Cultural and Religious Realities" in I.

Mukonyora, J. L. Cox, F. J. Verstraelen, (eds.), *Rewriting the Bible: The Real Issues: Perspectives from within Biblical and Religious Studies in Zimbabwe.* Gweru: Mambo Press, 1993.

Wachege, N. P. *Jesus Christ Our* Muthamaki *(Ideal Elder: An African Christological Study based on the* Agikuyu *Understanding of Elder.* Nairobi: Phoenix Publishers Ltd, 1992.

Waliggo, J. M. "African Christology in a Situation of Suffering" in J. N. K. Mugambi, L. Magesa, (eds.), *Jesus in African Christianity. Experimentation and Diversity in African Christology.* Nairobi: Initiative Publishers, 1989.

Waliggo, J.M., Roest Crollius, A., Nkéramihigo, T., Mutiso-Mbinda, J. *Inculturation: Its Meaning and Urgency.* Kampala: St. Paul Publications, 1986.

Walls, A. F. "Outposts of Empire" in T. Dowely, (ed*.), A Lion Handbook. The History of Christianity.* Bristol: Lion Publishing Reprinted, 1977.

"British Missions" in T. Christensen, W. R. Hutchinson, (eds*.). Missionary Ideologies in the Imperialist Era: 1880-1920. Papers from the Durham Consultation,* 1981. (Second Print). London: Aros, 1982.

"Rumination on Rainmaking: The Transmission and Receipt of Religious Expertise in Africa" in J. C. Stone, (ed.), *Experts in Africa.* Aberdeen: University African Study Group, 1980.

Waruta, D. W. "Who is Jesus Christ for African Today? Priest, Prophet, Potentate" in J. N. K. Mugambi, L. Magesa, (eds*.), Jesus in African Christianity: Experimentation and Diversity in African Christology.* Nairobi: Initiative Publishers, 1989.

Whitehead, A.N. *Science and the World.* Cambridge: Cambridge University Press, 1946.

Wilmore, G. S., Cone, J. H. (eds.), *Black Theology a Documentary History, 1966-1979.* Maryknoll, New York: Orbis Books, 1979.

Winzen, D. *Symbols of Christ.* London: Longmans Green & Co, 1955.

**Journals**

Boesak, A. "Civil Religion and the Black Community." *Journal of Theology for Southern Africa.* No. 19, June 1977, pp. 29-43.

Buthelezi, M. "Violence and the Cross in South Africa Today." *Journal of Theology for Southern Africa.* No. 29, December 1979, pp. 176-77.

Dandala, H. M. "SACLA: A Prophetic Event for South Africa." *Journal of Theology for Southern Africa.* No. 3, March 1980, pp. 54-68.

Dufour, L. "Jesus' Understanding of Death." *Theology Digest*, 24(3), 1976, pp. 193-300.

Dupuis, J. "The Christological Debate in the Context of Religious Plurality." J. Dupuis, (ed.), *Current Dialogue: World Council of Churches Dialogue with People of Living Faiths.* January 1991, pp. 13-29.

Fashole-Luke, E. "Christianity and Islam in Freetown." *The Sierra-Leone Bulletin of Religion,* IX, 1, 1967, pp. 10-11.

Fortune, G. "*Who was Mwari?*" *Rhodesian History: The Journal of the Central Africa Historical Association,* Vol. 4, 1973, pp. 1-20.

Goba, B. "Doing Theology in South Africa: A Black Christian Perspective. An Invitation to the Church to be Relevant." *Journal of Theology for Southern Africa,* No. 31, June 1980, pp. 27-33.

Goosen, C. J., I. S. Masola, P. Makhubu, "Cultural Backgrounds and Religious Education." *Journal of Theology for Southern Africa.* No. 33, December 1980, pp. 78-94.

Gwembe, E. (S.J.), "The Traditional Religion." *Crossroads.* No. 141, April 1994, pp. 13-15.

John Paul II, "Letter to Cardinal Agostino Casaroli, Secretary of State, 20th May 1982." *L'Osservatore Romano,* 28 June, 1982, pp. 7-8.

"Addressing First Plenary Assembly of SECAM." Kampala, 31st July, 1969, *AFER,* Vol. XI, No. 4, 1969, pp. 391-417.

Junod, H.P. "The Ethnological Situation in Portuguese East Africa." *Bantu Studies.* Vol.10, 1936, pp. 296-7.

Middleton, J. "One Hundred and Fifty Years of Christianity in a Ghanaian Town." *Africa,* Vol. 53, 1983, pp. 2-9.

Moyo, A. M. "The Quest for African Christian Theology and the Problem of Relationship between Faith and Culture-The Hermeneutical Perspective." *African Theological Journal,* Vol. 12, No. 2, 1983, p. 97.

"We Must be Examples of Love and Teachers after the Heart of Christ".

*L'Obsservatore Romano.* 29 th May, 1989. pp. 211-212.

Ranger, T.O. "The Meaning of *Mwari.*" *Rhodesian History: The Journal of the Central Africa Historical Association.* Vol. 5, 1974, pp. 5-17.

Roberts, R. S. "A New Series on Culture and Society in Central Africa." *Zambeziana,* Vol. IX, 1980, pp. 492-494.

Samartha, S. J. "In Search of a Revised Christology: A Response to Paul F. Knitter." *Current Dialogue: World Council of Churches Dialogue with People of Living Faiths,* 21st December, 1991, p. 33.

Van der Merwe, W. J. "The Shona Idea of God." *NADA,* Vol.34, 1957, p. 42.

Verstraelen, F. J. "Patterns of Missionary and Ecumenical Relationships in Zimbabwe." *Journal of Missiological and Ecumenical Research,* Vol. 24, No. 3, October 1995, pp. 189-221.

Von Sicard, H. "The Origin of Some Tribes in the Belingwe Reserve." *NADA,* Vol. 29, 1952, p. 55.

**Magazines and Newspapers**

Makoni Mission, St. Faith's Rusape. *Mashonaland Quarterly Paper, 1909,* 68, 22.

Mtobi, H. "Letters for the Children." *Mashonaland Quarterly Paper, 1900, 18, 3.*

Muradzikwa, H. T. "Guy Clutton-Brock Buried." *The Herald-Incorporating the Nation,* 12 August, 1995, p. 1, Cols. 1-4.

"Hwedza Member of Parliament (MP) Pressed to withdraw Motion". *The Herald-Incorporating the Nation.* 21 July, 1995, p.7, Cols. 2-3.

Owen, A. D. "The White Man's Burden as Affecting Medical Man." *Mashonaland Quarterly Paper,* 1901, 35, 16.

*The Missionary Magazine and Chronicle,* XXVIII, 1864.

*The Zambezi Record,* II, 15 January, 1902.

Peta, B. "Hatendi Quits Electoral Body." *The Financial Gazette,* 3-9 February 2000, P.1.

**Unpublished Sources**

Alderson, C. W. "The Diocesan Synod held at St. Michael's Harari (Mbare, Runyararo) under the Chairmanship of Bishop Cecil Alderson." Salisbury (Harare): St. Michael's Mbare, 3 May 1962.

Bakare, S. "Report of the Idolatry and Evangelism Commission. The Anglican Church, the Diocese of Harare." Harare: St. Mary's and All Saints Cathedral Hall, 7-8 May 1994, pp. 1-19.

Bourdillion, M. F. C. "Talk at the Anglican Cathedral: Some Background Information necessary for Dialogue with African Traditional Religion." Delivered to the Idol Commission, Anglican Diocese of Harare, May 1992. Harare: St. Mary and All Saint's Cathedral Hall, 5 October, 1992.

Braund, G. "USPG Travelling Missioner 1968-73." *Globespell, USPG's Tabloid Review of 1973*, p. 3

Broedrick, G. E. P. "History of the Diocese of Southern Rhodesia, Formerly Diocese of Mashonaland, 1874-1952." Salisbury (Harare): St. Mary and All Saint's Cathedral Hall, September 1953.

Dankwa, A. "Tradition and Christianity at Cross-roads." A Paper Presented at the Triennial Consultation Meeting of the Presbyterian Church, Aburi, September, 1982.

Gaul, W. T. "Bishop Gaul's Charge: Resolutions Passed at the 1903 Synod, The Church of the Province of South Africa, Diocese of Mashonaland (Zimbabwe)." Salisbury (Harare), 19 April 1903.

Gundani, P. "The Second Vatican Council and Beyond: A Study of the Transformation Process, Power, Transfer and Sharing in the Roman Catholic Church in Zimbabwe 1965-85." D Phil Thesis. Harare: University of Zimbabwe, 1994.

Hatendi, R. P. "Memorandum to all licensed Clergymen and Ordinands in Training." Diocese of Harare, 17 January, 1990.

"*AD CLERUM* of offences to all licensed Clergymen." Diocese of Harare, 6 October, 1990.

"Memorandum to all Clergy Incumbents, Churchwardens, and Chapel Wardens." Diocese of Harare, 19 December, 1990.

"Memorandum to all licensed Priests, all Chairmen of *Wabvuwi*, and Chaplains on the Decade of Evangelism." Diocese of Harare, 4 February, 1991.

"Memorandum on Healing and Deliverance from the Demonic Powers to all licensed Clergymen and all Heads of Diocesan Institutions." Diocese of Harare, 16 August, 1991.

"Memorandum on Ancestor Worship and Consulting *n'angas* to all members of the Synod and *Wabvuwi.*" Diocese of Harare, 24 August, 1992.

"Memorandum on Cross-Cultural Evangelism to all licensed Clergymen and Churchwardens." Diocese of Harare, 20 October, 1992.

"Agenda and Reports." Church of the Province of Central Africa, Diocese of Harare Synod, 1992. 12-13 September, 1992.

"The Bishop's Charge." Fifty Fifth Session of the Harare Diocesan Synod, 7-8 May, 1994.

"Christmas Message, 1992: Cross-Cultural Evangelism." Diocese of Harare, 20 October, 1992.

Machoko, C. G., W. K. Simbabure. "Report of the Idolatry and Evangelism Commission." Synod of the Anglican Diocese of Harare, 12-13 September, 1992.

______. "A Report for the Consideration of the Synod of the Anglican Diocese of Harare, 7th-8th May 1994." St. Mary's and All Saints Cathedral Hall, 14 April, 1994.

Shoko, T. "Health and Well Being: A Phenomenological Quest for the Essence of the Karanga Religion." D. Phil. Thesis. Harare: University of Zimbabwe, 1993.

Wernberg, G. S. "Idolatry and Evangelism." Chandra, D. (Diocesan Secretary) (ed.). Diocese of Harare, 55th Session of the Harare Diocesan Synod 7-8 May, 1994, Summary of Proceedings. Harare: St. Mary's and All Saints Cathedral Hall, 18 May, 1994.

# INDEX

# ENDNOTES

## *Introduction*

1 R. McBrien. *Catholicism*. Minneapolis: Winston Press, 1981, p. 605.

2 P. J. O. Tillich, *Systematic Theology*. London: Nisbert, 1953, p. 193.

3 K. Barth, (*Einfuhrung in die evangelische Theologie*). *Evangelical Theology: An Introduction.* Translated by G. Foley. New York: Holt, 1963, p. 237.

4 J. C. Beker, “Colossians,” J.L. Mays, (ed.), J Blenkinsopp, J.D. Levenson, W.A. Meeks, C.A. Newsom, D.L. Petersen, (associate editors), *Harper's Bible Commentary.* San Francisco, New York, Washington: Harper & Row, Publishers, 1988, pp. 1227-1228.

5 J. A. Fitzmyer, S. J.” Pauline Theology”. R.E. Brown, S.S., J.A Fitzmyer, S.J., R.E.Murphy, O. Carm. (eds.) *The Jerome Biblical Commentary.* Volume 1, the Old Testament. Volume 2, The New Testament and Topical articles. London: Geoffrey Chapman Publishers, 1968, p. 812.

6 J. I. Jones, “The Epistle to the Colossians”. F. Davidson,(ed.), *The New Bible Commentary*. London: The Intervarsity Fellowship, 1968, PP. 1045-1051.

7 E. Stauffer, "Ego". G. Kittel, (ed.), G.W. Bromiley, Translator and editor, *The Theological Dictionary of the New Testament,* Volume 2, Grand Rapids, Michigan: W M. B Eerdmans Publishing Company, 1964, p. 349.

8 Ibid, p.350.

9 A. Oepke, *Dia.* G. Kittel, (ed.), p. 67.

10 G. Kittel, *Logos.* G. Kittel, (ed.), pp. 106-107.

11 K. Rahner, (*Schrifren Zur Theologie). Theological Investigations*. London: Darton, Longman & Todd, 1974, p. 177.

12 W. Pannenberg, *(Grundfragen Systematischer Theologie). Basic Questions in Theology.* (Translated by George H. Kehm). London: SCM Press, 1970, 1971, p. 266.

13 J. Moltmann, *Theology Today: Two Contributions Towards Making Theology Present.* London: SCM Press, Philadelphia: Trinity Press International, 1988, p. 305.

14 W. Kasper, *An Introduction To Christian Faith.* New York, Paulist 1980, pp. 15-16.

15 J.B. Cobb, J.R. Cobb, "The Religions". R. King, P. Hodson, (eds) Foreword by S. Sykes, *Christian Theology. An Introduction to Its Traditions and Tasks.* London: SPCK, 1983, p.319.

16 E.C.F. Schillebeeckx, *(Jezus: het verhaal van een levende). Jesus An Experiment In Christology.* London Collins, p. 237.

17 J. Hick, *Problems of Religious Pluralism*. London: Macmillian, 1985, p. 63.

18 R. Panikkar, *The Unknown Christ Of Hinduism: Towards an*

*Ecumenical Christophany.* (Revised and Enlarged Edition). Maryknoll, New York: Orbis Books, 1981, p. 169.

19 P. F. Knitter, *No other Name? A Critical Survey of Christian Attitudes toward the World Religions.* Maryknoll, NewYork, Orbis Books, 1985, p. 19.

20 M.F.C. Bourdillion, *Where are The Ancestors? Changing Culture in Zimbabwe*. Harare: University of Zimbabwe Publications, 1993, p.39.

21 A.S. Chigwedere, *From Mutapa to Rhodes 1000 to 1890 A D.* London: Basingstoke and Harare: Macmillian Publishers Ltd. 1980, p.20.

22 D.N.D Beach, *The Shona and Zimbabwe 900-185: An Outline of Shona History.* Repr. Gweru: Mambo Press, 1984, pp. 247-253.

23 J.S. Pobee, *Toward an African Theology.* Abingdon/ Nashville, Tennessee: Parthenon Press, 1979, p. 66.

24 M. Dewey, *The Messengers; A Concise History of The United Society For The Propagation Of The Gospel.* London and Oxford: A.R. Mowbray & Co. Ltd. 1975, pp. 115-116.

25 B. H. Kato, *Theological Pitfalls in Africa.* Kenya, Kisumu, Evangelical Publishing House, 1975, 183; and P.T. Tienou, *The Theological Task of the Church In Africa*. Nigeria, Lobaya: Africa Christian Press, 1982, p.25.

26 S.J. Samartha, "In search of a Revised Christology. A Response To Paul F. Knitter—Pneumatology " J. Dupuis, (ed.) *Current Dialogue.* 21 December 1991. World Council of Churches. Dialogue with People of Living Faiths. Geneva. 1991, p.34.

# CHAPTER 1

1. M. C. Kirwen, *The Missionary And Diviner: Contending Theologies Of Christian And African Religions.* Maryknoll, New York: Orbis Books, 1987, p. 28.

2. M. F. C. Bourdillion, *The Shona Peoples: An Ethnography of the Contemporary Shona, With Special Reference To Their Religion.* Revised Edition. Gweru: Mambo Press, 1987, p. 277.

3. F. J. Verstraelen, "The Christian Bible and African Cultural and Religious Realities". I. Mukonyora, J. L. Cox, (eds.), F. J. Verstraelen (coordinator), *"Rewriting" The Bible: The Real Issues. Perspectives From Within Biblical and Religious Studies In Zimbabwe. Religious and Theological Studies Series I.* Gweru: Mambo Press, 1993, p. 243.

4. D. P. Abraham, "The Role of Chaminuka and the *Mhondoro* Cults in Shona Political History," In Stokes and Brown (eds.), *The Zambezian Past: Studies In Central African History.* Manchester, 1966, p. 33.

5. M. L. Daneel, *The God of the Matopos Hills:. An Essay on the Mwari Cult in Rhodesia.* The Hague, Paris: Mounton & Co., 1970, p. 36.

6. T.O. Ranger, "The Meaning of Mwari." R.S. Roberts, P.R. Warhurst, (eds.) *Rhodesian History: The Journal of the Central Africa Historical Association.* Vol.5, pp. 5-17.

7. W.J. Van der Merwe, "The Shona Idea of God." *NADA*. Vol.34, Salisbury, Rhodesia, 1957, p.42.

8. H. Von Sicard, "The Origin of Some Tribes in the Belingwe Reserve." NADA. Vol. 29, 1952, p.55.

9. G. Fortune, "Who was Mwari?" R.S. Roberts, P.R.Warhurst, (eds.) *Rhodesian History: The Journal of the Central African Historical Association*, Vol. 4, 1973, pp. 1-20.

10. A. S. Chigwedere, From *Mutapa to Rhodes 1000 To 1890 AD.* London, Basingstoke and Harare: Macmillan Publishers, Ltd, 1980, p. 63.

11. Ibid., p. 63.

12. Ibid., p. 64.

13. Ibid., p.145.

14. E. Aplers. *Aspects of Central African History*. T.O. Ranger (ed.), London: Heinemann, 1979. p. 66.

15. A.S. Chigwedere. *From Mutapa to Rhodes 1000 to 1890 AD.* London: Basingstoke and Harare: Macmillan Publishers Ltd. 1980. p. 45.

16. M.L. Daneel. *God of the Matopo Hills: An Essay on the Mwari Cult in Rhodesia*. The Hague, Paris: Mounton & Co. 1970.

17. J.S. Pobee, *Toward an African Theology*. Abingdon/Nashville, Tennessee: Parthenon Press, 1979, p. 23.

18. D.N.D. Beach, *Zimbabwe before 1900*. Gweru: Mambo Press, 1984, p. 18.

19. Ibid., p. 66.

20. S.M. Mutswairo, *Mapondera: Soldier of Zimbabwe*. Harare: Longman Zimbabwe Ltd., 1983, p. 89.

21. E. G. Parrinder, *African Traditional Religion.* London: Sheldon Press, 1976, p. 120.

22. O. Olajubu, A "Social-Cultural Analysis of *Celibacy* Among the Yoruba: Oyo Alafin's Servants as a Case Study." In Olson. C. (ed.), *Celibacy and Religious Traditions.* Oxford: Oxford University Press, 2007, p.278.

23. J.S. Pobee, *Toward an African Theology*. Abingdon/Nashville, Tennessee: Parthenon Press, 1979, p. 67.

24. M. C. Kirwen, *The Missionary And Diviner: Contending Theologies Of Christian And African Religions.* New York, Maryknoll: Orbis Books, 1987, p. 28.

25. E.G. Parrinder, *African Traditional Religion.* London: Sheldon Press, 1976, p.117.

26. A. Shorter, *African Culture and the Christian Church: An Introduction to Social and Pastoral Anthropology.* Maryknoll, New York: Orbis Books, 1977, p. 129.

27. M. C. Kirwen, *The Missionary And Diviner: Contending Theologies Of Christian And African Religions.* Maryknoll, New York: Orbis Books, 1987, p. 28.

28. Ibid., p. 48.

29. E. G. Parrinder, *African Traditional Religion.* London: Sheldon Press, 1976, p. 117.

## CHAPTER 2

1. C. F. Pascoe, *Two Hundred Years Of The SPG: An Historical Account Of The Society For The Propagation Of The Gospel To Foreign Parts. 1701-1900.* London: SPG, 1901, p. 4.

2. Ibid., p. 5.

3. Ibid., p. 9.

4. Ibid., p. 10.

5. Ibid., p. 932.

6. Ibid., p. 15.

7. W. Carey, *Enquiry Into The Obligations Of Christians To Use Means For The Conversion Of The Heathens. London: Baptist Missionary Society, 1792, quoted in: M. Dewey, The Messengers: A Concise History Of The United Society For The Propagation Of The Gospel.* London and Oxford: A. R. Mowbray & Co. Ltd, 1975, p. 9.

8. M. Dewey, *The Messengers: A Concise History Of The United Society For The Propagation Of The Gospel.* London and Oxford: A. R. Mowbray & Co. Ltd, 1975, p. 19.

9. Ibid., p. 84.

10. SPG 1921 Second Supplementary Charter From King George V", quoted in: M. Dewey, *The Messengers: A Concise History Of The United Society For The Propagation Of The Gospel.* London and Oxford: A. R. Mowbray & Co. Ltd, 1975, pp. 96-97.

11. Ibid., p. 95.

12. M. Dewey, The *Messengers: A Concise History Of The United Society For The Propagation Of The Gospel.* London and Oxford: A. R. Mowbray & Co. Ltd, 1975, p. 110.

13. "The Restless Ones, SPG 1957-1958 Report", London: SPG 1957-58. p. 37. quoted in: M. Dewey, *The Messengers: A Concise*

*History Of The United Society For The Propagation Of The Gospel.* London and Oxford: A. R. Mowbray & Co. Ltd, 1975, p. 112.

14. "Part Of A Letter From SPG in 1959 To All English Incumbents", quoted in: M. Dewey, *The Messengers: A Concise History Of The United Society For The Propagation Of The Gospel.* London and Oxford: A. R. Mowbray & Co. Ltd, 1975, p. 112.

15. Ibid., p. 113.

16. M. Dewey, *The Messengers: A Concise History Of The United Society For The Propagation Of The Gospel.* London and Oxford: A. R. Mowbray & Co. Ltd, 1975, pp. 115-116.

17. Ibid. p.121.

18. J. Kingsnorth, "Soon After The Merger Of SPG And UMCA", quoted by Peter Wyld in: "What On Earth?, The USPG 1969 Report", p. 8, quoted in: M. Dewey, *The Messengers: A Concise History Of The United Society For The Propagation Of The Gospel.* London and Oxford: A. R. Mowbray & Co. Ltd, 1975, p. 122.

19. G. Braund, "USPG Travelling Missioner 1968-73", (then overseas Secretary, in Globespell, "USPG's Tabloid Review of 1973", p. 3, quoted in: M. Dewey, *The Messengers: A Concise History Of The United Society For The Propagation Of The Gospel.* London and Oxford: A. R. Mowbray & Co. Ltd, 1975, p. 125.

20. "Dublin Report, Partners in Mission", London: SPCK, 1973, p. 53, quoted in: M. Dewey, *The Messengers: A Concise History Of The United Society For The Propagation Of The Gospel.* London and Oxford: A. R. Mowbray & Co. Ltd, 1975, p. 125.

21. B. Carr, General Secretary Of The All Africa Council Of Churches, quoted by John Kingsnorth in *Network*, June 1974, quoted

in: M. Dewey, *The Messengers: A Concise History Of The United Society For The Propagation Of The Gospel.* London and Oxford: A. R. Mowbray & Co. Ltd, 1975, p. 134.

22. J. Kingsnorth, loc. cit., quoted in: M. Dewey, *The Messengers: A Concise History Of The United Society For The Propagation Of The Gospel.* London and Oxford: A. R. Mowbray & Co. Ltd, 1975, p. 134.

23. Ibid., p.4.

24. A. F. Walls, "British Missions". T. Christensen, W. R. Hutchinson (eds.), *Missionary Ideologies In The Imperialist Era: 1880-1920. Papers from The Durham Consultation 1981.* (Second Printing). London: Aros, 1982, p. 160.

25. Ibid., pp. 160-161.

26. Ibid., p. 164.

27. Herald Reporter, "Guy Clutton-Brock Buried". T. Sithole (ed.) *The Herald—Incorporating The Nation* Harare: Saturday, 12th August, 1995, p. 1, Cols., 1-4.

28. Parliament Reporter, Parliament ZIANA. "Hwedza MP Pressed to Withdraw Motion". T. Sithole (ed.), *The Herald—Incorporating The Nation.* Harare: Friday July 21, 1995, p. 7.

29. L. Sanneh, Translating *The Message: The Missionary Impact On Culture. American Society of Missiology Series No 13.* New York, Maryknoll: Orbis Books, 1991, p. 39.

30. J. M. Waliggo, "Making A Church That Is Truly African." In J. M. Waliggo, A. Roest-Croellius, T. Nkeramihigo, J. Mutiso-Mbinda, (eds.). *Inculturation, Its Meaning and Urgency.* Kampala: St. Paul Publications—Africa, 1986. p. 11.

31. Ibid., p. 22.

32. R. Oliver, *The Missionary Factor In East Africa.* London: Longman, 1970, p. 245, quoted in: L. Sanneh, *Translating The Message: The Missionary Impact On Culture. American Society Of Missiology Series No 13.* New York, Maryknoll: Orbis Books, 1991, pp. 105-106.

33. "An Outline History Of The United Society For The Propagation Of The Gospel in CMC/USPG Consultation", 8-10 February, 1973, (Available from either Society), p. 11, quoted in: M. Dewey, *The Messengers: A Concise History Of The United Society For The Propagation Of The Gospel.* London and Oxford: A. R. Mowbray & Co. Ltd, 1975, p. 2.

34. M. Anderson-Morshead, *History of The Universities' Mission To Central Africa, 1859-1909.* (originally published by UMCA in 1897, revised for the Jubilee, and reissued in 1956 for the centenary as Vol. I. of a three volume history), p. 5, quoted in: M. Dewey, *The Messengers: A Concise History Of The United Society For The Propagation Of The Gospel.* London and Oxford: A. R. Mowbray & Co. Ltd, 1975, p. 56.

35. M. Dewey, The *Messengers: A Concise History Of The United Society For The Propagation Of The Gospel.* London and Oxford: A. R. Mowbray & Co. Ltd, 1975, pp. 54-56.

36. Ibid., p. 58.

37. Ibid., p. 59.

38. Anderson-Morshead, op. cit., pp. 53-54, quoted in: M. Dewey, The *Messengers: A Concise History of The United Society For The Propagation Of The Gospel.* London and Oxford: A. R. Mowbray & Co. Ltd, 1975, p. 60.

39. Anderson-Morshead, op. cit., p. 90, quoted in: M. Dewey, *The Messengers: A Concise History Of The United Society For The Propagation Of The Gospel.* London and Oxford: A. R. Mowbray & Co. Ltd, 1975, p. 63.

40. Anderson-Morshead, op. cit., p. 220, quoted in: M. Dewey, *The Messengers: A Concise History Of The United Society For The Propagation Of The Gospel.* London and Oxford: A. R. Mowbray & Co. Ltd, 1975, p. 64.

41. Anderson-Morshead, op. cit., p. 185, quoted in: M. Dewey, *The Messengers: A Concise History Of The United Society For The Propagation Of The Gospel.* London and Oxford: A. R. Mowbray & Co. Ltd, 1975, p. 65.

42. "SPG 1881 Report," quoted in: M. Dewey, *The Messengers: A Concise History Of The United Society For The Propagation Of The Gospel.* London and Oxford: A. R. Mowbray & Co. Ltd, 1975, pp. 68.

43. A. G. Blood, History Of The UMCA, Vol. II, p. 14, quoted in: M. Dewey, *The Messengers: A Concise History of The United Society For The Propagation Of The Gospel.* London and Oxford: A. R. Mowbray & Co. Ltd, 1975, pp. 88.

44. "Seeds Of Time", SPG 1953 Report, p. 75, quoted in: M. Dewey, *The Messengers: A Concise History of The United Society For The Propagation Of The Gospel.* London and Oxford: A. R. Mowbray & Co. Ltd, 1975, pp. 111.

45. M. Dewey, The *Messengers: A Concise History Of The United Society For The Propagation Of The Gospel.* London and Oxford: A. R. Mowbray & Co. Ltd, 1975, pp. 114.

46. Ibid., p. 112.

47. Ibid., p. 114.

48. Ibid., p. 114.

49. Ibid., p. 117.

## CHAPTER 3

1. E. W. Smith, (ed.), *African Ideas of God.* London: Edinburgh House, 1950, pp. 98-110, quoted in: W. R. Peaden, Missionary *Attitudes to Shona Culture 1890-1923.* R. S. Roberts, (ed.), *The Central African Historical Association Local Series 27.* Salisbury (Harare): A. W. Bardwell & Co. (Pvt) Ltd, 1970, p. 2.

2. G. W. H. Knight-Bruce, *Memories of Mashonaland.* London, New York: Edward Arnold publisher To the India Office, 1895, p. 20, quoted in: J. Farrant, *Mashonaland Martyr—Bernard Mizeki and the Pioneer Church.* Oxford: Oxford University Press, 1974, p. 126.

3. G. W. H. Knight-Bruce, *Memories of Mashonaland.* New York London: Edward Arnold Publisher to The India Office, 1895, p. 43.

4. Ibid., p. 141.

5. "The Missionary Magazine and Chronicle, XXVIII", 1864, p. 284, quoted in: G. Bhebhe, *Christianity and Traditional Religion in Western Zimbabwe 1859-1923.* London: Longman, 1977, p. 43.

6. "The Zambezi Mission Record, II", 15, January 1902, pp. 53-57 quoted in: G. Bhebhe, *Christianity and Traditional Religion in Western Zimbabwe 1859-1923.* London: Longman, 1977, p. 114.

7. W. T. Gaul, "Church of the Province Of South Africa. Diocese of Mashonaland (Zimbabwe)" *Bishop Gaul's Charge at the Synod of*

*1903*. (Resolutions Passed at the 1903 Synod. Salisbury (Harare): 19th April 1903), p. 3.

8. "Wesleyan Methodist Missionary Society S/M South Africa 1906 to 1911, Stanlake's Report of the Bulawayo and Tegwani Circuits", 31st December 1907, quoted in G. Bhebhe, *Christianity and Traditional Religion in Western Zimbabwe 1859-1923.* London: Longman, 1977, p. 111.

9. G. W. H. Knight-Bruce, *Memories of Mashonaland.* New York. London: Edward Arnold Publisher to The India Office, 1895, quoted in: J. Farrant, *Mashonaland Martyr—Bernard Mizeki and the Pioneer Church.* Cape Town, London, Salisbury (Harare): Oxford University Press, 1966, p. 143.

10. R. R. Langham Carter, *Knight-Bruce—First Bishop and Founder of the Anglican Church In Rhodesia.* Salisbury. (Harare): Christchurch, Borrowdale, 27th January, 1975, p. 21.

11. Ibid., p. 24.

12. H. Mtobi in "Letters For The Children 1900, 18, 3. Issued with Mashonaland Quarterly Paper", quoted in: W. R. Peaden, Missionary *Attitudes to Shona Culture 1890-1923.* R. S. Roberts, (ed.), *The Central African Historical Association Local Series 27.* Salisbury (Harare): A. W. Bardwell & Co. (Pvt) Ltd, 1970, pp. 30-31.

13. G. E. P. Broderick, *A History of the Diocese of Southern Rhodesia Formerly Diocese Of Mashonaland 1874-1952.* Salisbury (Harare): Cathedral of St. Mary and All Saints, September 1953, p. 126.

14. W. R. Peaden, Missionary *Attitude to Shona Culture 1890-1923*. R. S. Roberts, (ed.), *The Central African Historical Association Local Series 27*. Salisbury (Harare): A. W. Bardwell & Co. (Pvt) Ltd, 1970, p. 32.

15. "Makoni Mission, St. Faith's, Rusape", *Mashonaland Quarterly Paper,* 1909, 68, 22, quoted in: W. R. Peaden, Missionary *Attitudes to Shona Culture 1890-1923.* R. S. Roberts, (ed.), *The Central African Historical Association Local Series 27.* Salisbury (Harare): A. W. Bardwell & Co. (Pvt) Ltd, 1970, p. 33.

16. G. E. P. Broderick, *A History of the Diocese of Southern Rhodesia Formerly Diocese of Mashonaland 1874-1952.* Salisbury (Harare): Cathedral of St. Mary and All Saints, September 1953, p. 254.

17.1 Ibid., p. 273.

18. Historical Manuscripts Collection, Anglican Church, Missionary Conferences, 1914-1960, The Second Native Missionary Conference In The Diocese Of Southern Rhodesia-1918 (Hence cited as ANG 1/4/5), Section XII in the National Archives in Harare, quoted in: W. R. Peaden, *Missionary Attitudes to Shona Culture 1890-1923.* R. S. Roberts, (ed.), *The Central African Historical Association Local Series 27.* Salisbury (Harare): A. W. Bardwell & Co. (Pvt) Ltd, 1970, p. 35.

19. Historical Manuscripts Collection, Anglican Church, Missionary Conferences, 1914-1960, The Second Native Missionary Conference In The Diocese Of Southern Rhodesia-1918 (Hence cited as ANG 1/4/5), Section III, IV in the National Archives in Harare, quoted in: W. R. Peaden, *Missionary Attitudes To Shona Culture 1890-1923.* R. S. Roberts, (ed.), *The Central African Historical Association Local Series 27.* Salisbury (Harare): A. W. Bardwell & Co. (Pvt) Ltd, 1970, p. 36.

20. W. R. Peaden, Missionary *Attitudes to Shona Culture 1890-1923.* R. S. Roberts, (ed.), *The Central African Historical Association Local Series 27.* Salisbury (Harare): A. W. Bardwell & Co. (Pvt) Ltd, 1970, p. 36.

21. N. D. Atkinson, "The Missionary Contribution to Early Education in Rhodesia". J. A. Dachs, (ed.) Christianity *South of the Zambezi Vol. I.* Gweru: Mambo Press, 1973, p. 89.

22. Southern Rhodesia Report of The Commission of Native Education, 1925, paragraph 252, quoted in: W. R. Peaden, Missionary *Attitudes to Shona Culture 1890-1923.* R. S. Roberts, (ed.), *The Central African Historical Association Local Series 27.* Salisbury (Harare): A. W. Bardwell & Co. (Pvt) Ltd, 1970, p. 8.

23. "Southern Rhodesia Report of The Commission of Native Education, 1925, paragraph 232", quoted in: W. R. Peaden, *Missionary Attitudes to Shona Culture 1890-1923.* R. S. Roberts, (ed.), *The Central African Historical Association Local Series 27.* Salisbury (Harare): A. W. Bardwell & Co. (Pvt) Ltd, 1970, p. 9.

24. "Makoni Mission, St. Faith's, Rusape", *Mashonaland Quarterly Paper,* 1909, 68, 22, quoted in: W. R. Peaden, *Missionary Attitudes to Shona Culture 1890-1923.* R. S. Roberts, (ed.), *The Central African Historical Association Local Series 27.* Salisbury (Harare): A. W. Bardwell & Co. (Pvt) Ltd, 1970, p. 23.

25. National Archives Of Zimbabwe, Harare, N3/5/1/1, Fr. Fleischer—Native Commissioner, Inyanga, (Nyanga) 29X 1911, quoted in: W. R. Peaden, *Missionary Attitudes To Shona Culture 1890-1923.* R. S. Roberts, (ed.), *The Central African Historical Association Local Series 27.* Salisbury (Harare): A. W. Bardwell & Co. (Pvt) Ltd, 1970, p. 24.

26. National Archives Of Zimbabwe, Harare, N3/5/1/1, Fr. Fleischer—Native Commissioner, Inyanga, (Nyanga) 29X 1911, quoted in: W. R. Peaden, Missionary *Attitudes To Shona Culture 1890-1923.* R. S. Roberts, (ed*.), The Central African Historical Association Local Series 27.* Salisbury (Harare): A. W. Bardwell & Co. (Pvt) Ltd, 1970, p. 20.

27. G. W. H. Knight-Bruce, *Memories of Mashonaland. Rhodesiana Reprint Library. Volume Thirteen, Facsimile Reproduction of The 1895 Edition.* Bulawayo: Books of Rhodesia Publishing Co. (Pvt) Ltd, pp. 50-51. quoted in: J. Farrant, *Mashonaland Martyr—Bernard Mizeki And The Pioneer Church.* Oxford: Oxford University Press. 1974. p. 131, also quoted in: W. R. Peaden, *Missionary Attitudes to Shona Culture 1890-1923.* R. S. Roberts, (ed.), *The Central African Historical Association Local Series 27.* Salisbury (Harare): A. W. Bardwell & Co. (Pvt) Ltd, 1970, p. 17.

28. A. D. Owen, "A Plea for Medical Work as a Means for Increasing Missionary Influence," *Mashonaland Quarterly Paper*, 1899, 28 pp. 7-8, quoted in: W. R. Peaden, *Missionary Attitudes to Shona Culture 1890-1923.* R. S. Roberts, (ed.), *The Central African Historical Association Local Series 27.* Salisbury (Harare): A. W. Bardwell & Co. (Pvt) Ltd, 1970, p. 18.

29. M. Gelfand, "Medicine and The Christian Mission In Rhodesia 1857-1930," in J. A Dachs, (ed.) *Christianity South of the Zambezi.* Gweru: Mambo Press, 1993, p. 114.

30. "A Remarkable Letter From A Native Catechist", *The Zambezi Missionary Report,* 1922-1925, 7, 494, 492-493 quoted in W. R. Peaden, *Missionary Attitudes To Shona Culture 1890-1923.* R. S. Roberts, (ed.), *The Central African Historical Association Local Series 27.* Salisbury (Harare): A. W. Bardwell & Co. (Pvt) Ltd, 1970, p. 34.

31. E. F. Paget, *The Toroquay Directory and South Devon Journal Toroquay*: (containing Paget's visit to Britain) National Archives of Zimbabwe, Harare, ANG 1/1/1-66 (Anglican Church) Torquay: Wednesday, June 16, 1926, p. 5.

32. *Proceedings Of The Southern Rhodesia Missionary Conference.* Salisbury (Harare): 2nd to 5th August, 1926, p. 17. The Argus Printing and Publishing Company Limited.

33. Ibid., p. 31.

34. *Proceedings of the Southern Rhodesia Missionary Conference.* 26th-29th March, 1928, p. 9. National Archives Of Zimbabwe, Harare, ANG 1/4/5 (Southern Rhodesia Missionary Conference 1914-1960) Salisbury (Harare): The Rhodesia Printing and Publishing Company Limited.

35. *Proceedings of the Southern Rhodesia Missionary Conference.* Bulawayo: Chronicle, 26th-28th June 1930, p. 20. National Archives of Zimbabwe, Harare, ANG 1/4/5 (Southern Rhodesia Missionary Conference 1914-1960).

36. S. J. Christelow, *Diocese Of Southern Rhodesia: Circular To The Bishop And All Licensed Clergymen, From Director Of Missions,* 30th April, 1938, p. 1. National Archives of Zimbabwe, Harare, ANG 16/12/1/1-18 (Anglican Church) Salisbury (Harare).

37. D. V. Steere, *God's Irregular Arthur Shearley Cripps.* London: SPCK, 1973, p. 45.

38. See Julian on A. S. Cripps, *Cinderella in the South,* Oxford, 1918. pp. 119-136. Reverend Leonard Mamvura Interview, 4th September 1971, quoted in: M. Steel, "With Hope Unconquered and Unconquerable, Arthur Shearley Cripps. 1869-1952". T. O. Ranger and J. C. Weller. (eds.) *Themes in the Christian History of Central Africa.* London, Nairobi, Ibadan, Lusaka: Heinemann, 1975, p. 155.

39. E. Fashole-Luke, "Christianity And Islam in Freetown", *The Sierra Leone Bulletin Of Religion, IX,* 1 1967, pp. 10-11 quoted in: G.

Bhebhe, *Christianity And Traditional Religion In Western Zimbabwe 1859-1923.* London: Longman, 1977, p. 162.

40. C. W. Alderson, "The Diocesan Synod Held at St. Michael's Harare (Mbare), (Runyararo) On The 3rd Of May 1962, Under The Chairmanship Of Bishop Cecil Alderson". Salisbury (Harare): St. Michael's, Mbare, 3rd May, 1962, p. 1, quoted in: *The Link,* Diocese of Mashonaland, (Harare), Salisbury (Harare): June 1962, p. 6.

41. Ibid., p. 7.

42. J. P. Burrough, *Diocese of Mashonaland: Pastoral Regulations: Instructions and Counsel, Issued by the Bishop of Mashonaland for the Guidance of the Clergy in Their Pastoral Responsibilities and Priestly Obligations.* Salisbury (Harare): Cannon Press, May 1978, p. 15.

43. Ibid., p. 3.

44. R. P. Hatendi, "Shona Marriages and the Christian Church". *Christianity South of the Zambezi, Vol. I.* J. A. Dachs (ed.) Gweru: Mambo Press, 1973, p. 139.

45. Ibid., p. 139.

46. Ibid., p. 147.

47. Ibid., p. 148.

48. R. P. Hatendi, *Diocese of Harare* "*AD CLERUM* OF OFFENSES to All Licensed Clergymen of the Diocese". Harare: 6th October 1990, p. 1.

49. Ibid., p. 1.

50. R. P. Hatendi, *Diocese of Harare* "*AD CLERUM* on Apartheid in the Diocese". Harare: 8th December 1990, p. 1.

51. R. P. Hatendi, *Diocese of Harare* "Memorandum to All Clergy Incumbents Churchwardens and Chapel Wardens". Harare: 19th December 1990, p. 1.

52. R. P. Hatendi, *Diocese of Harare* "Memorandum to All Licensed Priests All Chairmen of Vabvuwi and Chaplain on the Decade of Evangelisation and Vabvuwi". Harare: 4th February 1991, p. 1.

53. R. P. Hatendi, *Diocese of Harare* "Memorandum: On Healing and Deliverance from the Demonic Powers, to All Licensed Clergymen and all Heads of Diocesan Institution". Harare: 16th August 1991, p. 1.

54. R. P. Hatendi, "Church of the Province Africa, Diocese of Harare Synod 1992 Agenda and Reports". Harare: 12th and 13th September 1992, p. 5.

55. S. Bakare, (Chairman), "Report of the Idolatry And Evangelism Commission. The Anglican Church, Diocese of Harare". Harare: St. Mary's And All Saints Cathedral Hall, 7th-8th May 1994, pp. 18-19.

56. S. Bakare, My *Right to Land—in the Bible and in Zimbabwe: A Theology of Land in Zimbabwe*. Harare: Zimbabwe Council of Churches, 1993, p. 48.

57. Ibid., p. 50.

58. Ibid., p. 52.

59. S. Bakare, *The Drumbeat of Life: .Jubilee in an African Context.* Geneva: Risk Book Series. World Council Of Churches (WCC) Publications. 1997, p. 15.

60. C. G. Machoko, W. K. Simbabure, "The Church of the Province of Central Africa, Diocese of Harare, Report of the idolatry and Evangelism Commission, which was set up by the Synod of the Anglican Diocese of Hararc which met in Harare from the 12th to the 13th September 1992. A Report for the Synod of the Anglican Diocese of Harare, 7th-8th May 1994 for its Consideration". Harare: St. Mary and All Saints Cathedral Hall, 14th April 1994, pp. 4-5.

61. G. S. Wernberg, "Idolatry and Evangelism." D. Chandra, Diocesan Secretary, (ed.) Diocese Of Harare 55th Session of the Harare Diocesan Synod 7 A M 8th May 1994. Summary of Proceedings". Harare: 18th May 1994, pp. 2-3.

62. R. P. Hatendi, "Fifty Fifth Sessions of the Harare Diocesan Synod the Bishop's Charge." Harare: 7th May 1994, p. 3.

63. "Vicar General Appointment is Unconstitutional." T. Sithole (ed.) *The Herald—Incorporating the Nation* Harare: Saturday, 20 th May, 1995, p. 5.

64. I. M. Maspero, "The Church of the Province of Central Africa (Anglican), Diocese of Mashonaland (Harare). The Acts of the Diocese Of Mashonaland (Harare) Including the Diocesan Regulations." Harare: 1 st August 1974, p. 44.

## CHAPTER 4

1. A. K. Busia, *The Position of the Chief in The Modern Political System Of Ashanti. A Study of the Influence of Contemporary Social Changes on the Ashanti Political Institutions.* London: Frank Cass,

1968, 1st published in 1951, p. 38. quoted in: K. Bediako, *Jesus In African Culture. A Ghanian Perspective*. Accra: Asempa Publishers, 1990, p. 25.

2. Ibid, p. 22.

3. A. F. Walls, “Ruminations On Rainmaking: The Transmission And Receipt Of Religious Expertise in Africa” in J. C. Stone. (ed.) *Experts in Africa*. (Proceedings Of A Colloquium Art The University Of Aberdeen. March 1980). Aberdeen: Aberdeen University African Studies Group, 1980, p. 148.

4. Y. A. Obaje, “Theocentric Christology”, J. S. Pobee (ed.) *Exploring Afro-Christology*. Frankfurt, A. M. Main, Bern, New York, Paris: Peter Lang, 1992, p. 145.

5. K. Dickson, *Theology in Africa*. New York, Maryknoll: Orbis Books, 1984, p. 13.

6. E. Durkheim, *The Elementary Forms of Religious Life*. London: George Allen & Unwin. Ltd, 1976, p. 186.

7. M. F. C. Bourdillion, *Talk at The Anglican Cathedral*. “Paper on Some Background Information Necessary for Dialogue with African Traditional Religion Which Was Delivered to the Idol Commission Which was set up by the Anglican Diocese of Harare in May 1992". Harare: 5th October 1992, p. 2.

8. M. F. C. Bourdillion, *Talk At The Anglican Cathedral*. “Paper on Some Background Information Necessary for Dialogue with African Traditional Religion Which Was Delivered to the Idol Commission Which Was Set Up By The Anglican Diocese Of Harare In May 1992". Harare: 5th October 1992, p. 2. quoted in: M. F. C. Bourdillion, *Where Are The Ancestors? Changing Culture in Zimbabwe.* Harare: University of Zimbabwe Publications, 1993, p. 39.

9. R. S. Rattray, Ashanti. London, 1923, p. 150. quoted in: F. J. Verstraelen, "Ghana, West Africa: Between Traditional And Modern." quoted in F. J. Verstraelen (General Editor), A Camps, L. A. Hoedemaker, M. R. Spindler, (eds.), *Missiology. An Ecumenical Introduction. Texts and Contexts of Global Christianity.* Grand Rapids, Michigan: William B. Eerdmans Publishing Company, 1995, p. 76.

10. N. Smith, *The Presbyterian Church Of Ghana, 1835-1960. A Young Church In A Changing Society.* Accra, 1966, pp. 241f. quoted in F. J. Verstraelen (General Editor), A Camps, L. A. Hoedemaker, M. R. Spindler, (eds.), *Missiology. An Ecumenical Introduction. Texts And Contexts Of Global Christianity.* Grand Rapids, Michigan: William B. Eerdmans Publishing Company, 1995, p. 76.

11. A. Dankwa, "Tradition and Christianity at Crossroads", A Paper at the Triennial Consultation Meeting of the Presbyterian Church, Aburi, September, 1982 quoted in J. Middleton "One Hundred and Fifty Years of Christianity in a Ghanaian Town" *Africa.* 53, 1983, pp. 2-19. Comments on Middleton's Work by Historian P. Jenkins, ("150 jahre Christliche prasenz in Akropong aus sicht eines ethnologen") and theologian J. S. Pobee, ("Akropong der Stolz der Basler Mission aus der Perspective eines Afrikanischen Theologen") are in "Zeitschrift fur mission 12, 1986, pp. 213-18, 219-25, quoted in F. J. Verstraelen (General Editor), A Camps, L. A. Hoedemaker, M. R. Spindler, (eds.), *Missiology. An Ecumenical Introduction. Texts and Contexts of Global Christianity.* Grand Rapids, Michigan: William B. Eerdmans Publishing Company, 1995, p. 76.

12. H. Lindsell, *A Christian Philosophy of Missions.* Wheaton, Illinois: Van Kampen Press, 1949, p. 200.

13. P. F. Knitter, No *Other Name? A Critical Survey of Christian Attitudes toward the World Religions.* New York, Maryknoll: Orbis Books, 1985, p. 163.

# CHAPTER 5

1. F. J. Verstraelen, "Mission and the Bible in Historical and Missiological Perspective". I. Mukonyora, J. L. Cox, F. J. Vestraelen (coordinator), (eds.), *"Rewriting" The Bible: The Real Issues. Perspectives from within Biblical and Religious Studies In Zimbabwe. Religious and Theological Studies Series I.* Gweru: Mambo Press, 1993, p. 142.

2. H. R. Niebuhr, *Christ and Culture*. New York, Evanston and London: Harper & Row, 1951, p. 118.

3. Ibid., p. 209.

4. J. S. Pobee, *Toward an African Theology*. Nashville, Tennessee: Abingdon Press, 1979, p. 94.

5. K. A. Dickson, Theology in Africa. London: Darton, Longman and Todd New York, Maryknoll: Orbis Books, 1984, pp. 197-198, quoted in: C. Nyamiti, "African Christologies Today" in R. J. Schreiter, (ed.), *Faces of Jesus In Africa: Faith And Cultures Series*. New York, Maryknoll: Orbis Books, 1991, p. 8.

6. K. Bediako, *Jesus in African Culture. (A Ghanaian Perspective)*. Accra: Asempa Publishers, 1990, pp. 41-42.

7. A. Akrong, "Christology from an African Perspective" in J. S. Pobee, (ed.), *Exploring Afro-Christology*. Frankfurt, AM Main, Bern, New York, Paris: Peter Lang, 1992, p. 125.

8. Y. A. Obaje, "Theocentric Christologies" in J. S. Pobee (ed.), *Exploring Afro-Christology*. Frankfurt, AM Main, Bern, New York, Paris: Peter Lang, 1992, p. 45.

9. E. J. Penoukou, “Christology in the Village” in R. J. Schreiter, (ed.), *Faces Of Jesus in Africa: Faith And Cultures Series.* New York, Maryknoll: Orbis Books, 1991, p. 38.

10. A. T. Sanon, “Jesus Master of Initiation” in R. J. Schreiter, (ed.), *Faces Of Jesus Christ in Africa: Faith and Culture Series.* New York, Maryknoll: Orbis Books, 1991, p. 93.

11. J. S. Pobee, *Toward an African Theology.* Nashville, Tennessee: Abingdon Press, 1979, p. 95.

12. H. Sawyerr, *Creative Evangelism: Toward A New Christian Encounter With Africa.* London: 1968, pp. 72 ff. quoted in C. Nyamiti, “African Christologies Today” in R. J. Schreiter, (ed.), *Faces Of Jesus Christ In Africa: Faith And culture Series.* New York, Maryknoll: Orbis Books, 1991, p. 6.

13. K. Bediako, Jesus *in African Culture. (A Ghanaian Perspective).* Accra: Asempa Publishers, 1990, p. 18.

14. C. Kolie, “Jesus as Healer” in R. J. Schreiter, (ed.), *Faces Of Jesus Christ in Africa: Faith and Culture Series.* New York, Maryknoll: Orbis Books, 1991, p. 148.

15. B. H. Kato, *Theological Pitfalls in Africa.* Kenya, Kisumu: Evangel Publishing House, 1975, p. 183.

16. T. Tienou, *the Theological Task of the Church in Africa.* Igbaja, Nigeria: Africa Christian Press, 1982, p. 25.

17. C. Nyamiti, *Christ as Our Ancestor. Christology from an African Perspective. Mambo Occasional Papers—Missio—Pastoral Series No 11.* Gweru: Mambo Press, 1984, p. 70.

18. J. Mutiso-Mbinda, "Anthropology and the Paschal Mystery," *Spearhead,* No. 59 Eldoret, Kenya: Gaba Publications, 1979, quoted in: Z. Nthamburi, "Christ as seen by an African: A Christological Quest" in R. J. Schreiter, (ed.), *Faces Of Jesus Christ in Africa: Faith And Culture Series.* New York, Maryknoll: Orbis Books, 1991, p. 67.

19. J. M. Bahemuka, "The Hidden Christ in African Traditional Religion" in J. N. K. Mugambi, L Magesa, (eds.), *Jesus in African Christianity: Experimentation And Diversity in African Christology.* Kenya, Nairobi: Initiatives Publishers, 1989, p. 13.

20. P. N. Wachege, *Jesus Christ Our Muthamaki (Ideal Elder) An African Christological Study Based on the Agikuyu Understanding Of Elder.* Kenya, Nairobi: Phoenix Publishers Ltd, 1992, p. 146.

21. L. Magesa. "Christ the Liberator in Africa Today" in J. N. K. Mugambi, L. Magesa, (eds.), *Experimentation and Diversity in African Christology.* Kenya, Nairobi: Initiatives Publishers, 1989, p. 87.

22. A. Nasimuyu-Wasike, "Christology and an African Woman's Experience" in J. N. K. Mugambi, L Magesa, (eds.), *Jesus in African Christianity: Experimentation and Diversity in African Christology.* Kenya, Nairobi: Initiatives Publishers, 1989, pp. 78-79.

23. Ibid., p. 79.

24. N. K. Mugambi, "Christological Paradigms In African Christianity" in J. N. K. Mugambi, L Magesa, (eds.), *Jesus in African Christianity Experimentation and Diversity in African Christology.* Kenya, Nairobi: Initiatives Publishers, 1989, p. 156.

25. Ibid., pp. 159-160.

26. J. M. Waliggo, "African Christology in a Situation of Suffering" in J. N. K. Mugambi, L Magesa (eds.), *Experimentation and Diversity in African Christology.* Kenya, Nairobi: Initiatives Publishers, 1989, pp. 106-107.

27. Z. Nthamburi, "Christ as seen say an African: A Christological Quest" in J. N. K. Mugambi, L. Magesa, (eds.), *Jesus in African Christianity. Experimentation and Diversity in African Christology.* Kenya, Nairobi: Initiatives Publishers, 1989, p. 58.

28. D. W. Waruta, "Who is Jesus Christ for Africans Today? Priest, Prophet, and Potentate" in J. N. K. Mugambi, L Magesa, (eds.), *Jesus in African Christianity: Experimentation and Diversity in African Christology.* Kenya, Nairobi: Initiatives Publishers, 1989, pp. 50-52.

29. B. Bujo, African *Theology in its Social Context.* (Trans) John O'Donohue. M Afr Africa: St. Paul Publications, 1992, p. 79.

30. F. Kabasele, "Christ as Ancestor and Elder Brother" in R. J. Schreiter, (ed.), *Faces of Jesus Christ in Africa: Faith and Culture Series.* New York, Maryknoll: Orbis Books, 1991, p. 123.

31. Ibid., p. 122.

32. F. Kabasele, "Christ as Chief" in R. J. Schreiter, (ed.), *Faces Of Jesus Christ in Africa: Faith and Culture Series.* New York, Maryknoll: Orbis Books, 1991, p. 104.

33. A. M. Moyo, "The Quest for African Christian Theology and the Problem of Relationship between Faith and Culture—The Hermeneutical Perspective". *African Theological Journal,* Vol. 12, No. 2, 1983, p. 97. quoted in: Z. Nthamburi, "Christ as seen by an African: A Christological Quest" in J. N. K. Mugambi, L Magesa, (eds.), *Jesus In African Christianity Experimentation and Diversity in African Christology.* Kenya, Nairobi: Initiatives Publishers, 1989, p. 56.

34. C. S. Banana, "Come and Share": *An Introduction to Christian Theology.* Gweru: Mambo Press, 1991, pp. 64-65.

35. C. S. Banana, *The Church and the Struggle for Zimbabwe. from the Programme to Combat Racism to Combat Theology.* Gweru: Mambo Press, 1996, p. 14.

36. C. S. Banana, *Gospel According to the Ghetto.* Gweru: Mambo Press, 1980, pp. 71 74.

37. G. H. Muzorewa, *An African Theology of Mission. Studies in History of Missions Vol. 5.* New York: Lewiston, The Edwin Mellen Press, 1990, p. 153.

38. B. Goba, "Doing Theology in South Africa: A Black Christian Perspective. An Invitation to the Church to be Relevant". J. W. de Gruchy (ed.), *Journal of Theology for Southern Africa.* Cape Town: Mills Litho (Pvt.) Ltd, No. 31, June 1980, pp. 27-33.

39. A. Boesak, "Civil Religion and the Black Community". J. W. de Gruchy (ed.), Journal *of Theology for Southern Africa.* Cape Town: Mills Litho (Pvt.) Ltd, No. 19, June 1977, p. 39.

40. C. J. Goosen, I. S. Masola, P. Makhubu, "Cultural Backgrounds and Religious Education". *Journal of Theology for Southern Africa.* No. 33, December 1980, p. 82.

41. H. M. Dandala, "SALA—A Prophetic Event for South Africa". *Journal of Theology for Southern Africa.* No. 3, March 1980, p. 61.

42. M. Mothlabe (ed.), *Essays on Black Theology*. Johannesburg: SCM Press, 1972, quoted in: M. Buthelezi, "Violence and the Cross in South Africa". *Journal of Theology for Africa.* December 1979, also quoted in: T. A. Mofokeng, *The Crucified Among the Cross bearers:*

*Toward a Black Christology*. Kampen, 1983, quoted in P. N. Wachege, *Jesus Christ our Muthamaki (Ideal Elder) An African Christological Study Based on the Agikuyu Understanding Of Elder*. Kenya, Nairobi: Phoenix Publishers Ltd, 1992, pp. 176-7.

43. E. Gwembe, S. J. "The Traditional Religion", in: "Crossroads" No. 141, April 1994 pp. 13-15, quoted in F. J. Verstraelen, "Patterns of Missionary and Ecumenical Relationships in Zimbabwe" in: *Exchange. Journal of Missiological and Ecumenical Research*. Vol. 24, 1995, No. 3, p. 211.

## CHAPTER 6

1. M. Nazir-Ali, *Mission and Dialogue Proclaiming the Gospel Afresh In Every Age*. London: SPCK, 1995, p. viii.

2. P. N. Wachege, *Jesus Christ Our Muthamaki (Ideal Elder) An African Christological Study Based on the Agikuyu Understanding of Elder*. Nairobi, Kenya: Phoenix Publishers Ltd, 1992, p. 1.

3. S. J. Samartha, "In Search of a Revised Christology. A Response to Paul F. Knitter". *Current Dialogue*. World Council of Churches. Dialogue with People Of Living Faiths. 1211 Geneva 2: Switzerland, 21 December 1991, p. 33.

4. J. N. K. Mugambi, *African Christian Theology an Introduction*. Nairobi: Heinemann, Kenya Ltd, 1989, p. 91.

5. O. Cullman, *The Christology of The New Testament*. London; SCM Press, 1959, pp. 271-72, quoted in; P. N. Wachege, *Jesus Christ Our Muthamaki (Ideal Elder) An African Christological Study Based on the Agikuyu Understanding of Elder*. Nairobi, Kenya: Phoenix Publishers Ltd, 1992, p. 136.

6. Ibid., p. 137.

7. Ibid., p. 138.

8. Ibid., p. 138.

9. P. N. Wachege, *Jesus Christ Our Muthamaki (Ideal Elder) An African Christological Study Based on the Agikuyu Understanding of Elder.* Nairobi, Kenya: Phoenix Publishers Ltd, 1992, p. 140.

10. O. Cullman, *The Christology of The New Testament.* London; SCM Press, 1959, pp. 83-107, quoted in; P. N. Wachege, *Jesus Christ Our Muthamaki (Ideal Elder) An African Christological Study Based on the Agikuyu Understanding of Elder.* Nairobi, Kenya: Phoenix Publishers Ltd, 1992, p. 142.

11. J. J. C. Dunn, *Christology in the Making.* London; SCM Press, 1980, pp. 306-07, quoted in; P. N. Wachege, *Jesus Christ Our Muthamaki (Ideal Elder) An African Christological Study Based on thee Agikuyu Understanding of Elder.* Nairobi, Kenya: Phoenix Publishers Ltd, 1992, p. 143.

12. W. Barclay, *Jesus as they Saw Him.* London, SCM Press, 1962, p. 37 quoted in; P. N. Wachege, *Jesus Christ Our Muthamaki (Ideal Elder) An African Christological Study Based on the Agikuyu Understanding of Elder.* Nairobi, Kenya: Phoenix Publishers Ltd, 1992, p. 144.

13. D. G. Dunn, *Unity and Diversity in the New Testament: An Inquiry into the Character of Earliest Christianity.* London: SCM Press Ltd, 1977, p. 58.

14. P. N. Wachege, *Jesus Christ Our Muthamaki (Ideal Elder) An African Christological Study Based on the Agikuyu Understanding of Elder.* Nairobi, Kenya: Phoenix Publishers Ltd, 1992, p. 235.

15. D. Winzen, *Symbols of Christ*, London, New York, Toronto: Longmans Green & Co, 1955, p. 14.

16. X. L. Dufour, "Jesus' Understanding of Death". *Theology Digest 24 (3).* London; 1976, pp. 193-300, quoted in: P. N. Wachege, *Jesus Christ Our Muthamaki (Ideal Elder) An African Christological Study Based on the Agikuyu Understanding of Elder.* Nairobi, Kenya: Phoenix Publishers Ltd, 1992, p. 193.

17. A. Jones, (ed.) *The Jerusalem Bible. The Gospel According to St. John.* London; Darton, Longman and Todd, 1966, p. 189, quoted in; P. N. Wachege, *Jesus Christ Our Muthamaki (Ideal Elder) An African Christological Study Based on the Agikuyu Understanding of Elder.* Nairobi, Kenya: Phoenix Publishers Ltd, 1992, p. 194.

18. Y. M. J. Congar, "I Believe in the Holy Spirit". London: Geoffrey Chapman, 1983, Vol. III. quoted in; P. N. Wachege, *Jesus Christ Our Muthamaki (Ideal Elder) An African Christological Study Based on the Agikuyu Understanding of Elder.* Nairobi, Kenya: Phoenix Publishers Ltd, 1992, p. 204.

19. Pope John Paul II, "We Must Be Example of Love and Teachers after the Heart of Christ". *Observatore Romano* 29 May 1989, p. 17, quoted in; P. N. Wachege, *Jesus Christ Our Muthamaki (Ideal Elder) An African Christological Study Based on the Agikuyu Understanding of Elder.* Nairobi, Kenya: Phoenix Publishers Ltd, 1992, pp. 211-12.

20. M. Nazir-Ali, *Mission and Dialogue. Proclaiming the Gospel Afresh in Every Age.* London: SPCK, 1995, p. 56.

21. Pope John Paul II, quoted in: "Letter to Cardinal Agostino Casaroli, Secretary of State", 20th May 1982, quoted from; The English weekly Edition of; *L'Osservatore Romano*, June 28, 1982, pp. 7-8, quoted by C. McGarry, (S.J.) *Preface,* Herkima College, Jesuit

School of Theology. Nairobi 1992 p. 7, quoted in; J. M. Walliggo, A. Roest Crollius, J. S. T. Nkeramihigo, J. S. J. Mutiso Mbinda, (eds.), *Inculturation: Its Meaning and Urgency.* Africa, Uganda, Kampala: St. Paul Publications, 1986, p. 7.

22. Pope John Paul II, in: *Evangelii Nuntiandi*, 63, quoted by C. McGarry, (S.J.) Preface, Herkima College, Jesuit School of Theology. Nairobi 1992, p. 7, quoted in; J. M. Walligo, A. Roest Crollius, J. S. T. Nkeramihigo, J. S. J. Mutiso Mbinda, (eds.), *Inculturation : Its Meaning And Urgency.* Africa, Uganda, Kampala: St. Paul Publications, 1986, p. 8.

23. IMBISA Secretariat, *Inculturaton: The Faith That Takes Root in African Cultures. IMBISA Study Document. The Seed is the Word of God.* Zimbabwe, Gweru: Mambo Press, 1993, p. 47.

24. J. M. Waliggo, "Making a Church that is Truly African". In J. M. Waliggo, A. Roest Crollius, S. J. T. Nkeramihigo, S. J. J. Mutiso-Mbinda, (eds.), *Inculturation: Its Meaning and Urgency.* Kampala, Uganda: St. Paul Publications, Africa, 1986, p. 22.

25. *Final Statement of the FABC Assembly,* No. 12. "His Gospel to our Peoples"—Vol. II. Manila, 1976. p. 332, quoted by: A. Roest Crollius, in: "Inculturation: Newness and Ongoing Process". J. M. Waliggo, A. Roest Crollius J. S. Nkeramihigo S. J. Mutiso-Mbinda, (eds.), *Inculturation: Its Meaning and Urgency.* Kampala, Uganda: St. Paul Publications, Africa, 1986, p. 37.

26. A. Roest Crollius, "Inculturation: Newness and Ongoing Process". In J. M. Waliggo, A. Roest Crollius J. S. Nkeramihigo S. J. Mutiso-Mbinda, (eds.), *Inculturation: Its Meaning and Urgency.* Kampala, Uganda: St. Paul Publications, Africa, 1986, p. 43.

27. Pope John Paul II, Addressing First Plenary Assembly of SECAM. Kampala, 31st July, 1969, quoted in: AFER, Vol. XI, No. 4,

1969, p. 404, quoted in J. Mutiso-Mbinda, "*Inculturation: Challenge To The African Local Church*". J. M. Waliggo, A. Roest Crollius, S. J. T. Nkeramihigo, S. J. J. Mutiso-Mbinda, (eds.), *Inculturation: Its Meaning and Urgency*. Kampala, Uganda: St. Paul Publications, Africa, 1986, pp. 75-76.

28. M. Nazir-Ali, *Mission and Dialogue Proclaiming the Gospel Afresh in Every Age*. London: SPCK, 1995, p. vii.

29. J. Dupuis, "Christological Debate in the Context of Religious Plurality". J. Dupuis, (ed.), *Current Dialogue*. Vol. 9. January 1991. World Council of Churches, Dialogue With Peoples Of Living Faiths. Geneva. 1991, p. 21.

30. Ibid., p. 23.

31. Ibid., p. 23.

32. Ibid., pp. 23-24.

33. S. J. Samartha, "In Search Of A Revised Christology. A Response to Paul F. Knitter—*Pneuma*tology". J. Dupuis, (ed.), *Current Dialogue*, 21 December 1991. World Council of Churches. Dialogue with People of Living Faiths. Geneva. 1991, p. 34.

## CHAPTER 7

1. S. Bakare, J. Weller, "Liturgy Lecture Notes". Harare: Bishop Gaul College, National Anglican Theological College in Zimbabwe (NATCZ), 1986.

2. J. R. Quinn, Sacramental. In T. C. O'Brien et al, (eds.), *New Catholic Encyclopedia, Vol. 12.* (Supplement 17) Washington D.C.Catholic University of America Press, 1981 pp. 790-92, quoting *Sacrosanctum Concillium, Art. 60.*

3. C. P. Price, L. Weil, *The Church's Teaching Series. Liturgy for Living. With The Assistance of a Group of Editorial Advisors under the Direction of the Church's Teaching Series Committee.* New York: The Seabury Press, 1979, pp. 13-14.

4. I.Bria, *Liturgy after the Liturgy. Mission and Witness from an Orthodox Prospective.* Geneva: World Council of Churches (WCC) Publications, 1996, pp. 1-35.

5. Zimbabwe Catholic Bishops' Conference (ZCBC). *Responsibility, Honesty, Solidarity. Joint Pastoral Statement by the Zimbabwe Catholic Bishops' Conference.* Harare: Social Communications Department of the ZCBC, 16th April 1997, pp. 7-8.